No Surprises

Paul Greenberg

No
Surprises

Two Decades of Clinton-Watching

Paul Greenberg

Brassey's
Washington London

Library of Congress Cataloging-in-Publication Data

Greenberg, Paul
    No surprises: two decades of Clinton-watching/Paul Greenberg.
        p.   cm.
    Includes index.
    ISBN 1-57488-005-5
    1. Clinton, Bill, 1946–   . 2. United States — Politics and government — 1993–
3. Arkansas — Politics and government — 1951–
I. Title.
E886.G744   1996
973.929'092 — dc20   95-26414

10 9 8 7 6 5 4 3 2 1

Printed in the United States of America

CONTENTS

PREFACE

I wrote this book because I wanted a copy of it. As the Clinton presidency took center stage, there were no surprises for someone who had followed the long, long overture in Arkansas year after year. Each event and non-event had a familiar feel. But it grew tiresome having to tramp down to the basement of the *Arkansas Democrat-Gazette* to thumb through past editorials and columns to refresh my memory. Often the search meant walking down the street to the old clinic now used to store the newspaper's records and then sorting through dusty cartons of old editorials from the *Pine Bluff Commercial* — the newspaper whose editorial page I had managed for some thirty years. It'll be a lot handier to have the best of all that old Clintoniana gathered into this one book. I can keep it on the shelf as a concise guide to the standard operating procedures of the Clinton Years.

Besides, there are a lot of other, more serious reasons for digging through those old cartons and this eye-glazing thing they call a database. We in Arkansas were the first and most consistent in our critique and challenge of the man who would be president. As a result, I was bombarded with inquiries from all over the world about our skeptical approach toward Bill Clinton, and about the evidence and experiences that supported it. Everywhere I speak, people still come up to me and wonder about our editorial position on the most famous couple from Arkansas. Here's hoping this selection of thinking and writing about the Clintons over two decades helps others better understand the most important family in America.

A confession: The title of this book — *No Surprises* — may be a slight exaggeration. To a remarkable extent, the current president of the United States is indeed turning out to be the governor of Arkansas writ large. But I was surprised by how soon things would begin to fall apart for the Clinton administration, and how quickly much of American public opinion would grow disillusioned with the bright, shiny presidential candidate who wowed the country in 1992.

Going back through these columns, I was impressed by how many times I had given Bill Clinton the benefit of the doubt, hoping for the best despite worrisome indications of the worst. The American public's impression of Bill Clinton may be much like my own these days, but it crystallized more quickly, taking only a couple of years to reach conclusions I had to grope for over a couple of decades.

A great many Americans must still be going through the process I did. They may be troubled by this president's politics but not able to put their finger on the unease he inspires. Many may still be hoping that next time, or the time after that, he'll come through like the different kind of leader all had hoped he would be. I can identify with them; they bring to mind some of my old editorials, which were of two minds about the future president. This book lets you follow one commentator as he tries to articulate those conflicting feelings even as an undeniable pattern emerges.

Putting together this collection of articles about our president also let me share my concerns about the spirit of his time — the current, clintonized culture of America in the '90s. It seems a remarkably spiritless spirit: full of sentimentality without emotion, leadership without direction, idealism without sacrifice, policy without decisions, great ambition without clear purpose, unending talk without much meaning or action . . . and a degree of self-absorption remarkable for even American society, which always seems to be taking its own temperature. The following snapshot commentaries from the '70s and '80s might help explain not only the development of Bill Clinton, but how the culture of the '90s took vague shape, and why it provokes such a powerful reaction from its critics. Bill Clinton didn't come from nowhere; he is a man of his — and our — times.

Frank Margiotta at Brassey's first approached me about this project and then nudged and prodded, encouraged and complained, exulted and groaned, and organized and reorganized these commentaries till a book emerged. He has been both encouraging and unrelenting, a combination of qualities any writer is fortunate to have in a publisher. I am particularly indebted to him for insisting that we preserve the original text of the editorials and columns as they appeared in the *Pine Bluff Commercial* and the *Arkansas Democrat-Gazette.* The text of many of the columns sent to the Los Angeles Times Syndicate are taken directly from the computer files of the *Democrat-Gazette.* Apart from the few explanatory phrases and occasional omissions clearly indicated in the text, these columns and editorials read as they did when written. So this book has proven something of a self-criticism, too, for few experiences can be as educational, or as chastening, as having to review one's old judgments in their original words. I am grateful to Brassey's for the opportunity to revisit a past that proved so instructive.

I am indebted to many others for their cooperation and encouragement, notably including the *Arkansas Democrat-Gazette* and the reference staff of the public library in Pine Bluff. It was the library's microfilmed files of the *Pine Bluff Commercial* that allowed me to track down the origin of the now familiar sobriquet, Slick Willie. Special thanks are due my son, Dan Greenberg, for spending part of a broiling Arkansas summer in a hot, dusty storage room rearranging boxes and boxes of old clippings in neat, chronological order, and then sifting through my siftings for columns and editorials of particular interest. The job took not only loving devotion but sheer physical stamina.

Special thanks to Lois Baron, the project editor who worked on this manuscript for Brassey's; to Arlene Starr, secretary-receptionist at the *Arkansas Democrat-Gazette,* whose help with this book went above and beyond her already hectic duties at the newspaper; to Clay Carson of the *Democrat-Gazette's* technical support team for transferring many of my old columns from the paper's electronic library to Brassey's in a computer-digestible form; and to the Brassey's production team for their patience and artistry in designing and producing the book you now hold in your hands.

Our objective was not only history's, which is to find a usable past, but to provide a good read. How well all of us succeeded, we now invite the reader to judge. And to enjoy.

"HE HAS MASTERED
THE ART OF
EQUIVOCATION"
AN INTRODUCTION TO
BILL CLINTON

A s election day approached in 1992, the *Arkansas Democrat-Gazette* did not feel strongly enough about any candidate to make an endorsement in the presidential race, but we did have sufficiently strong reservations about the one we knew best, Bill Clinton, to run what may have been a unique pre-election editorial — a non-endorsement. To many voters, the reasons for that decision may have sounded like exaggerated rhetoric from a newspaper going against the tide. But within a surprisingly short time, this analysis of the politics and character of Bill Clinton would become conventional knowledge. That may have been the only surprise about the Clinton administration to those of us who knew its leader. The speed with which the administration unraveled and the failure of his presidency did not shock us; the rapidity of the process did.

There is only one original tear sheet of this editorial left in the *Democrat-Gazette*'s library files. The demand for copies of the editorial was so great during the last week of the campaign, when passions inevitably mount, that it had to be reproduced in mass quantities. The demand for copies continued as the administration time and again followed the forebodings expressed in an editorial that had been published a week before Bill Clinton was elected president of the United States.

As I write these words Sunday, June 4, 1995, the major headline on the front page of the *New York Times* is no surprise, either: "Clinton, Facing Pressure, Plays Down Prospect of Using Troops in Bosnia." It is probably the most predictable of headlines about this president's policy, whether toward Bosnia or almost any other subject — from a middle-class tax cut to granting refugees asylum. Just fill in the blank and you've got a crystal ball that shows the future as well as the past of the Clinton administration: "Clinton, Facing Pressure, Plays Down ———." As this election-eve editorial noted, "He has mastered the art of equivocation."

NOT FOR BILL CLINTON
OCTOBER 28, 1992

Traditionally, this newspaper has not endorsed in presidential elections, but 1992 would have been a natural year to start a new tradition. A native son of Arkansas heads the Democratic ticket. He is congenial, ambitious, and a fighter who never gives up where his career is concerned. Bill Clinton is blessed (or maybe cursed) with an uncanny political intelligence. It is no fluke that he has come this far, no accident that other Democratic contenders didn't make the race or fell by the way, and that he should now be on the threshold of the presidency. His triumph Tuesday would not only boost this long underestimated state's pride, but doubtless provide some welcome patronage; even his campaign has enlivened the state's economy.

As for who Bill Clinton might be, what he stands for, what principles and policies he represents . . . none of that is as clear as his political pizzazz. Is he going to bring us together or set class against class? Tackle the deficit, embark on more spending programs, neither or both? Is he for real reform in education, or will he only repeat the platitudes of the teacher lobby? Is he against a litmus test for nominees to the Supreme Court, or would he appoint only justices pledged to uphold *Roe v. Wade* and the right to an abortion? Or both?

Would he continue this country's involvement in the world or shrink back from free trade and the defense of free institutions even while speaking fondly of both? To borrow an unforgettable construction of the governor's, would he go with the majority if the vote were close, or agree with the arguments of the minority, or, more probably, do both simultaneously?

Bill Clinton is a master politician, but what principles, if any, inform his politics? He embodies the glossy spirit of the times, but is it a spirit to be encouraged? Are there any steadfast principles — besides winning the next election — that he would never compromise to win popularity? Who knows? And if we don't, how can we recommend him to America as a leader?

What does Bill Clinton's track record in Arkansas foretell in a President Clinton? A purely rhetorical approach to issues that may please all, coupled with a tendency to side with those interests powerful enough to do him some political good. He may be running for president on a soak-the-rich appeal, but his tax policy in Arkansas has been to hand out exemptions to large corporations and soak the middle class. The state's tax structure is more regressive than ever after a decade of Clintonomics.

Education is his strong suit, and Bill and Hillary Clinton deserve thanks for finally giving Arkansas some tests and standards, which unfortunately show that we're not educating our young people well. About three-quarters of the crop will need remedial courses in the basics when they enter state universities. The governor has never mustered the courage to seriously tackle Job One in educational reform: school consolidation. It would have cost him some votes. In his administration, any reform that might encounter opposition (civil rights, environmental regulation) tends to be shunted aside to a study commission, where it either dies or emerges toothless.

A great campaigner, Bill Clinton has proven a mediocre administrator. He's leaving the state's Department of Human Services in disarray, its medical payments slashed and programs uncertain. He had to be sued before doing anything meaningful about the scandalous disregard of abused and neglected children in this state's "care." His attitude toward releasing prisoners has been equally irresponsible, and constitutional reform has languished on his watch. His environmental policy adds up to little more than delay and neglect.

In short, Mr. Clinton has been a great theorist of how government should operate, not a great practitioner. Arkansas has progressed, but not nearly so much as it would have if Bill Clinton had been the Bill Clinton of the campaign ads. Surely no one would confuse the Clinton

Years in Arkansas with the great burst of energy and spirit that charac-
terized a genuine reform administration like Winthrop Rockefeller's.
For that matter, the Bumpers and Pryor administrations showed more
gumption when it came to basic reforms in government.

Finally and sadly, there is the unavoidable subject of character in a
presidential candidate. Surely even his supporters, or at least those not
entirely blinded by the Clinton glitz, can see that — whatever one
thinks of young Clinton's adventures with the draft and antiwar demonstrations — he regularly dissembled about both over the course of some
twenty years. Nor would they deny that he broke his enthusiastic
promise not to run for president this year but to stay on and discharge
the duties of governor, as he solemnly swore to do. But it is not the
duplicitousness in his politics that concerns so much as the polished
ease, the almost habitual, casual, articulate way he bobs and weaves.
He has mastered the art of equivocation. There is something almost
inhuman in his smoother responses that sends a shiver up the spine. It
is not the compromises he has made that trouble so much as the
unavoidable suspicion that he has no great principles to compromise.

Let us hope that, after the landslide victory the polls project, the
mythic crucible of the presidency will equip Bill Clinton with conviction and grant him success, for all of our sakes. But hope alone is not a
sufficient basis on which to make an endorsement for president of the
United States and, yes, commander-in-chief of the armed forces.

And the other candidates? George Bush has not impressed as a campaigner, and his record at home has been less than successful. Yet the
president deserves high marks in foreign policy, where he inspires confidence whatever our cavils. Besides, reports of the death of the American economy are premature, even if the recessionary blues still linger.
Other indicators — low interest rates, a low inflation rate, yesterday's
report on last quarter's economic growth — are more hopeful. If he is a
president on the way out, as the polls say, George Bush will take with
him a predictability that may be missed almost as soon as his conces-
sion speech is completed.

Ross Perot? Strange man. Strange on-again, off-again campaign. His
appetite for squirrelly conspiracy theories amounts to a craving. How
would you like to have a president whose eyes narrow whenever he
serves up some yarn from Fantastic Spy Stories? Or finds it "interesting" and "fascinating" that two plus two should equal 3.8, maybe. Even

stranger, this least serious of the candidates is the only one who takes a serious approach to the country's biggest economic problem, the national debt. Hey, what a country. Hey, what a campaign.

So consider this a non-endorsement. Some traditions may be worth keeping.

Chapter 1

SLICK WILLIE

Politicians aren't given nicknames; they earn them. At some point, an almost audible click can be heard as a name catches in the public mind — Old Hickory, The Rail Splitter, Tricky Dick, The Great Communicator. . . . Slick Willie had a long incubation period. The *Pine Bluff Commercial* was in the habit of assigning sobriquets to various local and state figures since Patrick J. Owens, my predecessor as editorial page editor, initiated that style at the *Commercial* in the early '60s. Governor Orval Faubus was Peerless Leader and, later, Eternal Incumbent. As early as 1979, the editorial column was trying out several such titles for the brash, yet indecisive, newcomer in the Governor's Mansion. Most played on Bill Clinton's youth; he was the youngest governor in the Union at the time. Among the failed experiments: Kid Clinton, Boy Governor, Young Smoothie. . . . but nothing clicked till Slick Willie made his debut during Governor Clinton's reelection campaign of 1980, one of the only two important elections he would lose. (The other came in an earlier race for congressman against John Paul Hammerschmidt, who would prove unbeatable in the state's sole Republican stronghold: hilly Northwest Arkansas.)

As best I can determine from the microfilmed copies of the *Commercial* at the public library in Pine Bluff, Slick Willie first appeared in our editorial columns on Saturday, September 27, 1980. And a star was born. The name had been inspired by Governor Clinton's attempt to place himself in the reform tradition of modern, post-Faubus Arkansas governors while at the same time trying to out-demagogue his Republican opponent that year, Frank White, on the issue of how best to handle the wave of Cuban refugees that hit Arkansas in the summer of 1980. Shipped to an army base — Fort Chaffee outside Fort Smith, Arkansas — the refugees' arrival touched off widespread fears and a nativist reaction that both candidates would exploit as election day approached. Occasional incidents involving a small percentage of the Cubans — usually the young and unruly — didn't help.

Let it be noted that Bill Clinton had welcomed the Cubans warmly when the first contingent arrived in May. "The Cuban refugees who are now temporarily housed in Florida," he said in a welcoming statement, "came to this country in flight from a communist dictatorship. I know that everyone in this state sympathizes and identifies with them in their desire for freedom. I will do all I can to fulfill whatever possibilities the president imposes on Arkansas to facilitate the refugees' resettlement in this country." By September, he would be badmouthing Jimmy Carter for sending the Cubans to Arkansas, and threatening to defy the whole United States Army if Washington sent more.

The heat had mounted, literally, through July and August. The drought of 1980 produced one of the hottest summers in Arkansas history. I remember it well; my father was dying down in Shreveport, my home town, with cancer of the colon. Each weekend we would load the kids into the old Ford station wagon my wife's parents had given us and drive the 184 miles from Pine Bluff to Shreveport.

That was where the governor's office found me when Bill Clinton called to ask what I would do about the Cubans — perhaps because the *Commercial*'s editorials had praised a previous governor, David Pryor, when he extended a helping hand to the Vietnamese refugees who had passed through Chaffee a few years earlier. As the son of immigrants who themselves had found refuge and opportunity in America, how could I have written anything else? I remember standing in the hallway of the house at 544 Forrest, listening to my father breathing laboriously in the bedroom, while the governor explained that a lot of people, meaning voters, were growing uneasy with the presence of these foreigners in Arkansas. There was trouble brewing and I sensed the governor was looking for some politically savvy, maybe even morally acceptable, way to finesse a political problem — which is all the Cubans had become to him. I didn't have an answer for his problem. All I could do was tell him to do the right thing. I urged him to explain that these newcomers and their children would soon be Americans, too, and we ought to welcome and support them. I don't think he was too happy with my counsel. At any rate, it was the last time he asked for it. My father died August 18, 1980, the sixth day of Elul, 5740.

The Young Pretender
September 27, 1980

Bill Clinton's playing the role of Progressive Young Governor gets even hokier as election day approaches. Last weekend, he arrived at the Democratic state convention at Hot Springs to say that his reelection was necessary to assure continued progress for Arkansas under progressive Democratic leadership. It is understandable that at a Democratic convention, the originator of the recent progressive trend in Arkansas history should go unnoted. This is, after all, the party that chose Jim Johnson and Marion Crank to oppose Mr. Rockefeller, and there are some memories best left undisturbed.

But what made the young governor's aligning himself with the Rockefeller-Bumpers-Pryor tradition even more piquant was his having blown into Hot Springs just after demagoguin' the Cuban issue in the best, or worst, tradition of Orval E. Faubus — who might well be his mentor when it comes to appealing to the worst in the electorate. Nor is that the only disturbing similarity between Slick Willie and old Orv. In many ways, Bill Clinton represents a return to faugressive* government after more than a decade of progress: in his ethical insensibility, as shown in his tolerance for closed meetings and Code of Ethics statements that don't get filed. In caving in to special interests like the truckers after saying he wouldn't on the subject of highway weight limits. And in the whole array of Clinton Scandals that stretch back to his leaving the office funds in a mess when he ended his stint as attorney general.

But in his own eyes, or at least speeches, Bill Clinton is a shining progressive. How he manages to leave that impression with the unwary was demonstrated at Hot Springs, where he took credit for lifting the sales tax on medical prescriptions. That was a worthy contribution — but a limited one. He found no reason to recall that first he waffled and then opposed dropping the sales tax on *both* medicine and groceries

---

*The *Commercial* habitually referred to Orval Faubus's style of governing, especially in regard to its dubious claims and numerous scandals, as Faugress. Hence the adjective, faugressive.

when that proposal was on the ballot in 1978. By later dropping the tax on prescriptions only, his administration left one of the most regressive features of this state's tax code on the books — just as it was in Orval Faubus's time.

The governor also trumpeted a homestead exemption for the elderly (regardless of income) that he had supported. No need to emphasize that he now supports Amendment 59, one of the biggest tax breaks ever offered rural interests in Arkansas, including planters and timber corporations. When it comes to framing basic tax legislation, he has abandoned the approach to equity represented by homestead exemptions and switched to a system that values some kind of property — notably farms, pastures, and timber lands — at a more favorable rate than residences or businesses. His progressive tax policy consists mainly of sops, while his sweeping concessions to powerful interests find their way into the basic law of the state.

It's a great act when the governor squeezes himself into this state's newly budding progressive tradition and the governor can hope that not until after election day will many voters notice that his idea of progress bears a striking similarity to Faugress.

Bill Clinton did indeed come back strong in 1982 to win another term as governor — but not, as I had thought, because he realized that he'd been too slick. But because, after a painful two-year period during which he must have come as close to introspection as a Bill Clinton can, he had reexamined every political mistake he had made in his first term as governor — major, minor, and in between — and apparently decided that he'd lost in 1980 because . . . he hadn't been slick enough. That's the last time he would make that mistake. To judge by the unbroken string of political triumphs that followed, and how he achieved them, Bill Clinton seems to have solemnly resolved during those two years in exile that never again would he offend a single voter:

Portrait of Dorian Clinton
August 30, 1980

Perhaps it speaks well of David Pryor that the junior senator from Arkansas appears incapable of believing anything ill of his fellow man, or at least of his fellow Democrat in a general election. Speaking to the Young Democrats' rally at Hestand Stadium in Pine Bluff the other evening, Senator Pryor presented this novel theory of why Bill Clinton bobbled his reelection as governor two years ago: "I don't believe Bill Clinton made a major political mistake. Bill Clinton was a man of such great dedication to presenting the truth . . . that he lost the race because he decided to run a clean campaign on his record."

That is a version of the 1980 campaign that only Bill Clinton himself might recognize. Airbrushed out of this recollection is that less-than-high point of his campaign when, diving to Frank White's level if not below, Governor Clinton threatened to defy the whole Yewnited States guvmint if it insisted on sending any more Cubans to Chaffee. It was a performance worthy of Orval E. Faubus, the guest of honor at his inaugural.

To describe Mr. Clinton's hollering Cuban as running a clean campaign on his record shows how well Mr. Pryor has mastered senatorial courtesy in his years on the Hill. The Slick Willie of 1980 is scarcely present in Senator Pryor's description two years later, and neither is the mean spirit of the 1980 gubernatorial campaign.

Mr. Clinton was also at the rally, and he had his own theory to explain his defeat two years ago: "Frank White got elected by deception and I was too dumb to fight back." Whatever Bill Clinton is, or says he is, it isn't easy to think of him as dumb. Of all the criticisms made of his political conduct (manipulative, shallow, immature, more ambitious than thoughtful, too slick, too sharp, and so on) surely being dumb may be the least convincing. Dumb, he ain't. And that he should think of himself as a dumb dupe of a sharp pol, or at least ask others to think of him that way, may be another tribute to that old gap in perception that Robert Burns made poetry of when he spoke of the rare gift to see ourselves as others see us.

Bill Clinton may have failed of reelection for any number of reasons, but not because he waged a noble campaign on behalf of the oppressed and persecuted, the stranger and the widow. He was right out there Cuban-baiting and Fed-defying along with Frank White. Mr. White may have proved better at wallowing in that sort of thing, but not because Mr. Clinton didn't compete.

If Bill Clinton hadn't risen to the bait in 1980, he might have lost even more resoundingly, but he would have lost with honor. And to hear him described as an innocent victim of demagoguery, rather than simply as another pol who got out-demagogued, outraged memory. But in one way that description is appropriate at Hestand Stadium [home of local rodeos] where over the years a lot of bull has been tossed around.

When the election of 1980 was over, and Bill Clinton had been the surprise loser to an equally stunned Frank White, I thought it had happened because the young governor had been too slick for Arkansas's populist tastes, and that he would now wise up, find some solid principles to tie to, and come back strong:

SWAMPED BY THE TIDE
NOVEMBER 6, 1980

After Tuesday's election results, Bill Clinton must feel like the oldest thirty-four-year-old governor in the country. But is he wiser? For a remarkably intelligent young governor, Mr. Clinton demonstrated a curious inability in office to learn from his mistakes. He appeared so intent on rationalizing those mistakes, or even presenting them as triumphs, that he scarcely had time to learn from them. He seemed a smooth model of political calculation, treating every error as another political problem to be offset by the proper maneuver. It was the Jimmy Carter Syndrome.

This may still be a problem, to judge by the variety of explanations out of the governor's camp the morning after the election: It was the fault of inflation, it was those car-tags-and-Cubans, it was the frustration vote that had done it. . . . There was no intimation that it might have been Bill Clinton who did the most to do in Bill Clinton — from the time he embraced Orval Faubus at his inaugural and then proceeded to embrace Mr. Faubus's political techniques.

For all his sophistication, Bill Clinton never seemed to grasp the impression he was creating month after month, the impression of a Slick Willie. He may never have grasped the sensibilities he was rubbing, or how plain people saw the turnabouts and evasions he was so clearly handling to his own satisfaction. Somewhere along the way, he lost touch with the populist tradition in this state, and any politician who does that runs a risk of paying for it sooner or later. In Mr. Clinton's case, it was sooner.

Those seeking an explanation of Bill Clinton's great fall Tuesday need to look beyond the Reagan Tide and the dyspeptic times. Those factors may have aided and abetted, but they were not sufficient to deny reelection to another well-known Democratic candidate — Dale Bumpers. Senator Bumpers of course had a great ally in the quality of his opposition, but he still won in a walk — well, a brisk stroll. And that was despite all the irritating factors operating in this our autumn of discontent. Because however unpopular his decisions, Dale Bumpers has been able to give his public service the stamp of character. He comes across as a confessing man, not a politician on the make.

So it isn't only the exigencies of a campaign, or the spirit-of-the-times, or our stars, Dear Brutus, that may explain the most surprising upset in modern Arkansas history. That upset was a couple of years in the making, even if almost no one saw it coming. Monroe Schwarzlose out in Cleveland County did. Last summer, long before Arkansas's own Cuban Crisis, he was saying that no matter how well he did against the governor in the Democratic primary, Frank White would be a cinch to win. Ol' Monroe never had to worry about losing touch with the populist tradition; he's a natural embodiment of it. Not even George Gallup or Lou Harris has that advantage. And so Cleveland County's favorite son was able to call this election months in advance.

One notes with some satisfaction, even exhilaration, that Arkies remain a perfect mystery on these occasions to the state's public opinion polls. It's as though people in these latitudes accorded pollsters the same welcome and confidence traditionally given revenooers. In those unpredictable years when the populist tide is rolling, it's a wonder the professional poll takers even get the date of an election right. . . .

Arkansas remains one of the most, if not the most, unpredictable, rambunctious, and eclectic electorates in the Union. Remember when we confounded the networks by electing Winthrop Rockefeller, George Wallace, and J. William Fulbright the same night? There was a weird logic to it, but maybe you had to be an Arkie to understand it. Populism is alive and well and living in Arkansas, where it makes occasional public appearances under the name of both reform and reaction. As dangerous and muddle-headed and rancorous as it can be, it can also be a terrible swift sword, putting pols in their place (or out of their places) and upsetting the best laid, and best financed, plans.

Bill Clinton is still young, and he still has promise — if he will take this opportunity to look within for some hard and fast principles that don't change out of political calculation. If there is anything tragic about his defeat, it is only that, even if it had been unavoidable, he could have gone down with honor. He didn't have to exploit the Cuban issue before switching to the high road when that seemed more likely to pay off.

One of the anomalies of Bill Clinton's career is that he has seemed more impressive outside the state than in. And the further out, the more he glittered. The *Washington Post*'s David Broder only recently named him — along with Jack Kemp — as the young politician most likely to be a future president of the United States. (Being classed with Jack Kemp should have told Mr. Clinton something.) If only he could be reelected in Arkansas, it seemed, he might be president someday. Ah, but would he have been reelected president? Or would a national electorate have delivered the same judgment Arkansas did Tuesday? The state's voters may have done Bill Clinton a service by giving him time to stop and reflect.

———————

When a convict out on Arkansas's early-release program killed a storekeeper in little Dumas, Arkansas, Uriah Heep could not have done a more unctuous job of distancing himself from the event than Bill Clinton, who as governor had seen to it that the state's prison board would take the responsibility if the wrong prisoners were released.

Some of us still remember the innocent victim, Laverne Sanderlin. The name of Bill Clinton's own Willie Horton was Larry Dean Robertson. But to make the connection between a governor and the responsibility he dodged requires knowing something about the history of early release in Arkansas:

THE HISTORY OF A CRIME
APRIL 24, 1987

Bill Clinton may not have some of the obvious qualifications for the presidency of the United States — like maturity, decisiveness, leadership, responsibility, great attachment to principle, or a splendid record in his home state — but he's got the nerve for the job. He has demonstrated that much once again, this time by his fulsome comments on the gruesome killing of a sixty-seven-year-old woman in her store at Dumas.

As a just-released convict was being arraigned in connection with the case, the governor called the killing a "terrible tragedy" that raised questions about the early release of prison inmates. It *was* a terrible thing, and it does raise such questions. But one would never guess from the governor's words or his manner that he himself was the pivotal figure in the policy that allowed the Board of Correction to release convicts early.

In his public comments, the governor was oh-so-understanding about the decision to release this suspect — as if this policy had originated with the prison board or Director Art Lockhart. "To be fair to the board and to Lockhart," he volunteered, "I don't think they saw it as a political thing. They were doing their best to do their job." Indeed they were — a job the governor had foisted on them. He kept talking about this case as if it were some unavoidable act of nature, rather than a clearly foreseeable consequence of his own policy.

It didn't require a clairvoyant in the fall of 1986 to see where the governor's manipulation of prison policy would surely lead. Even a little country newspaper like the *Pine Bluff Commercial* could spot the danger once legislators began talking about early release as the solution to the problem of prison crowding:

Warning: Easy Outs Ahead

The easy way to solve the problem of prison crowding is to let the prisoners out. It's easy on the prisoners, that is. It may be tough on society. But despite the danger, politicians will be tempted to release convicts rather than build more prisons and therefore have to ask for more taxes. It may seem economical to shorten sentences; think about all the state can save on their maintenance. But think again — about all the crimes that repeat offenders and parole violators commit — and it's clearer that early release is no bargain. . . .

If more prisons are needed, build them. If that means higher taxes, raise them. As an alternative to this simple approach, early release may look easy and economical — but it ain't necessarily so.

— *Pine Bluff Commercial*, November 30, 1986

Nor was it hard to spot Bill Clinton's slick hand when this transfer of authority was being made formal in the early weeks of the legislature:

Slick Willie Lives

How do you free more convicts from the state's prisons when the governor won't take the responsibility, and heat, for ordering their early release?

No problem. . . . You just rewrite the Prison Overcrowding Emergency Powers Act, which gives the governor power to declare an emergency and speed up paroles or authorize early release. You transfer that power to the Board of Correction. It isn't as accountable to the people, who tend to grow irked at the number of felons walking around after having served only a laughable fraction of their sentences. Now voters won't be able to blame the governor for that spectacle; he can pass the buck to the Board of Correction.

Under Senate Bill 233, sponsored by Clarence Bell and Jerry Bookout, the prisoners get out and the governor gets off the hook. Senator Bell, who described his proposal as an administration bill, explained its purpose and motive in a moment of colorful candor on the Senate floor: "It takes away the responsibility of the governor . . . Leroy don't want that ball." And neither does Slick Willie.

— *Pine Bluff Commercial*, February 8, 1987

This was the session when the governor managed to pass his responsibility for the early release of prisoners to an appointed body unaccountable to the public. Under this new set-up, the prison board had no real choice but to start releasing inmates when the governor and legislature failed to appropriate sufficient funds to hold them all. And the scene was set for inevitable tragedy. . . .

Larry Dean Robertson is not the only convicted felon to be granted early release under this new law. The prison gates have been opened for hundreds of others, and hundreds more are doubtless to follow. How many Laverne Sanderlins will pay for this policy? Considering the odds in favor of crimes being committed by repeaters, the decision to release these prisoners is a crime in itself — a crime in the broader sense of a grave offense against sense and society. And it is only aggravated by the governor's trying to pass the responsibility for it onto appointed officials beyond the reach of the people.

Except for an occasional ray of candor about this abdication of responsibility ("It takes away the responsibility of the governor . . . Leroy don't want that ball"), early release has been made to look as if it were the result of some impersonal mechanism, of some unavoidable bureaucratic necessity rather than the result of very human judgment, or rather misjudgment.

In the end, neither the governor who put this heedless policy into motion nor the legislators who assured its culmination can evade their responsibility for it. The Board of Correction and its director are the least to blame for what happens when scores of prisoners must be released early month after month. These appointed officials have been put in an untenable position by politicians in the legislature and in the Governor's Mansion. What we have here is not an act of God but of a governor who abandoned his duty and a legislature that refused to accept its. One of the abiding mysteries of Arkansas politics remains how, in the wake of such events, the state's governor and legislature can sleep o' nights.

Artful Dodger
April 4, 1990

Oooweee. Bill Clinton didn't like all those nosy reporters flocking around when he filed for re-re-re-reelection as governor and asking if he intended to complete his term if elected — rather than run for senator or president in 1992.

The governor showed little patience with these picadors from the press: "I have told you repeatedly that Dale Bumpers will run for reelection and I don't believe in running against an incumbent senator that's doing a good job. I am not going to run for another office. . . . Dale Bumpers doesn't have to worry about me and George Bush is about 80 percent in the polls. You think there's going to be a presidential race in '92?"

If the Democrats are brave enough to ask Bill Clinton to be their keynote speaker in '92, wouldn't that last line make a great opener? "George Bush is at 80 percent in the polls. You think there's going to be a presidential race in '92?" That would certainly get things off to a rousing start. And this guy has just been elected chairman of the Democratic Leadership Council. As a cheerleader, he makes a pretty good undertaker.

The governor might have been more patient with us inky wretches of the press if he had remembered that his oh-so-earnest assurances about what he would not run for haven't always panned out. Didn't he also leave the impression — repeatedly — the last time he ran for governor that he wouldn't run for the term he's now seeking? Could that have something to do with how pesky the press is on this subject? It's not as if his word were his bond in these matters.

Besides, before the question period and ordeal was over, the persistence of the press had paid off. Asked if he would rule out running for president, Slick Willie replied he couldn't "even imagine" that prospect, and he didn't have "any intention" of entering the presidential race. But he never actually said he wouldn't. What is *not* said in these exchanges tends to be more telling than what is.

Until the governor does tell the voters he'll stick out this term if he can, the questions will continue, and should.

If a single personal experience with Bill Clinton would make me never trust him again, it had to be a comment he made in the most offhand fashion in the fall of 1991. The scene was the annual luncheon for us country editors at the Governor's Mansion just as he was preparing to enter the coming presidential campaign. With Americans still in an exultant mood over victory in the Persian Gulf, Bill Clinton spoke — for what seemed forever — about what he wanted to do as president. At one point he mentioned almost in passing that he had supported George Bush when the president asked Congress to authorize the use of force in that crisis. I was shaken. That wasn't the way I remembered it at all. Could I have been mistaken? I asked him if he was sure about that, and he looked at me in the calmest way — I'm certain his heart didn't skip a beat — and said of course he was. That was what finally tore it for me:

SLICK WILLIE AND THE WAR
SEPTEMBER 20, 1991

This is a story about how political myths are made in time for presidential campaigns.

The other day, at a luncheon for editors at the Governor's Mansion in Little Rock, Bill Clinton referred to himself as an early supporter of the war in the Persian Gulf. Strange. I had remembered his saying he agreed with those who had *opposed* authorizing the president to use military force against Iraq last January.

When I expressed some surprise, the governor fixed me with his sincere look and explained that, no, he had sided with the majority on this issue.

The question could be of considerable interest, since Mr. Clinton shows every sign of running for president next year.

As soon as I got back to the office, I checked the files and, sure enough, there it was — an Associated Press story on Page 7a of the *Commercial* for Tuesday, January 15, 1991 — three days after the fateful vote in Congress:

Clinton Waffles on War Decision

LITTLE ROCK (AP) Gov. Bill Clinton says he understands both sides of the argument over whether to give President Bush the authority to attack Iraq, although he agrees with the side that lost.

Congress voted Saturday to allow Bush to use force against Iraq. Clinton declined to say how he would have voted.

"I agree with the arguments of the people in the minority on the resolution — that we should give sanctions more time and maybe even explore a full-scale embargo . . . before we go to war," Clinton said Monday.

The United Nations set today as the deadline for Iraq to get out of Kuwait. Clinton said the U.S. should support the unprecedented action. . . .

I read the crucial paragraph again to make certain I hadn't imagined it: "*I agree with the arguments of the people in the minority on the resolution — that we should give sanctions more time and maybe even explore a full-scale embargo . . . before we go to war," Clinton said Monday.*

The next step was to call the AP and make certain this was actually its story, not some strange fabrication in the pages of my newspaper. Sure enough, it was — word for telling word. Yet now the governor was being equally clear and emphatic in explaining why he had agreed with the majority and supported the president's position on the war.

Can the AP's account have been a misquote? I've seen misquotes before, but seldom one so long, so detailed, and in direct quotes.

Well, reporters do get confused. So do politicians, of course, and everybody's mind can play tricks. It took one of my friends some time after the war in the Gulf had been fought and won to speak of it as a just war. Victory tends to shed light on one's judgments, and Bill Clinton has never seemed one who would desert a president in his hour of victory.

Reading back over the original story, one can see how the governor's position could be interpreted after the fact to reflect either position. Emphasize some portions, omit others — especially that direct quote about agreeing with the arguments of the minority against using military force last January — and a flexible candidate could go either way nine months later.

I had seen stories that described the governor as an early supporter of the war, and assumed they were written by people who simply hadn't kept up with the news. Now, after hearing him make the same claim before a roomful of newspaper editors, I begin to suspect that those stories originated with the governor himself. What Bill Clinton had been was an early waffler on the war. If it had proved a disaster, he could easily have contended that he had opposed it all along, and cite that direct quote as prophecy. They don't call this guy Slick Willie for nothing.

However this confusion originated, it's good to have the governor finally and clearly on record in support of the president at a crucial juncture — even if the crucial juncture passed some time ago. But his waffling, and then saying he didn't, raises a more troubling question about his presidential ambitions than how he stood on the war: Is his ex-post-facto support for the war a lapse of memory or of character? (I have always had the greatest respect for the governor's memory.)

What is clear about this quick and convenient revision of history is that we have a campaign myth in the making — another triumph of imagination over history, and of merchandising over truth. Which may be one more reason Americans have come to hate politics.

Bill Clinton's presidential campaign of 1992 was a beautifully orchestrated mix of perfect waffles, classic clinton clauses, and Slick Willie-isms galore. A choice selection follows:

ON THE CAMPAIGN TRAIL
OCTOBER 13, 1991

"I want to lead the way," said Bill Clinton as he opened his presidential campaign, "because that's what we've tried to do in Arkansas. We've balanced the budget every year and we're improving services. . . ."

No need to go into detail, namely, that a governor of Arkansas has little choice but to balance the budget. This state's exemplary Revenue Stabilization Act (Ben Laney's great contribution to Arkansas history) makes an unbalanced budget illegal.

Speaking of improving services here in Arkansas, within two days after Bill Clinton announced for president, his administration was announcing that the state budget would have to be cut by $25 million to meet the requirements of the Revenue Stabilization Act.

About $2.4 million may be lost to the long neglected Division of Children and Family Services. It took a lawsuit before Bill Clinton moved to revamp that operation after a series of scandalous stories about abused children in foster care. That didn't keep him from saying in his announcement for president: "It is our ability to take care of our own at home that gives us the strength to stand up for what we believe around the world."

The ironies just keep coming. Forty-eight hours into the Clinton campaign, and the contrast between the bright young idealistic candidate for president and the slick customer who's been governor of Arkansas for more than a decade was already oppressive. . . .

JANUARY 10, 1992

Which is the real Bill Clinton?

Is it the one who blamed the absence of a national economic plan for General Motors's decision to close twenty-one of its plants? "I'm convinced this day would not have come," he said, "if our nation had a clear strategy to compete in the world economy. . . . We have got to have a plan. . . ." (Just what America needs as Communism collapses around the world: a planned economy.)

A few days later, candidate Clinton was back in his statesman mode on *ABC News,* saying he didn't want to play the "blame game" with

George Bush. Odds are he'll keep alternating between the high and low road, above-the-battle and in-the-thick-of-it, partisan and non-, all depending on his audience and the flow of the news.

So which is the real Bill Clinton?

The answer, one begins to suspect from a long history of smooth shifts, is that there is no real Bill Clinton.

Bill Clinton No. 2, the presidential candidate, has been billing himself as The Champion of the Middle Class. Bill Clinton No. 1, the governor whose regressive taxes have squeezed the middle class in Arkansas, apparently has been retired for the duration. Lest we forget, this state remains one of only eighteen in the Union that collects a sales tax on food and clothing. And that tax has been climbing and climbing during the Clinton Years. Under his plan, the poor got an overdue break on the state income tax, industry after industry got tax exemptions on an impressive scale, and the middle class got hit.

Candidate Clinton has a standard excuse for Governor Clinton's tax policy: a constitutional quirk that requires only a majority vote in the legislature for sales taxes but a three-quarters vote for the most progressive kind. The governor also notes that he once backed a constitutional amendment that would have addressed the problem, but the voters turned it down.

The usual innocent from the *New York Times* repeated this version of history in a wrap-up of the Clinton record the other day. No need to go into detail, namely: Governor Clinton quit after one try at reforming the state Constitution years ago. It took several attempts to extend his gubernatorial term to four years, yet his attitude toward tax reform seems to be: If at first you don't succeed, give up.

FEBRUARY 2, 1992

We would have had to revise our entire opinion of Bill Clinton's slippery politics, and maybe consider retiring the image of Slick Willie, if the governor had extended executive clemency to Rickey Ray Rector, who was executed last weekend after being convicted of killing a policeman. Clemency in this case would not have been the politically expedient thing to do three weeks before the New Hampshire primary.

To quote an AP dispatch: "The execution could help Democratic presidential candidate Clinton distance himself from his party's soft-on-
crime liberal image, said some political observers in New Hampshire."

Friday night's was a more than usually difficult execution. For a
painful time, the team assigned to it was unable to find a suitable vein
in which to inject the fatal dose, although the condemned man tried to
help. The way in which he died only added to the difficulties of his case,
for Rickey Ray Rector had shot out part of his own brain after killing
Bob Martin, a veteran Conway police officer. That was after he had
murdered a man and wounded two others in a senseless restaurant
shooting; Rickey Ray Rector had a long and violent record. And now
the state — that is, all of us — has convicted and executed a self-lobotomized defendant.

Yet none of this would have surprised more than Bill Clinton's deciding to grant clemency in this case, and thereby do something politically inexpedient. Now *that* would have been a shock.

MARCH 17, 1992

What Bill Clinton thinks, or says he thinks, about an issue may
depend on when and where you catch him in his career trajectory, and
what constituency he's courting at the moment. The one sure thing
about his policy *du jour* is that it will be designed to maintain his
"political viability within the system." The phrase is from a letter he
wrote as a twenty-three-year-old Rhodes Scholar, and in that regard he
hasn't changed a bit. Moderate or liberal, trickle-down conservative or
wild-eyed populist, in Arkansas or out, he is faithful in his fashion. Bill
Clinton's lode star has always been his own political advancement.
Such an ambition saves a man from tragedy because it saves him from
significance.

In Howard Nemerov's verse play about the Witch of Endor, a minis-
ter to poor King Saul, having watched the king learn his fate from the
witch, asks to be told his, too. Shall he fight with the Israelites on the
morrow, or join the Philistines in victory? The witch explains that it
scarcely matters:

> I think
> Men of your sort, though they have lives and deaths,
> Never have fates. Maybe because they have

Their cleverness instead, their light, dry minds
Which blow in the wind of fortune back and forth,
They can have many meanings, no one meaning.

Poor Bill Clinton: He's So Misunderstood

April 23, 1992

There long has been a barely perceptible whine when Bill Clinton speaks of his political fortunes, and how people have mistreated and misunderstood him. But not before his speech at a Little Rock fundraiser Monday evening did he transform that deep natural sympathy for himself into a campaign theme. This is not a good omen — for him, his campaign, or the country. Our governor and native son would do better to take his cue from Harry Truman, who gave 'em Hell rather than confuse self-pity with a campaign tactic. He's not running for the lead in a melodrama but for president of the United States, and the criticism and scrutiny have hardly begun.

"A lot of people criticize me," he told his supporters, "because I get along with people." This was his way of referring to accusations that he's too cozy with the state's special interests. His defense: "I thought the object of politics was to get things done. The object of politics in Washington for too long has been to ignore getting anything done but always make sure you're postured right on the evening news."

He doesn't get it, does he? It's not what Bill Clinton has done so much as what he has failed to do that bothers some of us — like failing to lift Arkansas above the forty-ninth rung in the Union when it comes to median income.

Beyond the wonderworld of campaign brochures and slick PR, the list of what Bill Clinton has *not* done in Arkansas is pretty darned impressive: He has not reformed an unfair tax structure; he's actually aggravated it considerably for that middle class he talks so sympathetically about. Outside a few, well-publicized cases, he has not consolidated our multitudinous school districts. He has not built a great university or passed civil rights and fair-housing laws, tightened up on prison furloughs and early releases, or reformed the Constitution. He has not avoided conflicts of interest, or kept our rivers and streams and air pure, or cracked down on crime despite his election-year enthusiasm for executions . . . though he has always managed to talk a great game about almost everything.

When it comes to posturing himself, on the evening news or anywhere else, Bill Clinton is no slouch. He started out as a moderate speaking for a New Covenant of responsibility between government and the governed. He put that idea in temporary storage when he positioned himself as a Southern populist against Paul Tsongas, preparatory to changing back into his Practical-Pol-Who-Gets-Things-Done costume when his opponent was Governor Moonbeam [a reference to California's Jerry Brown].

Is there an interest, special or ordinary, that Bill Clinton hasn't pandered to by now? In the New York primary, he came as close to being all things to all men, women, children, and ethnic groups as any politician who ever told the people exactly what they wanted to hear. Even now it's not clear whether he's for or against Right-to-Work, or for or against limiting welfare benefits to single parents, or was really for or against the war in the Persian Gulf. . . . It all seems to depend on when and where he's talking, and to whom.

"I have proved one thing —" says Bill Clinton. "I'm not very slick: I often say something I shouldn't. It makes the evening news just a little bit off-kilter so that characterization they like to make of me can be reinforced one more time." Not bad. Indeed, a fairly artful way to dodge the charge that he's an artful dodger. But what other candidate would be sufficiently slick to talk his way past the weekly, almost daily, scandals, near-scandals, and non-scandals that have come raining down on his parade?

If the newspaper that first identified the governor's inseparable alter ego as Slick Willie may offer still another piece of gratuitous advice: Sir, avoid the word "slick" in any campaign speech, just as you would not mention rope in the house of a man who was hanged. It does not help. On the contrary, it encapsulates all it is in your political interest to suppress.

We remember listening to the governor go on for hours — it seemed days — about exactly how he would have answered each and every accusation against Michael Dukakis. (Now there was a fellow who deserved some pity, though he never sought any.) The striking thing about Slick Willie's critique of the Dukakis campaign that long, long afternoon in 1988 was that it concentrated solely on rhetoric, on what Mike Dukakis should have said and how he should have said it, and not at all on the substance of the campaign.

One issue of substance is already emerging in the campaign of 1992: character. When Bill Clinton isn't dismissing it as not a "real" issue, he seems unable to get a grip on it. As if in all innocence he can't understand what it is about him, or rather about his slippery turns and neat evasions, that seems to bother voters, including many who cast their ballot for him in the primaries. He just doesn't get it. It's as if he were trying to communicate with the American people across some unbridgeable gap, some sensibility that he himself hasn't much developed, and therefore doesn't think is "real." Like character.

A pioneer in the theater of the absurd once wrote a play about six characters in search of an author. For sheer absurdity, an American presidential campaign would put any piece of mere fiction to shame. It now seems to have produced a leading candidate in search of his character.

Bill Clinton said one more thing at Little Rock the other evening: "It is time that we grew up and recognize that we have to make tough choices." Good advice. He almost always seems to *say* the right thing.

SLICK WILLIE DENIES IT
JULY 29, 1992

Here's hoping Bill Clinton is feeling all right.

Usually he glides past tough questions with the greatest of ease, stretching and bending the truth perhaps, but rarely if ever indulging in simple, straightforward, honest falsehood. I might feel better about him if he did; it would be less slick.

There is a certain charm in the story about one of the Longs of Louisiana who, when an angry delegation showed up to complain that he had not fulfilled some campaign promise, told his press secretary just what to say: "Tell 'em I lied!"

Such candor is not the Clinton style, which tends toward the disingenuous rather than the lie outright. Maybe it's the lawyer in him. Anyway, just before his triumph at the Democratic National Convention, the governor ran into this tough question in an interview with

Newsweek magazine: "You have promised to name a pro-choice justice if you're elected. If Bush said outright that he had a pro-life litmus test, something you've criticized, is having a pro-choice standard any different?"

Good question.

But instead of trying the usual end-run that so many of us Clinton-watchers have come to know and despise, The Candidate chose to brazen it out: "The only point I have made about this whole issue," he claimed, "is that I want to appoint somebody who has an expansive view of the Bill of Rights and believes in the right to privacy." Not true. Almost immediately after the Supreme Court of the United States handed down its latest decision in the ongoing abortion controversy, Bill Clinton made the point that his nominees to the Supreme Court would be Pro-Choice: "I would appoint judges to the Supreme Court with a long history of advocacy of the Bill of Rights, including the right of privacy and including the right to choose."

As if to remove any doubt about his litmus test for appointees to the court, Bill Clinton proceeded to tell a rally in favor of a right to abortion: "As president I won't make you worry about the 'one justice away' on the Supreme Court of the United States." (The court had just upheld the general principle of *Roe v. Wade*, the magna carta of abortion, by only one vote.)

And finally, in an interview with *NBC News*, The Candidate named the one specific decision his nominees to the Supreme Court would have to uphold: "I would want to know that *Roe v. Wade* would be secure."

Now he says the only point he made was that nominees should be attached to the Bill of Rights and the right to privacy. The Candidate's acute memory is well known; this chain of statements illustrates that he also has a powerful forgettery when convenient. Instead of talking his way out of an unwise commitment, he has simply denied making it. A rare forthrightness.

Maybe he was overworked just before the convention. By the time it was over, The Candidate was back on the road — on a slow bus through Pennsylvania — and pacifying a questioner who didn't seem to think *Roe v. Wade* should be the final word on abortion after all.

"In a democracy," Bill Clinton [said], "not everything that is wrong can be made criminal. My belief is that you should have the right to argue that all day long. When you've got the American people split down the middle . . . I believe you should let them argue it out." Not exactly a reversal on *Roe v. Wade,* but not exactly the same ringing endorsement he had given it earlier, either. This was more like the familiar Bill Clinton, the great broken-field runner who can slip and slide his way past any issue great or small, legal or ethical.

Oh, yes, that interview with *Newsweek* contained another particularly delicious quote from the governor. It came in answer to the question, "How do you respond to the charge that you're 'Slick Willie'?"

His reply: "It is a bum rap. It is a bogus, bum rap."

So emphatic a denial hasn't been heard since another great American statesman, Richard Nixon, declaimed: "I am not a crook."

REPUBLICANS JUST DON'T GET IT
AUGUST 7, 1992

The sum total of the political savvy, historical tradition, creative juices, and general intelligence of the Republican Party of the United States, which in the past has produced leaders and martyrs like Lincoln, sources of raw energy like Teddy Roosevelt, pillars of integrity like both Tafts, and landslide winners on the order of Dwight Eisenhower and Ronald Reagan, may best be described this year by a simple phrase that I used to hear applied to certain of my fellows when I was growing up in these Southern latitudes:

"Not only don't he know much, but he don't suspect a helluva lot." . . .

George Bush has accused his rival of secretly being — horrors! — a liberal. This was doubtless supposed to shock and alarm. What it did was bore. The dreaded L-word ain't what it used to be. The Republican Party's mainly titular leader in this campaign seems unaware not only of the lateness of the hour, but of what year it is. Does George Bush think he's still running against Michael Dukakis in 1988? He acts as if he's running in 1980 — not against a demoralized, increasingly irrelevant Jimmy Carter but *as* Jimmy Carter that year: malaise personified.

The charge that Bill Clinton is a closet liberal does him too much credit. It implies that somewhere he has an identifiable political philosophy. Who would believe that? Open his political closet and there's nothing there. Or rather, it's crammed full of political identities for every occasion.

Back in March, when the presidential campaign was still young, David Shribman of the *Wall Street Journal* chronicled just a few of Bill Clinton's fast changes:

> The candidate who began the race defending himself against charges that he was a "warmed over Republican" scored his breakthrough against Paul Tsongas in part by questioning the Democratic credentials of the former Massachusetts senator. The man who started out as a Democratic moderate found himself courting the Democratic left. The Arkansas governor who positioned himself as a friend to business criticized his rival as being a creature of Wall Street. The contender who called for shifting spending from defense to domestic matters came out two weeks before the Connecticut primary in favor of continuing production of the Seawolf nuclear submarine, which was to be built in Connecticut, and which even the Bush administration now opposes. . . .

And that was just back in March.

As the campaign changed, so did Bill Clinton, at every turn. He ran against Tom Harkin as a moderate, against Paul Tsongas as a liberal, and against Jerry Brown as a conservative. His political coloration changed with every challenge. What he thinks, or says he thinks, seems to depend on where you catch him in his political trajectory.

The one predictable aspect of Bill Clinton's philosophy *du jour* is that it will be designed "to maintain my political viability within the system." That revealing phrase is from a letter he wrote as a twenty-three-year-old Rhodes Scholar to explain why he wasn't going to act on his beliefs and openly resist the draft. The student was father to the man.

Then and now, Bill Clinton's chief political principle has been his own political advancement. Moderate or liberal, in Arkansas or out, trickle-down conservative or populist orator, young or less young, he has never deviated from that single, obsessive goal. Such ambition saves a fellow from being a liberal — or anything else. No wonder George Bush's accusation fell flat.

People earn their names, just as George Orwell said we earn our faces after forty. Certain sobriquets become public currency not because they are particularly clever or artful, but because they're inescapable. Everett Dirksen had to be the Wizard of Ooze, and Thomas E. Dewey the little man on top of the wedding cake, and no one was ever much in doubt about the identity of Tricky Dick. The same with Slick Willie.

Credit for the popularity of Slick Willie as shorthand for the political persona of Bill Clinton must go chiefly to Bill Clinton himself; he vindicated that title through years of diligent effort. To claim that his vacuous zigs and zags are really only a cover for liberalism, or for any other coherent political philosophy, is to miss the central theme of his career, and to overlook what is most vulnerable about his appeal this year.

The GOP now has accused Bill Clinton of having character, if only a liberal one. His opponents are taking careful, deliberate aim at his strongest points, ignoring his weakest. But that's the Republicans so far in this campaign: They don't seem to know much, or even suspect a helluva lot.

BILL CLINTON VS. HISTORY
AUGUST 10, 1992

Bill Clinton would have made a great editor; he never tires of changing words about.

It happened again the other day, when a spokesman for the Bush campaign finally caught on to the game Bill Clinton was playing in January of '91, when the country was debating whether the president should use force against Saddam Hussein in the Persian Gulf. While others were debating this question in good faith, whatever position they took, Bill Clinton discreetly agreed with both sides.

Only later, when the president's policy proved successful, would The Candidate endorse it without reservation. Bill Clinton is not a man to desert his country in its hour of victory. [When his actual views at the time were exposed] Slick Willie swung back almost immediately with his blue pencil, deftly editing history to make his mushy stand for, against, and neutral on the war look like some kind of Churchillian foresight. Anybody who didn't remember his exact words — and I had to look them up — might have been fooled. . . .

Which does not make his falsehood notably different from many of the things other politicians say, and doubtless from some things you and I have said and lived to regret. What appalls, what makes the hair on the back of my neck stand up, is that it is almost true, that it is so neatly, almost surgically, edited a falsehood. . . .

If only Arkansas's governor were not running for another position just now, he would make a great addition to the staff of the Ministry of Truth in George Orwell's *1984*. That was the outfit charged with constantly updating history to make it conform to current aims. Bill Clinton's newspeak is perfect.

Winston Churchill used to claim that history would justify his policies, particularly because he intended to be the one to write it. In Churchill, that was a witticism. In Bill Clinton, it's a policy.

For months now, Governor Clinton has been falsifying his position on the war. Rather than face up to what he really said, and what he declined to say, he has simply added to the chain of falsehoods, getting smoother at it each time. And deeper into a kind of automythology. It's scary. There is something scarier about these games, and that is the possibility that The Candidate has become so practiced at falsity, he's not aware of what he's doing — that it has become natural for him. The first time I saw him pull this routine about how he had supported the president on the war — at the Governor's Mansion last September — I could swear his innocent, blue-green eyes didn't even blink. I certainly was fooled — until I raced back to consult the files at the newspaper. His latest and even smoother rendition is enough to bring back a passage from Henry Adams's novel, *Democracy:* "The audacity of the man would have seemed sublime if she had felt sure that he knew the difference between good and evil, between a lie and the truth; but the more she saw of him, the surer she was that his courage was mere moral paralysis, and that he talked about virtue and vice as a man who is color-blind talks about red and green. . . . Was it politics that had caused this atrophy of the moral senses?"

Whatever the cause — and there are enough two-bit psychoanalyses of Bill Clinton floating around media-land these days to fill a copy of *Cosmopolitan* — this is still no way to treat words. Or history. Or truth. Or oneself.

Perhaps the most honest and certainly the most revealing document Bill Clinton ever wrote was his letter to the ROTC colonel who unwittingly helped him avoid military service. Two decades later, a presidential candidate, he would do his best to ignore, reinterpret, disown,

*and generally dismiss that remarkable document. He may even have
thought the only copy remaining had been safely destroyed years
before. How was he to know that Colonel Eugene J. Holmes had kept
his own copy all those years?*

All the Candidate's Men
September 21, 1992

It is like a Southern novel, namely *All the King's Men* by Robert
Penn Warren. Not for the first time in these latitudes, where events seldom occur only once, history imitates art. One can never know when
it will happen, only that it will. And sure enough, one slow September
evening when the nation's attention is elsewhere, there arrives a letter
from an old colonel about a young presidential candidate, and the familiar story of honor and dishonor, power and corruption, unfolds again.
Jack Burden steps off the page and one can almost hear his ironic voice:

> So I had it after all these months. For nothing is lost, nothing
> is ever lost. There is always the clue, the canceled check, the
> smear of lipstick, the footprint in the canna bed, the condom on
> the park path, the twitch in the old wound, the baby shoes dipped
> in bronze, the taint in the blood stream. And all times are one
> time, and all those dead in the past never lived before our defini-
> tion gives them life, and out of the shadows their eyes implore us.
>
> That is what all of us historical researchers believe.
>
> And we love truth.

Fifty years after the words were written in a Louisiana still under
Huey Long's shadow, an editor at a newspaper in Little Rock, Arkansas,
reads a letter in the form of a FAX transmission, and silently watches
the evidence and counter-evidence unscroll on his computer screen as
The Candidate's camp responds. The technology and times are different, but nothing fundamental has changed.

Politics can be a low and sordid carnival, and the journalism that
feeds on it lower and more sordid still. Jack Burden knew he was in a
wretched if necessary trade, having found what he sought but did not
want to find. Yet there come times, like Thursday evening, as one
watches the fragmented trust unfold more than twenty years later,
when even a newspaperman may feel some inkling of what the ancients

called awe. Truth is a fearsome thing, patient but inexorable, and to watch it close in is to be in the presence of a kind of majesty.

Whenever another string of his story would unravel, Bill Clinton would say that everyone, or almost everyone, or "the principals" involved in his negotiations with the draft twenty years ago were all dead. Eugene J. Holmes, Colonel, U.S.A. (Ret.), isn't. Not yet. Though he is already living with ghosts. They crowd this letter of his — the faces of his comrades from Bataan and the Death March, "the fine young soldiers whose deaths I have witnessed," his fellow prisoners of war in Japanese camps for three and a half years, and his brother Bob — killed during the Second World War and buried in England at twenty-three, the age of Bill Clinton when he was a Rhodes Scholar at Oxford and playing games with the colonel and the ROTC program at the University of Arkansas.

On the computer screen, the Clinton campaign's fine defensive ends were already going into practiced action. It would have been a mistake to attack the colonel. Even the misspellings, the Army syntax, the ragged prose of his letter added to its impression of veracity. Instead, the Clinton team cited the politic excuses the colonel had made for the governor earlier, before The Candidate's story had unraveled, and his presidential campaign knitted. . . . "It is very sad that someone has exploited the failing memory of a fine military leader," went Thursday's line. Governor Clinton was reported attending a fund-raiser hosted by Barbra Streisand somewhere in California at the time, and was unavailable for comment.

Perhaps it was just as well. Whom would you believe — the shaky old colonel with his ghosts, or the young and nationally acclaimed candidate whose blue-green eyes don't even flicker when he tells less than the truth?

I know whom I believe.

Yes, all in all, it was better strategy to have Betsey Wright, the best explainer in the business, insist: "There was no deceit." Bill Clinton himself was more honest, at least when he was twenty-three and wrote the colonel, "I began to think that I had deceived you, not by lies — there were none — but by failing to tell you all the things I'm writing now." The boy was father to the man; even now Bill Clinton is seldom if ever so straightforward as to lie outright.

The Candidate and his candidacy doubtless will get by this week's revelation without being overly inconvenienced, so the campaign can get back to "real" issues — by which is meant anything other than truth and character and history. After all, what is the word of an old colonel in today's mod America?

But who doubts that there will be other revelations? Will they come before or after Mr. Clinton's inauguration as president of the United States and commander-in-chief of the armed forces?

Does it matter just when the next break in the story comes? For the presidency of the United States is not only a political distinction. Such is its history (History again!) that the office cannot be exercised without some minimal moral authority. Just ask Richard Nixon. Watching Bill Clinton in these still opening phases of his denial, one cannot escape a mild seizure of Déjà Vu. Here is another skillful, clever politician who has woven a tangled web. How long before he, too, is issuing the next in a long succession of "final" statements on this story that will not go away? . . .

———————

No definition of Clintonism would be complete without noting its lack of definition, which allows its chief practitioner to take any side of any issue as needed:

BILL CLINTON *Is* A PRESIDENTIAL DEBATE

OCTOBER 2, 1992

Anyone still worried that the country will miss out on presidential debates this election year needn't fret. Bill Clinton, the president-presumptive according to the polls, has taken enough diametrically opposed positions on various issues to provide material for a whole series of debates — with himself.

The Bush-Quayle campaign has compiled an extensive list of Bill Clinton's contradictory positions on everything from free trade to school vouchers, which is no great feat. They're all part of the voluminous record. What impresses is that the Republicans were able to stop after citing only twenty or thirty such self-refutations. Talk about restraint. Clinton vs. Clinton could go on interminably. And often does. The Comeback Kid is never sharper than when he takes on the Democratic presidential nominee. For example:

"I would present a five-year plan to balance the budget," Clinton told Larry King's listeners early in June. A couple of weeks later, he strongly disagreed: "My plan will cut the deficit in half within four years."

"I want to make it very clear," he said in January, "that this middle-class tax cut, in my view, is central to any attempt we're going to make to have a short-term economic strategy, which is part of getting this country moving again." To which Governor Clinton responded forcefully in March: ". . . to say that this middle-class tax cut . . . is the center of anybody's (economic) package is wrong."

Any confusion was really the media's fault, one of the Bill Clintons responded in June: ". . . I would emphasize to you that the press and my opponents always made more of the middle-class tax cut than I did."

In October of 1990, Governor Clinton described himself as "fascinated" by the idea of government vouchers to finance attendance at private schools. In June of this year, the other Governor Clinton shot back in a speech to the teachers' lobby: "We shouldn't give our money away to private schools (and) undermine the integrity of the public school system."

Bill Clinton can denounce class war ("No more division by race, no more division by income, no more class warfare" — March 18, 1992) on the same night his campaign engages in it. ("In making the rich pay their fair share, Bill Clinton — he'll put people first." — Clinton campaign ad, March 18, 1992.)

"I wouldn't rule out term limits," the Democratic presidential nominee said last January, but he was rebutted by the governor of Arkansas in a July interview with the *Boston Globe:* "I'm against term limits because I think that it takes choices away from the voters."

Bill Clinton has debated Bill Clinton on any number of other topics — productivity, federal spending, the free-trade agreement with Mexico, welfare. . . . Some psychiatrists would kill for this kind of interior dialogue; imagine the material it would provide for articles in the leading psychoanalytical journals. *The Three Faces of Eve* had nothing on The Campaign Stands of Bill, which ought to be published in loose-leaf form.

Much depends on which audience the distinguished nominee or his sleazy alter ego, Slick Willie, is addressing at the time. (It's getting harder and harder to tell them apart.) On such occasions, he's less a speaker than a reflecting mirror of his audience's most cherished prejudices. Before a campus crowd at Drexel University in April, The Candidate emphasized fuel-efficient cars for the future ("forty miles per gallon by the year 2000, forty-five miles per gallon by 2020") but was rebuffed by his old moderate self before the Detroit Economic Club in August: "I don't think it's fair to impose a burden on an American fleet that has bigger cars in it than foreign competitors do. . . ."

As for his multitudinous collection of Final Statements on the draft, put them together and you've got an entire encyclopedia of arguments pro, con, both, neither, relevant and irrelevant, true and false on the subject. You casts your vote and you takes your choice: Patriot or something else, fighter for his beliefs or slick pol, Bill Clinton or Bill Clinton. He opposed the draft and supported it, gave up his ROTC deferment and had it withdrawn, never received a draft notice, and got one late, didn't have an ROTC deferment and gave it up, subjected himself to the draft out of concern for fairness and solely to preserve his "political viability," was told about his uncle's pulling strings to keep him out of the draft and it was all news to him, didn't get any special treatment but only the sort reserved for young men with his education and connections. . . .

Ditto, the various Clintons explaining his (non)stand on the war in the Persian Gulf, a conflict one opposed, the other supported, and still another left to David Pryor and Dale Bumpers to handle.

Bill Clinton could have a two-man, maybe a three-man, debate on a wide variety of issues in this presidential contest all by himself. When accused of being a slick, unprincipled, double-dealing pol, he has an effective answer in this modern age: George Bush is another. Didn't the president break his promise not to raise taxes?

There may have been an age, biblical or even as late as medieval, when the species was capable of distinguishing between a broken promise (like Bill Clinton's pledge not to run for president this year) and a lie, but it is long since past. Who's got time for that kind of detail in this Age of Teevee? It would be like trying to explain the difference between Augustine and Aquinas in a twenty-second sound bite.

The trick is just to mention Read My Lips, Iran-Contra, and the economy, the economy, the economy, and hurtle on. Then nobody'll notice, and if anybody does, make it seem too complicated to explain — or explain it at such length that everybody will be relieved to drop the subject. Bill Clinton is one of those rare and gifted politicians who can make boredom an ally. It's worked beautifully so far.

THE BONELESS WONDER

OCTOBER 9, 1992

Surely to no one's surprise, Bill Clinton now has come out for and against free trade. He's for it in principle but against the current free-trade agreement with Mexico, though not entirely. He would change it but, he assures, not renegotiate it. (Which should be a neat trick.) He would add just a few clauses, commissions, controls, and programs here and there, and leave it to somebody else — in this case, his running mate — to work out the details.

It all sounds familiar to anybody who has watched my absentee governor operate in Arkansas. Back home, he's all for tax reform, and has appointed so many commissions to study it that the state's tax code has become more regressive than ever. Mainly because, in his even-handed way, he's okayed tax exemptions at a record clip and raised the sales tax to new heights in order to balance his talk about tax fairness.

Other examples of the crushing Clinton touch abound:

He's so much for the environment, and has appointed so many committees to study it, that nothing much has been done to protect it. He has, however, managed to keep the state's environmental commission relatively free of environmentalists.

He's all for school reform but school consolidation has scarcely progressed. Consolidating some of this small state's 300-plus school districts being (a) the chief requirement for an efficient educational system, and (b) politically sensitive, the whole subject has been given a good leaving-alone.

As chairman of the lily-white Lower Mississippi Delta Development Commission, Bill Clinton handed out millions in patronage for rehashes of old studies without much noticeable effect on the Lower Mississippi Delta, which continues to bear an unsettling resemblance to the Third World. Somewhere one of his commissions is supposed to be writing a civil rights law for the state, which still doesn't have one after a decade of Clintonesque rhetoric about his devotion to the cause of racial justice.

He's been so interested in health care that the state's Department of Human Services has been put through one fiscal crisis after another during his frequent absences. Result: Both those who provide the care and those who receive it keep getting shortchanged despite the most solemn promises, which the Clinton administration now has forgiven itself for making.

Just as Al Gore is going to handle free trade in the Clinton administration, Bill Clinton's lieutenant and acting governor, Jim Guy Tucker, has been left to tie up loose ends in Arkansas. On balance, he might prefer to tackle the Augean Stables.

Bill Clinton is all for law enforcement, too, but one couldn't tell it by the continued crowding in the state's prisons. The chronic crisis in the prisons is being alleviated by turning convicts loose on the public at an alarming rate. Occasionally they may maim or kill, whereupon Governor Clinton will send his condolences and hint strongly that something is wrong with the way the prisons are being administered — as if he were just visiting the state. Which of course he is these presidential days. The governor and presidential candidate, certainly not in that order, tends to be too busy analyzing problems like crime actually to do much about them. The crisis over how to pay attorneys who defend the indigent in criminal cases, for example, continues to produce courtroom confrontations between judges and county government. But, what, Bill Clinton worry? He's only governor.

Now he's taken another (non)stand calculated to please all and unlikely to accomplish anything. Those opposed to the trade agreement with Mexico can take comfort from his shilly-shallying; those in favor of free trade can be assured that Bill Clinton is with them in principle, which in his case means little.

What a show.

The Candidate is most impressive when he puts his sax aside and goes into his statesmanship number. Just listen to those phrases roll: "The most difficult problem in modern politics, and therefore in this presidential election, is this simplistic and superficial labeling of complex issues."

For the most difficult problem in mod politics, others might nominate those leaders who have never met an issue they couldn't finesse or a special interest they couldn't entice. Result: The country is given no direction, no leadership, and plenty of high-minded guff.

Surely no one is better at complicating the simple than Bill Clinton, at least when opposing political forces are arrayed on both sides of an issue. The classic example: He might have voted to authorize the use of force in the Persian Gulf in a close vote, he said, but he agreed with the arguments of those who opposed it, he also said.

Now he's all for this trade agreement with Mexico if secondary agreements can be attached to create controls, commissions, and complications. You can imagine how much this must assure the Mexicans — or anybody who had planned to buy, sell, work, hire, or invest in this new and once promising free-trade zone. The treaty's actually taking shape in any form other than study commissions and bureaucratic promises may have to be postponed for the duration of the Clinton Era.

Bill Clinton is proving about as much use when it comes to this agreement with Mexico as Woodrow Wilson found the Republican reservationists in the Senate when he was trying to get the League of Nations approved. They didn't want to destroy the League, just gut it. Bill Clinton doesn't want to derail this historic expansion toward free trade, just place a lot of clauses, commissions, and controls on the tracks.

Our mod leader remains masterful at drift, definitely for indecision, and determined to be indeterminate. Mounting his horse and riding off in all directions, Bill Clinton proposes to lead us anywhere we want to go unanimously. He's ready to take on the world so long as he doesn't offend a single interest or voting bloc. If he were not the star of a presidential election but the feature of some other tasteless exhibition, there would be no problem about how to bill his act: The Boneless Wonder.

ONE MORE BETRAYAL
JULY 23, 1993

Bill Clinton now has announced a policy toward homosexuals serving in the military that is waffling, tricky, and without honor. It amounts to one more breach of faith with those who believed his campaign promises. Naturally he described his new policy as practical, principled, and honorable. At least he spared the country any reference to character.

The president and commander-in-chief spoke of his (not so) new policy as a compromise. He would have been closer to the mark if he had described it as compromised — politically, legally, ethically.

Politically, this is no mere retreat; it's a rout. One might as well call Napoleon's departure from Russia a strategic withdrawal. During the campaign, Bill Clinton said he was going to ban discrimination against homosexuals in the armed services — not stitch it carefully into the country's military policy with clauses, sub-clauses, rebuttable presumptions, and the same old double standard.

Homosexual conduct (unlike the heterosexual variety) will remain grounds for separation from military service. Even homosexual speech may prove grounds for dismissal.

A homosexual who wants to stay in the service better not act like one, or even talk like one. Homosexuals will not be asked formally to deny their sexuality on entering the service, but any statement to that effect will be held against them. It will be a "rebuttable presumption." This from the candidate who solemnly promised to treat homosexuals as equal citizens.

Under the new Clinton Plan, just as under the old system he attacked during the campaign, homosexual conduct will be taboo. Someone like Colonel Margarethe Cammermeyer would still be forced to leave the ranks after years of distinguished service. Legal action against homosexuals in the military, put on hold for the past six months, presumably will be reactivated. Thanks, Mr. President.

Legally, the latest Clinton Waffle invites confusion. Already federal courts have ruled against precisely the kind of discrimination now formally approved by the commander-in-chief. The surest effect of the president's announcement Monday will be a lengthening body of contradictory case law. Courts military and civil will now have to deal with questions like: When is an admission of homosexuality grounds for dismissal? When does speech become conduct? Whenever sound judgment and moral leadership are absent, niggling rules and regulations will multiply.

There is nothing to prevent a commander with a thing about homosexuals from hounding them out of the service under these new and easily twisted rules. Witch hunts haven't been abolished; they will just have to be conducted more cleverly. Informers are explicitly relied on under this "new" policy.

"As your commander-in-chief," Mr. Clinton told his audience at the National War College, "I charge all of you to carry out this policy with fairness." A question: How to carry out an unfair policy fairly? No doubt the same way one carries out a confused policy clearly. Barry Goldwater, Mr. Conservative himself, never stood taller than when he came out unequivocally for respecting the rights of homosexuals in the military.

Ethically, this abandonment of still another group of gullibles was particularly smooth. Mr. Clinton's familiar alter ego, Slick Willie, never seemed so much in charge of White House decisions, or rather machinations.

The Clinton Policy scatters traps everywhere — in the name of eliminating them. At least the previous policy of hunting down homosexuals in the military made no pretense of fairness; they knew what to expect. Now they're told they're free from suspicion — except when they talk or act like homosexuals, or someone else thinks they do. Rules that were clear but unfair have been replaced by rules that are cloudy but unfair. No doubt this will be described as a great moral and ethical advance.

If he had kept his campaign promise, the president argues, Congress would only have reversed it. So he reversed it himself. In the Age of Clinton, this is called leadership. None yet dare call it character or justice, but the new, clintonized vocabulary should soon subvert these concepts, too. Words like "honorable" and "fair" are pretty much gone even now.

The Candidate who promised to do away with discrimination against homosexuals in the military has begun his tenure as commander-in-chief by negotiating away his authority — to the Joint Chiefs, to his own secretary of defense, and to congressional powers like Sam Nunn. In the newly clintonized vocabulary of American politics, this will be called leadership, vision, progress, idealism. . . . You can feel old words lose their meaning and force every day of this administration.

"It is not a perfect solution," the president acknowledges. He's right about its not being perfect; he's wrong about its being a solution. It's a craven mishmash disguised as a policy. It's the same old persecution of homosexuals clouded over by a lot of High Popalorum and Low Popahirum. Bill Clinton's legalisms on this occasion would have done justice to Tricky Dick Nixon at one of his more moralistic moments. Spokesmen for various homosexual groups sound shocked — shocked! — to discover that the president can't be trusted. "We elected a leader and got a barometer," complains Tom McFeeley of the Human Rights Campaign Fund. Like this is news.

The policy of Don't Ask, Don't Tell represents "a capitulation to bigotry and political expedience," says Thomas B. Stoddard of the Campaign for Military Service. The most surprising aspect of such comments is how surprised those making them sound.

Didn't these guys notice what has been happening since the election
— to the Haitians, to the middle class, to Lani Guinier, to anybody who
believed what The Candidate said about campaign reform or Bosnia or
getting tough with Red China . . . or you name it?

Only when their own, particular interest was betrayed did they catch
on. Which is what the smoothest of political operators count on —
being able to sneak out of one commitment after another without jeop-
ardizing their support in general.

They say you can't cheat an honest man. Well, you can't fool people
who care about the integrity of the political process, about character
and honesty — or at least you can't fool them more than once. But those
who care only about their own single issue, and will accept every other
cave-in as smart politics, are the natural prey of the Slick Willies of the
world. Tom McFeeley and Thomas Stoddard have no beef. They backed
this guy, and they didn't complain when justice was denied others. Why
should they think they were going to be the exception? The pity is that
such a performance no longer surprises, that it hasn't surprised in some
time. What's so unusual about Bill Clinton's turning still another clear
issue into a complex machiavellian negotiation? His politics is simple
enough to summarize: Don't Ask, Don't Tell, Don't Keep Your Word.
That the president has broken another vow is scarcely the stuff of ban-
ner headlines. Such "news" no longer excites or even repels. What continues to trouble is the politics he represents — a politics without
meaning or trust or any purpose except to please everybody a little and
get reelected.

To quote a source condemned to report on Bill Clinton's career over
the years,

> "it is not the duplicitousness in his politics that concerns so much
> as the polished ease, the almost habitual, casual, articulate way
> he bobs and weaves. He has mastered the art of equivocation.
> There is something almost inhuman in his smoother responses
> that sends a shiver up the spine. It is not the compromises he has
> made that trouble so much as the unavoidable suspicion that he
> has no great principles to compromise."
>
> — *Arkansas Democrat-Gazette,* October 28, 1992

THE GHOST OF CHRISTMAS PAST
DECEMBER 20, 1993

It was last year just about this time. A new shining president-elect was putting his promises into . . . more promises. A distinguished transition team was at work right here in little ol' Little Rock. Briefings for the press were held in the old M. M. Cohn building off Metrocentre Mall. Day after day, the little alley that borders the building was lined with limos.

Night after night brought new announcements as the victors distributed the spoils, though the process was never described so bluntly or accurately. On the contrary, the press releases rang with new Guidelines and Parameters that would forever banish corruption from Washington. Reform was in the air; you could almost smell its sweetish odor, like that of something already beginning to decay.

In the temporary capital of the universe, dignitaries marched in and out, duly covered by other dignitaries from the media. All the faces were familiar, though a little less lifelike than on the tube. Reality will have that effect on the prominent and their promises. Authenticity seems a privilege reserved for those fame has not touched.

Oh, what a Christmas season that was. If you look carefully on dark nights, you can still see the Ghost of that Christmas Past hovering over what was once a side entrance to the department store that became part of a presidential transition, and now stands as empty and dusty as the promises made there. Remember all those rules that were finally going to divorce governing from lobbying?

Well, forget 'em.

Two top-ranking White House aides quit this month to become big-time lobbyists:

- Howard Paster, the Clinton administration's congressional liaison, walked through the familiar revolving door between government and lobbying to emerge as chairman and chief executive of Hill & Knowlton. That's the lobbying and public relations firm he was with before joining The White House, Inc. The job is said to be in the million-dollar-a-year range.
- Roy Neel, deputy White House chief of staff, is to become president of the United States Telephone Association, which coordinates the lobbies for regional and local phone companies. That job pays $500,000 a year. Before coming to the White

House, Mr. Neel was Al Gore's adviser — on communications issues, of course.

Who says public service leads nowhere?

Most impressive, these changes will be perfectly consistent with the Guidelines and Parameters and Toughest Rules on Lobbying Ever Announced — once you've read the fine print and clinton clauses.

Mr. Paster explains that he won't be doing any lobbying with government agencies himself, just directing others in their lobbying efforts. See the difference?

Neither does Washington-watcher Charles Lewis, who directs a group called the Center for Public Integrity. "They can attempt to finesse it all they want," he says, "but two of the most important figures in the Clinton White House have gone into the lobbying community, and that's the bottom line."

This is what reform looks like a year later, and smells like. Why am I suddenly nostalgic for old-fashioned corruption? Maybe because it didn't come with a lot of idealistic talk about how ethical everything was going to be.

Surely the Clinton administration is no worse than others at this game. What sets it apart is not the usual, dubious deals but the pretense that its way of governing/lobbying is so much more refined than what has gone before. There is always a good reason for these little departures from what was promised a year ago.

Back at the turn of the century, Finely Peter Dunne's fictional Irish barkeep, Mr. Dooley, observed much the same pattern in American politics, but refused to attribute it to hypocrisy. "It must be a good thing to be good or ivrybody wudden't be pretendin' he was," he philosophized. "But I don't think they'se anny such thing as hypocrisy in the wurrld. They can't be. If ye'd turn up the gas in the darkest heart ye'd find it had a good raison for th' worst things it done, a good varchuous raison, like needin' the money. . . ."

The more things change, the more relevant Mr. Dooley remains.

As a candidate, Bill Clinton promised to shut the revolving door that sent public officials spinning "from public service to private enrichment."

As president-elect, he declared: "I want to send a signal that we are going to end politics as usual."

Well, Pamela Gilbert got the signal. She's director of a private watch-dog group (Congress Watch) and can reach only one conclusion after this latest bait-and-switch: "The administration has made a very big deal about stopping business as usual, and this is exactly business as usual." The administration's spokesmen rolled out the usual explanations. George Stephanopoulos (remember him?) explained that the new rules and regulations were "infinitely better than what we had before." Just because there seems to be no difference in practice shouldn't get in the way of admiring the preaching. (Is this the way the Clinton Health Plan will work out, too?)

Dee Dee Myers, who was left to pick up the pieces again, did her best on behalf of the White House: "There is a standard, the president expects everybody to abide by it, and beyond that, I don't have anything to say about it." Richard Nixon couldn't have stonewalled any better.

As for the president himself, who usually has so much to say about practically anything, has anyone heard a peep out of him on this embarrassing subject?

None of this should come as a surprise. The transition team itself had all kinds of Guides and Parameters, but was headed by a couple of the best-connected influentials in the country, Warren Christopher and Vernon Jordan. A combined list of their law clients and corporate directorships would read like a Who's Who of corporate America, yet they weren't subject to the new rules. George Stephanopoulos had an explanation for that one, too.

The transition period is definitely over. The explanations will continue.

Chapter 2

CHARACTER

Since the 1970s, a persistent question runs through these commentaries about Bill Clinton, a question that continues to puzzle the pundits when they now write about President Clinton: Who is Bill Clinton?

And when the answer emerges, it turns out to be another question: Is there a Bill Clinton?

Again and again his ability to grasp the issues, his understanding of political positions, his personable style, his articulate explanations, and his potential for leadership are praised. But again and again, the disappointment can be sensed as the same question is asked, with increasing impatience: When will this leader take a firm position and lead?

At least since he left a fiscal mess behind when he moved up from attorney general of Arkansas to governor, Bill Clinton has looked on administration as essentially a problem in public relations. As an executive, he's a great campaigner.

Many of the Clinton administration's misadventures in Washington could have been predicted (and were) by those familiar with his executive style back in Arkansas. There was his tendency to hold onto subordinates long after they needed to resign; a preference for negotiation over leadership even within his own administration; an emphasis on patronage rather than competence; a reliance on expertise rather than anything so pedestrian as common sense; the unceasing urge to tinker and explain and change policies after they have been set rather than follow them; a habit of rising above rules and regulations; and — most predictable of all — a tendency to shift the blame, preferably to the press, when problems can no longer be denied. There seems to be no fixed set of values, no core of character.

THE GOVERNOR OVERTURNED
MAY 11, 1979

Despite a cocksure opinion from Bill Clinton last month, the state attorney general's office ruled this week that state officials obliged to file a Code of Ethics statement must do so within 30 days of taking office — and not wait a year or so, as the governor contended. Mr. Clinton did more than contend last month, he announced that it was "patently false" (wonderfully magisterial phrase) to say that his director of State Building Services, Martin Borchert, should already have filed a Code of Ethics statement in order to comply with state law.

When Mr. Borchert's conflict of interest broke into public view (although Governor Clinton has yet to recognize it) the young governor produced a press conference starring himself, Secretary of State Paul Riviere in a not very supporting role, and Mr. Borchert as a silent film star. The governor was willing to grant that neither he nor his appointee was "blameless in all this," but that was only as a preface to expressing outrage at "the shotgun, unfair and inaccurate stories to which Mr. Borchert has been subject." Mr. Clinton has yet to specify those stories. After this latest opinion from the attorney general's office, it's hard to see how he could. In light of this opinion, he owes an apology to those in the press corps he has maligned.

But from the first, the young governor has handled this affair in the highest, or lowest, tradition of Peerless Leader himself, Orval E. Faubus. The faugressive ground rules have been applied at every juncture, if with a certain amateurish backing and filling when the going got tough.

When this conflict of interest first arose, Mr. Clinton ignored and dodged it until he couldn't do so any longer. Whereupon he resorted to Phase II of faugressive strategy: Blame it on Them Lyin' Newspapers. Those who called attention to this problem in his administration, rather than being thanked for doing their duty, got cussed. The young governor seemed outraged that not all of the Arkansas press was prepared to treat him with the one-eyed deference of an editorial in the *Arkansas Gazette*. And he struck back by making some shotgun, unfair and inaccurate accusations in the perfervid style Orval Faubus resorted to when desperate. Now that the attorney general's office has agreed that his administration had a problem with the law, Modest William may revert to Phase III: Ignore it and hope the public forgets. . . .

To avoid further embarrassment, and obey the law, the governor needs to resist that urge and learn to treat criticism as criticism, not the Patently False charges of some nefarious conspiracy. That Nixonian view of the world does not become Mr. Clinton, and it may not prove effective for very long. As this attorney general's opinion indicates. No amount of brazenness under pressure may substitute for grace.

CASE OF THE AUGEAN BOOKS
MAY 15, 1979

That fiscal mess Bill Clinton left behind in the attorney general's office may not be forgotten after all. The Legislative Joint Auditing Committee wants to talk to him about it, and well it should. The committee has been presented with what must be the Augean Stables of bookkeeping, with the attorney general's office funds having been split up into nine or ten accounts, not counting the part held by the state treasurer. And auditors were left scratching their heads in an attempt to trace commingled funds. When one fund grew short, evidently another was used to bail it out, and so on until trying to trace the money got to be like unraveling a bunch of tangled fishing lines.

Governor Clinton's response is that he sees no point in appearing before the legislative committee: If the multi-discrepancies can't be reconciled, then he or his staff can pay the state any money that can't be accounted for and — ultimate objective — the matter closed. It's the old Just-Send-Me-the-Bill school of political responsibility in which there is nothing a checkbook cannot cure. One is reminded of that *New Yorker* cartoon set in Hell in which a surprised and slightly indignant new arrival tells the admitting devil: "But I thought that when you paid the IRS the penalty, that was all there was to it!"

Mr. Clinton has been formally solicitous about the matter when not ignoring it. "I have been terrifically upset about it," he said — after the Legislative Joint Auditing Committee expressed an interest in talking to him. Though not upset enough to change fiscal officers. Or even reprimand anyone noticeably. His chief fiscal officer in the governor's office is Diane Evans, who left his accounts as attorney general in this indecipherable shape. Mrs. Evans already has paid back $535 that can't be traced, though she said she thought all the cash funds were "hidden quite well" in the office's file cabinets.

Another member of the attorney general's staff when Bill Clinton headed the office has submitted claims for more than 41,000 miles of travel in his private automobile last fiscal year, on top of authorizing impressive purchases of gasoline for the attorney general's state car. Members of the legislative committee estimated that, even if this staffer had worked six days every week of the year, he would have had to average 130 miles every working day to pile up that much mileage. He says he did. The supervisor of the audit, basing his estimate on the mileage put on the attorney general's state car and the amount of gas bought for it, estimates the small car would have had to get 6.9 miles a gallon, which is remarkable even in these gas-guzzling days. This aide is now an administrative assistant to the director of Mr. Clinton's new Economic Development Department.

Governor Clinton somehow manages to spotlight the lower-downs in his administration when scandal hits ("Our people were wrong") while expressing the greatest concern for them. It's a neat trick, but Bill Clinton pulls it off every time. His language could come out of the literature of Watergate; it is Tough and Competent before scandal hits, then it collapses into the passive and third-person. The latter mode is the natural lingo of bureaucrats, since it defies any pinpointing of responsibility. It is not *I was wrong* or *I am responsible* but, to quote the governor, "Our people were wrong. I'm confident there was no wrongdoing. It was negligence. . . ." Huh?

Or as Mr. Clinton said of an embarrassing conflict of interest in State Building Services: "Finally, let me say that Mr. Borchert and I are not blameless in all this in that Mr. Borchert became inaccessible to the press, and that I did not anticipate the problem of the appearance of conflict of interest. . . ." The governor is always at least once removed from the problem in his own locution. "I think it's obviously something I should have paid closer attention to," he says of these Augean Books, whipping out a checkbook. He comes away from the mangled wreckage of this train of events expressing great solicitude for those directly involved, as if he were not among them. That way, people may mistake the engineer for an innocent, even generous, passenger.

The governor now grows fond of a bill, sponsored last session by the Joint Budget Committee, that would have required all state funds to be channeled through the state treasurer. If it had passed, he now says, "It would have been easier on Diane Evans." Not to mention, pointedly, himself.

Strange that bookkeeping and conflicts of interest should escape the attention of a governor who can roll out the exact percentage by which he carried even the least significant county last election. Or perhaps not so strange. If one is building a political machine on a faugressive scale, one may have to work so hard putting all the patronage together for 1980 that it's not easy to notice just what the thing is doing in the meantime. By now state government begins to resemble a roster of Bill Clinton's Oldest Friends & Political Supporters. And to make way for them, workers who have not had to pay the state any money for unaccountable funds may have to go, particularly if their record includes a cardinal sin like supporting Joe Woodward in the Democratic primary.

Mr. Clinton can neglect to supervise the state's money, or overlook a budding conflict of interest (reports of such can always be blamed on Them Lyin' Newspapers) but he never forgets a favor or a friend. The resemblance between Young Will and Old Orv [Orval Faubus] grows eerie in some respects. It wouldn't be too surprising if, after scandals like the Borchert Affair and the Augean Books, he should emerge one election year, like Peerless Leader [the *Commercial*'s nickname for Orval Faubus] himself, basking in the reputation of a "scandal-free" administration.

Not Too Puzzling, Really
June 3, 1979

Bill Clinton sounded irked when the question of firings in his administration came up at his press conference Wednesday. Asked why the questions upset him, the governor explained that he wasn't angry (he could have fooled a reporter or two) but that he couldn't understand why people seemed to presume that a firing in his administration would be based on some political motive rather than an attempt to improve the workings of government.

The explanation is fairly simple, if the governor will admit to seeing it: His administration is rapidly coming to look like a reunion of Friends of Bill Clinton. It's as though he were bent on converting state government into the most impressive political machine since Orval Faubus's faugressive time. To every victor belongs the spoils, but Mr. Clinton seems to have the sharpest eye for them since Peerless Leader. Equally impressive has been his willingness to overlook a conflict of interest — indeed, blatantly to deny both conflict and a clear reading of the state's

Code of Ethics Law — when one of his appointees was concerned. See the Affair of Martin Borchert. His handling of that affair could scarcely be justified on any grounds but blind and arrogant machine politics.

As any businessman or Army officer might be able to explain, the leader of an operation sets the example. It should come as no surprise when the underlings follow that example. That's how leadership, good and bad, works. If Bill Clinton is going to surround himself with cronies, naturally enough his cronies can be expected to surround themselves with theirs. And that, governor, is why people seem to presume that firings in state government would be based on a political motive rather than an attempt to improve the workings of government.

If Mr. Clinton ever does get admittedly angry about that widespread assumption, and maybe he should, it would behoove him to sit down sometime and have it out with the fellow responsible. Himself.

THE CLANK OF THE MACHINE
JUNE 11, 1979

Bill Clinton, still trying to put down that controversy over the firings of state employees in his administration, says he's planning to institute a new personnel policy: State employees fired would be asked whether they mind having the reasons made known. That might depend on which reasons the administration will choose to make known, of course. While he's consulting these firees, the governor might also consult the public and ask if the taxpayers would like to know the reason when public servants are fired. After all, these are not his employees but the state's. Or at least that's the way they ought to be thought of.

In addition, Mr. Clinton might consider telling the public the reason many of his appointees were hired in the first place. In case after case, their outstanding qualification seems to have been their role in his life and/or campaign.

To be specific in the matter of hirings and firings: Why, other than for supporting Joe Woodward [the governor's opponent] in the Democratic primary, was Dorothy Palmer fired as the public information officer in the state's Local Services Department? There were no indications of any deficiencies in her work, and the administration isn't suggesting any. And why, besides being an old friend and campaign worker of Bill Clinton's, is Rose Crane best qualified to head the state's Natural and Cultural Heritage Department?

Other such questions abound in this administration. The obvious answer is patronage on an impressive scale. When the governor talks about personnel policy, he appears to be using a euphemism for a burgeoning Clinton Machine.

The Augean Books Closed
January 26, 1980

After a year of poking into the financial mess Bill Clinton left behind in the attorney general's office before moving on to bigger things, the legislature's Joint Auditing Committee has closed its overflowing file on the case of The Augean Books. Not because the legislators ran out of questions — those still abound — but because they despaired of ever getting answers from Young Smoothie.

Among the questions one wishes the governor had made time to address directly: How to explain those salary overpayments to some of his staffers and those debatable moving expenses to another? Why didn't he check to see if accounts were being kept straight? And how could one of his aides get away with claiming 41,000 miles of reimbursable travel in his private car while at the same time buying impressive quantities of gasoline for a state car on his office credit card? And perhaps most trenchant: Why did the governor promote these same staffers to responsible positions in his administration as he went from attorney general to governor?

The committee did not conceal its disappointment at Mr. Clinton's declining its invitation to visit about such matters. To quote its candid letter to the governor: "For unknown reasons, you have declined to appear before our Committee or offer any direct correspondence from you personally on this matter. It was the feeling of the Committee that this type of conduct cannot be condoned. . . ."

If the governor couldn't make it over to the legislature, or just send a letter, at least he could have dispatched John Danner to explain it away. That is Mr. Danner's specialty; he once wrote a famous memo on the subject. In his capacity as the governor's PR whiz, Mr. Danner might resort to a technique he alluded to in that memo: Invite a handpicked group of people from across the state, the sort who would be flattered by such attention, to some posh watering hole, where it would be explained how well administered the attorney general's funds were under Mr. Clinton's care. By the time Mr. Danner was through, his boss might be made to look like a clean-desk man and a C.P.A. to boot.

The Joint Auditing Committee is not amused. The committee protected its good name by refusing to accept this audit of the attorney general's office funds. The report will simply be filed. And, if Young Smoothie's luck holds, forgotten. Until perhaps some unforgettable scandal strikes and the public demands to know why it wasn't forewarned. It was, of course — by the Joint Auditing Committee. But no one seems to be listening.

It isn't easy to divine any central principle in Bill Clinton's executive philosophy, but the closest thing may be a memo penned by John Danner. These techniques for cultivating political power remained a stand-by of Clinton administrations state and national even after Mr. Danner himself moved on, his embarrassing memo having found its way into the press. As early as 1980, the Danner Memo had come close to framing a mission statement for Clinton administrations past and future, namely: Win the next election.

In a remarkably candid letter that he wrote to an ROTC colonel at the University of Arkansas, in which he explained why he would not be entering that program after all, a youthful and remarkably candid Bill Clinton had summed up the same Summum Bonum in two words: political viability.

THE DANNER MEMO
JANUARY 27, 1980

When politicians go on a retreat, it would be only natural that they meditate on how to get reelected. After a retreat for Bill Clinton's Cabinet, one of his aides — John Danner — drafted a six-page memo explaining how the governor can get more political mileage out of his Cabinet. Except for its having become public, the memo seems a most workmanlike plan. Mr. Danner could have come straight from Madison Avenue, or the White House. He seems to be conversant with techniques that it may take reporters years to notice being pulled on them.

The memo explains that the administration needs to do more to convey its "good deeds" to special interest groups and the public. That's only natural for any administration, but it's hard to conceive of one that would be more bent on publicizing its good points, or brushing aside its bad ones, than this one with its free tapes for radio stations, brigades of aides, and general PR gloss.

All Mr. Danner left out was a bit of advice that UA-PB's Herman B. Smith [chancellor of the University of Arkansas at Pine Bluff] has handed out from time to time and hasn't done a bad job following: "To improve the image, improve the reality." If the Clinton administration can avoid some of the faugressive tactics it pulled the first year in office, and do more constructive things than concentrate on how best to publicize itself, it might turn every reporter in the state into its PR agent — simply by having to pass on the news of its achievements.

Members of the governor's staff also are advised in this memo to establish a "regular telephone liaison" with leaders of opinion on particular issues. During the Nixon administration, this was called Stroking. It's a prudent technique, but Mr. Danner is taking no chances on its getting out of hand. This memo includes a sample script for such calls. That's unfortunate. It may breed a certain suspicion when the governor's people read their conversations over the phone. Mr. Danner would have done better to suggest that the Clinton people simply study an old master at the art like David Pryor [governor, congressman, and senator from Arkansas before he announced his retirement in 1995], who was using this technique long before he spent his first term in Congress. Mr. Pryor could call up folks who were *against* him and ask them for ideas and advice. By the time he hung up, they either were on his side or half-wished they were.

It's difficult to see how the governor's staff will be able to carry out one of Mr. Danner's recommendations, namely, try to "exert more control over our own public image." The Clinton Image is now so controlled it creaks a little around the elbows. A few cracks may have appeared here and there since last January, when the state's press was swooning over the new governor, but in general The Bill Clinton Show has retained its glamorous image. Come to think, the glamour is so thick it is starting to become part of the problem. Arkies may prefer their glamour in smaller, more economical doses. Perhaps Mr. Danner would have done better to recommend less control, more candor.

Mr. Danner also recommends, surely gratuitously, that the governor's staff stage its own information programs rather than leave that sort of thing to the less controllable press. Surely no administration has to be told to try to control the flow of news for its own benefit. (Another word for that kind of news policy is manipulation.)

Borrowing a leaf from Jimmy Carter's voluminous book, Mr. Danner suggests that the state administration hold some of those posh background-briefings-for-selected-citizens. He suggests that "most people would be flattered to receive such an opportunity." And flattery can get politicians further than most reasonable people might fully realize. Remember how even Nobel Prize winners flocked to the White House for a chance to sup with Jack Kennedy? Now there was glamour personified. Only William Faulkner commented that it was too fur a piece to go for dinner.

Another great advantage of such set-ups, as Mr. Danner notes, is that they "also give us the ability to hand-select both our audience and our agenda — something not usually possible when responding to speech or trip invitations from others." Most politicians may already be aware of that, but Mr. Danner has put the expressed motives for such briefings in unmistakable, if crass, words — and for that a pre-warned Arkansas public can be thankful. He suggests "well rehearsed presentations" in "prestigious settings." One immediately thinks of the way Jimmy Carter briefs Community Leaders on the Panama Canal, or SALT, or whatever he's selling at the time. . . . Nothing like the appearance of being let in on The Inside Dope to impress the tourists, and have them go back home and do the selling for you.

The Danner Memo also recommends that members of the governor's Cabinet visit at least two counties every month. It points out that such trips could be "invaluable as a political early warning system as well as for later campaign scheduling." But the governor wouldn't be the only one to benefit by his staff's staying in touch with the locals. The folks at home need to be heard, and listened to. This part of the Danner Memo has an altruistic side that should not go unnoticed. . . .

It's clear from the Danner Memo that the writer knows his job. Now all he has to learn is how to keep this administration's more manipulative plans out of the public prints.

KID CLINTON'S COMEBACK
MARCH 10, 1981

To no one's surprise, Bill Clinton is back in politics — if he was ever out. The boy ex-governor of Arkansas has just been named chairman of the division of the Democratic National Committee that deals with local and state elections. It's on the latter level that Mr. Clinton just this November had an experience that should have been most instructive. Making him responsible for the national party's role in state elections is a bit like electing the kid who just failed math (but only just barely) class treasurer. It makes a certain kind of sense: He may be so determined to pass this time that all may benefit by his zeal.

At this point in his education, the slightly aging *Wunderkind* of Arkansas politics already seems to have mastered the superficial lessons of his defeat — namely, that he could have done better at organizing and advertising his campaign. This conclusion comes from one of the most photogenic politicians and well-advertised campaigners in recent Arkansas history. But it was to be expected; experts often conclude that what's really needed is what they're expert at. That's one of the principal rules of effective consultsmanship. By now Mr. Clinton has delivered a whole series of post-mortems on his electoral performance, the burden of which seems to be that it was the fault of a badly misled public.

Here is Dr. Clinton's Rx for a Democratic comeback in 1982: "What we have to do is develop a way of communicating with people so that no Democratic candidate is defeated solely by advertising developed by the opposition. A lot of what the party needs to do is work on mass mailing . . . and building an organization to protect Democratic candidates from what has been a superior Republican" effort.

There doubtless is something to that — every party needs a computerized mailing list these days — but perhaps not so much as Mr. Clinton might think. Lest he forget: In the Democratic primary, he lost 30 percent of the vote to a retired turkey farmer out in Cleveland County. Where were Monroe Schwarzlose's television shorts and mass mailings? . . .

Mr. Clinton might look back on his own brief record in the Governor's Mansion and ask: What solid principles emerged from those two years, what themes that people could grasp and hold on to, what assurance, what message that would revive their faith in politics, what vision of their future? What emerged besides the same tired slogans, the same zigzags and compromises that were supposed to keep everybody happy but in the end satisfied too few?

Maybe Mr. Clinton needs to consult fewer polls and more with himself; his own record as governor offers an outstanding example of what has soured the Democratic appeal nationally. Why did his administration offer so little of substance or vision, so little mental or emotional traction? In trying to recall something of it, a line from Gertrude Stein about Oakland comes to mind: There is no there there. It's hard to remember just now what his administration was about. Jimmy Carter had the same problem. There were lots of words and policies, but one would be hard put to find The word for it, or The policy it embodied. There was no there there. And after a while, the old liberalism seemed indistinguishable from the new gliberalism. And voters across the country turned against it.

Even now there is little sign of any such introspection on Mr. Clinton's part. It's a lot easier to blame it all on not enough advertising or too few mailings. Having lost on his own hook, Mr. Clinton now blames his defeat on lack of party backing. Just as having been out-demagogued, he may be tempted to pose as some kind of martyr to political passion — although he gave his Republican opponent a good run at railing against the federal government for housing the Cuban refugees at Fort Chaffee. And now his advice to the national party, like his administration, remains mechanical and superficial.

The Clinton Years in Arkansas, both of them, offer a microcosm of the national party's four years in the White House. There was the same wavering leadership, the same tendency to fall back on empty slogans, an inability to win the allegiance or confidence of ordinary people. Strangely enough, it is the Republicans these days who offer faith and vision, or rather *a* faith and *a* vision, who speak of a new beginning, and it is their Democratic critics who deride such faith, without going so far as to offer a clear, workable alternative. If Republican ideas are faulty, at least they have some.

The Democrats may have to do more than rationalize their defeat to stage a comeback in 1982. The new chairman of the party, Charles T. Manatt, a Los Angeles lawyer, welcomed Bill Clinton aboard by describing him as "one of the bright young people in the party who have so much to offer the country in the years ahead." That's just what Arkansas voters thought. Two years ago. But for those years ahead, the Democratic Party needs more than a facelift. It needs a mindlift and a heartlift. Before plunging into any advertising campaigns, the party's leaders might want to sit down for a spell and decide just what it is they are advertising.

Same Young Bill Clinton
July 10, 1981

Just when one was growing hopeful about Bill Clinton, he delivers a sermon like the one he gave last Sunday at a Baptist church in Little Rock. In it, he expressed some doubt that Abraham Lincoln or Thomas Jefferson could be elected today — because "they were too weird." Actually, they were too weird for lots of people in their day, too. Both suffered more than one political defeat — but they bounded back, rather than blame the spirit of the age for not appreciating them sufficiently. Too often Mr. Clinton sounds as though he were blaming the public for not being perceptive enough to reelect him governor. It is not an appealing pose.

Jefferson and Lincoln, Mr. Clinton told his audience, "were different. They weren't like everybody. They said things which weren't popular. And you could never get the essence of their ideas in a thirty-second television commercial." Unfortunately, Mr. Clinton may have chosen the two most inappropriate examples for his lecture against brevity, which can be the soul of politics, too.

It doesn't take long to recite the key thesis of Jefferson's political life — "We hold these truths to be self-evident, that all men are created equal, that they are endowed by their Creator with certain unalienable Rights, that among these are Life, Liberty and the pursuit of Happiness. That to secure these Rights, Governments are instituted among Men, deriving their just powers from the consent of the governed, that whenever any Form of Government becomes destructive of those ends, it is the Right of the People to alter or abolish it, and to institute new Government. . . ."

It may take a while for men to *understand* that principle, and to act on it, but it doesn't take long to say it. And it was Abraham Lincoln who rephrased the same creed in the Gettysburg Address, which is short enough to be memorized by many a schoolboy, perhaps even to be aired on television. When he chose his own epitaph, Jefferson identified himself as the author of the Declaration of Independence and the Virginia statute of religious freedom, and father of the University of Virginia. The founder of America's oldest political party did not mention a *single* public office he had held, including the presidency.

Nor did Lincoln and Jefferson disdain popularity. On the contrary, they seemed deliberately to express their ideas in such a way that those ideas would become not only popular but irresistible. When called on to speak, they tended to grasp the opportunity to argue for their beliefs rather than explain away earlier defeats or complain that the good old days of American politics had passed.

When Lincoln did refer to his own political fortunes, it was usually in jocular fashion. He knew Americans did not tend even then to take seriously those who take themselves too seriously. That elemental grace is missing from too many of Bill Clinton's political performances. His endless post-mortems grow boring. And so does his concentration on the outcome of an election instead of the consequences of ideas.

Even with all his sophistication, Bill Clinton can display a rare innocence. A more subtle politician would let a little more time elapse before discussing morality after having demagogued the Cuban refugee issue during the last campaign. But not Mr. Clinton. Raising memories of the Little Rock Crisis in 1957, he said of himself then: "I was forced to ask myself, 'Do you believe that everybody, black and white, ought to be able to go to school together and have all the same rights and responsibilities or not?' It was a moral question that had become a political question." And it was one he dodged when he embraced Orval E. Faubus at his own inaugural and declined any judgment on Mr. Faubus's leadership during the Little Rock Crisis.

It takes little courage or judgment to see the Crisis of '57 clearly *now*. Mr. Clinton needed both in 1981 when the Cuban issue was foremost and a rival, Frank White, was demagoguin' it to beat the band. But instead of confronting the moral issue, Mr. Clinton politicked as usual. At one point, when he threatened to defy the whole Yewnited States Army, he sounded like Orval E. Faubus in 1957.

Whatever his thoughts about the Little Rock Crisis of '57, Bill Clinton seemed to have learned nothing from it when the moral and political test of 1980 arose. And he flunked both. He might have lost the election even if he had done the right thing — as Congressman Brooks Hays did in the Little Rock Crisis — but he would not have lost ignobly. And his sermons now would not be so embarrassing.

Maybe Arkansas didn't do Bill Clinton any favor, electing him governor so young, exposing him first to adulation and then rejection. But the right man would learn from it, and learn the right thing: Not that he wasn't tricky enough the first time out, but that he was too tricky, too smooth, too calculating.

We worry about Bill Clinton from time to time — when he always seems to be concentrating on the next election instead of the next idea. At his worst, he acts like his own most prominent groupie, hooked on the latest political small talk, devoid of vision. Rather than pushing a program or belief, he seems to be forever selling himself.

Somebody — an old buddy, a family friend, somebody he loves and trusts — ought to take the boy aside and quietly tell him to stop acting like just another self-absorbed pol and find out what he *believes*. And then tell the rest of us. We'll listen. He has such great potential — intelligence, education, and a modicum of experience in government, including the usually maturing experience of defeat. What worries us is the thought that one day those coffee-shop conversations about Bill Clinton's chances next year will begin, "He *had* such great potential. . . ."

NOT AGAIN, MR. CLINTON
SEPTEMBER 19, 1981

When Bill Clinton left the attorney general's office on his way to the Governor's Mansion in 1978, he left behind a littered trail of financial records that was never satisfactorily explained, though a legislative committee invited Mr. Clinton to do so. Now the trail has emerged at the Governor's Mansion. An audit of its accounts shows that, as governor, Mr. Clinton arranged to have the state pay for a nurse (for his newborn child) by having the nurse fill a slot reserved for a security guard.

This is the sort of job-juggling that the state's Uniform Classification and Compensation Act was designed to prevent in other parts of state government, but the act exempts the Governor's Mansion. Even so, as state Senator Bill Walmsley commented, "hiring a nurse is pretty blatant."

Mr. Clinton claims it's justified. He said both the Department of Finance and Administration and the Mansion Committee approved the substitution. He reminds one of any other politician who has been caught in a pickle and immediately produces a pile of documentation to show that it was all within the letter of the law. That doesn't make it right.

And neither does Mr. Clinton's dragging in David Pryor. "The DFA people told me that of course I could," he said of his decision to have the state pay for the nurse, and "that David Pryor had used security police to escort his teen-aged kids around." But they were still security

police, not nursemaids. And an understandably favorable opinion from
the state administration he headed doesn't transform guards into nurs-
es. If Mr. Clinton wanted a nurse in the Mansion, he should have paid
for that service himself or changed the designation in the budget
unequivocally from security guard to nurse. Either way, he would have
avoided being embarrassed later.

It's no big deal, perhaps, but once again Mr. Clinton has proved more
adept at rationalizing a dubious decision than at avoiding it in the first
place. However slick his technicalities after the fact, he would have
done better to follow the simple, safe Lou Holtz Rule from the first: Do
right. [Lou Holtz was the football coach at the University of Arkansas
who, when a student player defended some impropriety on the ground
that no specific rule forbade it, replied that he had a standing rule: Do
right.]

---

*In 1982, when Bill Clinton was making his comeback after having
been defeated for reelection as governor in 1980, he was forced into a
runoff not by Jim Guy Tucker — who shared the Clintonesque charisma as a young, dynamic candidate — but by a plain-vanilla public servant by the name of Joe Purcell, who had done a workmanlike job as
attorney general — and had about as much charisma as a cup of warm
tea. The* Pine Bluff Commercial *had supported Mr. Purcell, but without much hope he would actually give either Clinton or Tucker much
of a race. But the Arkansas electorate surprised the pundits again. The
day after the first Democratic primary, this surprising turn needed to
be explained:*

THE MORNING AFTER
MAY 26, 1982

Arkansas voters did it again, confounding the pollsters, the huck-
sters, the oh-so-sophisticated analysts, and just about everybody else
who'll dare tell you they know how Arkies will behave on an election
day. The candidate who had nothing going for him but maturity, experience, and an untarnished career of public service over two decades —
all the blah attributes that are supposed to be out of it in mod politics
— winds up forcing the smooth, savvy favorite into a runoff. The glib
predictions that Bill Clinton would win without a runoff, the polls that

showed Plain Joe Purcell back in the pack with 7 percent or maybe even 12 percent of the vote . . . all that is now yesterday's news, or, to be more exact, yesterday's speculation. . . .

Bill Clinton last night looked like a worried man trying hard to sing an unworried song. How's he going to campaign against Joe Purcell, who doesn't campaign against anybody but just for himself? Should he emphasize Plain Joe's age and arthritis — in a state full of old folks? And old folks who may out-think, out-fight, and, yes, out-vote younger ones. . . .

The contrast between the two candidates in the coming runoff couldn't have been clearer. There was ol' Joe, his voice hoarse, his glasses slipping down on his nose, not letting himself be hurried by importunate interviewers, still pounding away at the dullest issues, as if people were really interested in the nuts and bolts of government . . . and there was Bill Clinton, full of slightly strained pizzazz, and looking incomplete without his political twin, Jim Guy Tucker, to quarrel with. Surely the most excruciating scene of the evening was Mr. Tucker's semi-concession. Even in these untoward circumstances, he was obliged to repeat his standard campaign speech, look handsome, simultaneously jiggle an earphone for the convenience of the teevee types, and generally tough it out. That vignette was a small but painful summation of the refinements in barbarism accorded political leaders by technologically advanced American civilization.

It was hard to soften yesterday's basic message to Jim Guy Clinton: The people of Arkansas grow weary of getting to choose only between haircuts. What is it that Joe Purcell has that eludes the Jim Guy Clintons? It isn't sophistication, or intelligence, and it sure ain't looks or youth. And it isn't only the fine record, the dogged career of public service, the unimpeachable old-fashioned integrity. What is it that this old fellow with his uneraseable Arkansas mannerisms and mispronunciations has that sets him apart from the unlined, stamped-out, coiffeured candidates of the glossy ads? To use a 75-cent word that Joe Purcell would not and need not use — it's *authenticity*. He is simply himself — tenacity, twang, touch of arthritis, and all.

Bill Clinton may be as far from that authentic quality as he was two years ago, when the voters were sending him a message by the irrepressible agency of Monroe Schwarzlose. Doubtless Mr. Clinton has learned some lessons since, but it remains to be seen whether they were the right ones — lessons of substance rather than style, of character rather than charisma.

FORGET THAT DEBATE

MAY 28, 1982

Of course Bill Clinton wants to debate Joe Purcell in the runoff for governor. That kind of confrontation would emphasize his greatest strength — style — and minimize Plain Joe's — substance. Even while seeking a televised finale, Bill Clinton was playing down his well-known charisma: "I don't think charisma is a particularly good thing to have these days," he said. If he didn't know that before the election results Tuesday, he should know it now. When a charisma-less candidate like Joe Purcell can win a spot in the runoff, plain vanilla is in and boysenberry-rum-tutifruti out.

Trying — hard — to set up that debate in living color, Mr. Clinton explained, "It's not a question of charisma, but of knowledge, concern, and competence." Uh huh. But it's not a question of knowledge, concern, and competence; those are not the most evident qualities teevee brings out in its subjects. It's a question of charisma. And Bill Clinton, whether he wants it known or not, has it. There were times during his brief tenure as governor when that seemed all Mr. Clinton had — as when he was undercutting the Freedom of Information Act, or trying to get out from under the mess that his staff left behind in the attorney general's office accounts, or explaining away a number of other missteps. He may have been short of knowledge, concern, and competence on those occasions — but not of charisma. And that's what a televised debate would feature. Can't hardly blame him for wanting to reduce this runoff campaign to a televised face-off between a Robert Redford and a Buddy Ebsen.

But what would such a debate prove? Who is the best debater, perhaps, but not who would make the best governor. Many a good political leader has proven a poor debater. Dwight Eisenhower, who could command great armies and national mandates, could never take control of his own syntax. While many a slick rhetorician has proven a disastrous leader. For an example in this state's history, one need not look past that ornament of Frank White's administration, Orval E. Faubus.

[Former Governor Orval Faubus served in Governor Frank White's administration.]

Slick Willie has not been above borrowing a page or two from Peerless Leader's book. All it takes is a little editing to bring demagoguery up to date. At one point in his last campaign, Mr. Clinton threatened to defy the whole U.S. Army — over Cubans this time, not Negroes — but it was as elevating a performance. Now he says that if Joe Purcell won't debate him, that would raise "serious questions" about Mr. Purcell's candidacy. No, it would raise trivial questions — like who has the more boyish smile, the more winning style, the more comprehensive grasp of the high school debater's bag of tricks — from pregnant pause to rapid-fire delivery.

No doubt Slick Willie could teach Plain Joe a lot about debating. Plain Joe would be the despair of any speech coach. Only if Mr. Purcell had accepted this invitation to debate would some legitimate question about his general competence, and grasp of reality, have been raised. But Plain Joe may have learned some lessons along the way that Slick Willie hasn't — lessons about maturity and leadership, integrity and responsibility. And yes, about knowledge, concern, and competence. Unfortunately, an hour's encounter on television may not be the best arena in which to demonstrate them.

To sum up, as well-organized debaters should, Joe Purcell made a fine — and economical — attorney general (and nobody questioned the accounts he left behind), and he made a knowledgeable and competent lieutenant governor. He could make an outstanding governor. Bill Clinton didn't.

LOOKING FOR HIS SELF
JUNE 4, 1982

Even those who have grown skeptical about Bill Clinton's politics, feeling their suspicions harden into distrust with each slick little maneuver, may begin to feel a sliver of sympathy for Slick Willie in this campaign. How run against a fella like Joe Purcell? An opponent who says anything critical about Plain Joe looks mean, self-serving, unsportsmanlike.

Suddenly Bill Clinton is reduced to running not against somebody but for himself. After all those hectic years of photogenic gladhanding, articulate evasion, ad-agency iconography, poll-dictated policies . . . the young, blown-dry candidate is suddenly asked to produce an inner self, matured by years of responsibility and stewardship, tempered by defeat and disappointment, a self in no hurry to please or pose. . . .

But where is it? Where is that inner self? It seems unfair to ask Bill Clinton to produce one on demand. For he has been given so little time to develop one, and so little inducement to grow by the politics of imagery he has had to play. Suddenly, his New Politics begins to look very old.

———————

Bill Clinton would get past Joe Purcell in the runoff for the Democratic gubernatorial nomination in 1982 and go on to defeat his old nemesis, Republican Governor Frank White, in the general election that year. There would follow a decade in the Governor's Mansion as he won election after election. Even as he launched his presidential campaign ten years later in 1992, the eternal candidate was still remodeling his political persona. And he was also having to deal with questions about another Arkansas personage who had suddenly become prominent in the national news — Gennifer Flowers.

ON A CAMPAIGN TRAIL
JANUARY 21, 1992

There is a Gresham's Law in journalism, too. Just as bad money drives out good money in economics, so trash stories drive out real news. The latest example is the minor furor in the tabloids over Bill Clinton's personal life, all of it based on a story in the kind of supermarket newspaper that specializes in cheap fiction presented in the guise of news. These stories about Bill Clinton's bedside manner have all the credibility of the ones about Space Aliens Eat Baby and 100-Year-Old Newspaper Carrier Gives Birth to Illegitimate Child.

Much of the material for this latest round of Clintonmania comes from a less-than gruntled state employee who got fired and suddenly became a source. The time and energy that's going to be wasted on this muddy detour might have been better spent delving into something relevant — like the candidate's politics. Instead, the American public gets a trash bath. It's unlikely any of it will stick, but it's unfortunate any of us have to waste even the brief time it takes to see through this gunk.

In one of his thirty-second spots in the New Hampshire primary, Bill Clinton takes a not very subtle dig at a couple of his opponents — Tom Harkin and Bob Kerrey — who voted to raise their Senate salaries. "In eleven years as governor," he says, "I've never had a pay raise." Of course not. The state Constitution limits his salary. (No need to go into his expense account, allowance for the Governor's Mansion, and other perks.)

The governor also used to talk about how he had managed to balance the state budget every year — as if he had a choice. The state Constitution also mandates a balanced budget.

Slick Willie can look at a television camera and tell only part of the truth with the most practiced sincerity. A thoughtful candidate, why should Bill Clinton dump the whole truth raw on the voters when he can serve half of it expertly marinated with the juices of self-admiration?

FLASH: Bill Clinton now says he wants a state civil rights law. He hasn't demanded one for a decade in office as governor, but running for national office can open a politician's eyes. Or at least mouth.

You can fool some of the press all of the time, and all the press some of the time, but slowly, slowly the media pack begins to catch on to the shining persona Bill Clinton has become adept at projecting. Jonathan Alter in *Newsweek* actually refers to the governor the way a lot of the Arkies have learned to — as Slick Willie. Mr. Alter's comments in the January 20 edition didn't exhibit the usual gullibility one has learned to expect from the national press corps where Bill Clinton is concerned:

"Bob Kerrey was quite right last week to attack Bill Clinton for campaigning on substance but not proposing a real health-care plan. This is more than just the hot issue of the moment; without figuring out the specifics of health, all of the welfare and budgetary issues that Clinton talks about don't cohere." Neither does Governor Clinton's image as some kind of straight-talking reformer.

Jonathan Alter's conclusion: "Bill Clinton can't have it everywhichway. If he tries, he'll lose his edge and make that slick nickname stick." On the other hand, Bill Clinton's had it everywhichway in Arkansas —

election after election. Perhaps because less often he's been opposed by less palatable pols, and always by less smooth ones. This guy could make Machiavelli look a little naive.

Bill Clinton isn't engaged in a race just with his opponents but with his record back home. Distance from it lends enchantment. Will it catch up with him before November? Can the false impressions he's so carefully cultivated stay ahead of the inconvenient facts?

He's also painted himself as an early supporter of the war in the Persian Gulf when he was more of an early waffler. Yet one keeps running across that widespread misconception ("... he was the only Democratic candidate to support the Persian Gulf War unequivocally." — Margaret Carlson in the January 12 issue of Time). Unequivocally? Why, Equivocation could be Bill Clinton's middle name.

Perhaps not since Willy Loman has an American character striven so hard to be liked. Bill Clinton can mirror the opinion of whatever audience he's addressing at the moment without ever technically lying. If the audience is divided he may even be able to leave all sides with the impression that he agrees with them. There was a wonderful moment in New Hampshire not long ago when he managed to come out for, against, and neutral on Right-to-Work laws.

As this campaign progresses, so will the efforts to plumb Bill Clinton's depths. Only slowly will the suspicion mount that he has none.

IN SEARCH OF BILL CLINTON
MARCH 11, 1992

Hail, hail, the press gang's all here — or soon will be as Bill Clinton leads a now diminished pack of Democratic hopefuls out of the Southern primaries. The national press corps, if you could call anything so disorganized a corps, will soon hit Arkansas in even greater numbers, cameras in hand and word processors in tow. Assignment: Find the real, the genuine, the authentic Bill Clinton. Good luck. Even with all the great resources and bad manners of the media-ocracy, it won't be easy.

In full swarm, the Media will begin the search for the essence of The Hollow Man by covering itself. Instead of seeking interviews, the *Commercial* now has been granting them at a rate that has increased in direct proportion to the governor's successes in the primaries. The *Philadelphia Inquirer* called the other day to ask the same, inevitable, unanswerable question: What is Bill Clinton really like? That incessant query finally had got to us about three weeks before, when it was the *New York Post* asking, and we burst into a laugh that may have sounded maniacal because it was. (How often can one be asked the same question without an occasional breakdown?)

The young lady from the *Post* guessed we were laughing because she was a novice on the Clinton Trail while we had been reporting and appraising Bill Clinton, a.k.a. Slick Willie, since shortly before The Flood. Her supposition hurt our feelings. We like to think we would never be so rude as to laugh at a stranger asking directions.

It's like this, we explained: Here we have been trying to answer that same question ourselves since circa 1976 with little success. The experience is like visiting a carnival midway and wandering through the House of Mirrors for about fifteen years. Unable to find the way out, one day you come back to the same exact point where you entered the mirrored maze years before, only to hear a voice from the *New York Post* inquire, "Could you please show me the way to the exit?" What else is there to do at that point but laugh?

To think that Edmund Burke mistook the disparate, disheveled, thoroughly disoriented legion that is the press for a Fourth Estate! His overused description has to be one of the few misjudgments of an otherwise luminous mind. An assortment of scouts and stragglers, bushwhackers and camp followers, pundits and suckers recently descended on a special session of the Arkansas legislature to observe Bill Clinton *in situ.* They could not have chosen a better observation point, even if their presence was bound to affect what they observed. (There is a Heisenberg Effect in politics, too, and nothing may determine a politician's message or even his style like proximity to the press. The legislature, its company manners in place, never seemed so ruly.)

The most observant and least obsequious of our visitors soon understood that they were seeing a typical performance by our ordinarily absent governor. The state had to be deluged with horror stories about child abuse and hit by a lawsuit before his attention was caught. This special session addressed the crisis in Arkansas's child-welfare system only partially, and, more to the point, only after it had become *politically embarrassing.* Then, true to form, some reform legislation was wheeled into place.

The action taken was far from complete, and it will not be easy to tell how effective it will prove, yet one thing's for certain: It will be hailed by the governor and others eager that he look presidential as a "model" program, groundbreaking in its sweep, noble in its compassion, the best in the country, and an outstanding example of how the political system can be made to work again. The New Covenant in action! (A Bill Clinton Production. Costumes from the East.)

Arkansas's governor is one of those highly skilled political operatives usually found behind the scenes instead of out front; he is an updated Lee Atwater, James Farley, and Mark Hanna all rolled into one. There hasn't been an all-around political talent like his since Richard Nixon trod the boards. He's his own best press agent, and as a campaign manager he outshines the pros he's surrounded himself with. Who else could have emerged as the front-runner in a Democratic presidential race even before winning a single primary?

With so many political abilities, of course there's no room for a person in Bill Clinton's bulging persona. Whatever his political principles may be — and they are the subject of intense but fruitless search these days — they definitely are not Edmund Burke's ("The principles of true politics are those of morality enlarged . . ."). We tend to become what we do, and what Bill Clinton does is politics — or, more precisely, political advancement. That much should be clear by now. And still this madding crowd from distant points keeps asking what's inside after all the layers have been peeled away from the onion.

BUT IS HE A MENSCH?

APRIL 10, 1992

Bill Clinton can't seem to win for winning these days. He won all four Democratic primaries Tuesday, yet he does not have the air of a winner. In only one state (Kansas) did he capture a majority of the vote, and then it was a bare 51 percent. In populous New York, he got 41 percent of the vote against one candidate who had formally suspended his campaign (Paul Tsongas) and another (Jerry Brown) who still talks like Governor Moonbeam. . . .

Why all this distrust of Bill Clinton at a time when he should be cresting the political waves? The answer may lie in one word. Governor Clinton used it in his New York campaign: *mensch*. Crossing the language barrier, he told a radio talk show that the word "bubba" is

"Southern for *mensch.*" Those who don't know any better may find the comment captivating. In that sense, it was typical of Bill Clinton's political appeal.

Bubba, however, is not Southern for the Yiddish word, *mensch,* which means Person. With a capital P. *Mensch* has to do with human dignity, with self-respect and respect for others. A small child taking his first proud steps may move his mother to comment, "See? He walks like a *mensch.*" Or if a grown man should bend over to help an invalid, or give something to a beggar, he, too, is acting like a *mensch,* a real Person.

Perhaps the most workable definition of *mensch* is someone who tries to do the decent thing under all circumstances. That is, the word encompasses character and integrity, the very qualities that seem to inspire that unerasable doubt about Bill Clinton as a presidential candidate.

The assumption that those made uneasy by Bill Clinton's candidacy are concerned about his private life, or by what he smoked at Oxford, or his exact draft status in 1969, is one of those simplistic assumptions the too-sophisticated fall into. Rather, voters may be concerned not about his actions but the remarkably tangled explanations of those actions he's given over the years. His glibness may say something about how, as president of the United States, he would face moral crises, or whether he would.

The closest that Yiddish may come to "bubba" is *grubbe jung* — literally, fat kid. Or figuratively, callow youth. "Bubba" has to do with friendship, informality, a lack of pretension, maybe even a certain capacity for less-than-serious mischief. It is a good-hearted word but it has little to do with *menschlichkeit,* any more than *mensch* is related to bubbahood. A good ol' boy can certainly be a *mensch,* and vice versa, but the two terms are *not* synonymous.

Those who find such distinctions wearisome or even irrelevant (they're only words, after all) will make good Clinton voters. But to those of us who think words are important, that they have to do with things like truth and honor, it comes as hopeful news that, even if not all those troubled by the way Bill Clinton approaches truth can articulate exactly why, there seem to be large numbers of them out there. Despite the current atmosphere of disillusion and disgust with politics, and a general cynicism about where the country is heading, it's a good sign if words still matter.

HOW CALCULATION REPLACES CHARACTER

JUNE 1, 1992

Politics had nothing to do with it, Bill Clinton explained when asked why he hadn't come out before against Arkansas's quaint antisodomy law, which really belongs next to the suits of armor in a museum, not in the state's criminal code. The only reason he waited this long to oppose it, he explained, was that "nobody asked me about it" before.

Is this the kind of leadership the country can expect from a President Clinton? If nobody asks him about poverty or crime or Haitian refugees or ethnic massacres in Yugoslavia, will he maintain a politic silence?

Of course not, his admirers contend. Once he's in the White House, the real Bill Clinton will finally emerge. Yes, there is one. It's just that the Real Bill has to be kept under wraps till then lest he offend. But after he takes that inaugural oath, Bill Clinton will jettison Slick Willie and emerge as a shining idealist who'll talk straight to the American people.

Uh huh. Where have we heard that before? Of course. It's what every young politician or civic leader tells himself when he's making friends and influencing people by never risking an unpopular position. Once he's gathered the support he needs, and is elected to the next higher office, or attains the next rung on the corporate ladder, then he'll use that position to take some courageous stands and make some real changes.

We've all seen what really happens. Once the acquisition of political capital becomes the goal, there's no end to it. The careerist forgets what all the support he's gathered over the years was supposed to be for; he just goes on hoarding it. It's the same process that produces misers. And when he retires at the end of a long and distinguished if empty career, and someone wonders why Our Hero never took a stand that might have cost him something, he can explain that "nobody asked me about it."

Even if, at the height of his power, such a "leader" reached into his hope chest to pull out his true self, he might find it moldy. Character must be exercised regularly, or it will atrophy. Careerists understand that the accumulation of power and prestige must become a habit, and that if they do not advance, they will begin to decline. What they may forget is that idealism is a habit, too. It can't be stored away for a decade or two for some special occasion, then rolled out afresh to meet some great moral test. One might as well try to freeze-dry the spirit of youth.

No, the odds are that someone who believes character can be stored for future use wouldn't recognize a moral test if he saw one, mistaking it for just another issue to finesse. Moral tests actually come frequently in life; it's just that we tend to cease noticing them after a time, a process we wrongly call maturity. It's why children seem to have such a strong sense of justice; they haven't yet learned how not to see some things. The moral consciousness-lowering that adults perfect requires time and training, or just a lot of ambition. But eventually calculation can supplant character.

Vaclav Havel, now Czechoslovakia's president, says he found it easier to hold onto his idealism as one of its political prisoners. As he put it: "When a person behaves in keeping with his conscience, when he tries to speak the truth and when he behaves as a citizen even under conditions where citizenship is degraded, it might lead to anything, yet it might not. But what surely will not lead to anything is when a person calculates whether it will lead to something or not."

Ah, but nothing like that's going to happen to Bill Clinton, his fans keep assuring me. Once he gets to the White House, he won't have to pretend or maneuver any more. He'll be able to speak out. No more doubletalk, no more slick excuses. After all, once you've reached the pinnacle, who's there to appease any more?

Well, he'll want to win a second term, won't he? And after that, surely he won't want to offend anybody who could keep him from becoming secretary-general of the United Nations, or collecting the Nobel Peace Prize, or. . . .

THE CANDIDATE: PACKAGING BILL CLINTON

JUNE 4, 1992

These days it pays to be an outsider in a presidential election — as both Jimmy Carter and Ronald Reagan discovered.

One of Bill Clinton's attractions as a presidential candidate is that he's perceived nationally, if at all, as an outsider. That's according to Stephen Hess of the Brookings Institution, the West Point of gliberal think tanks. "Since people outside of Arkansas haven't heard much about Bill Clinton," he explains, "he can form his own persona."

And that's just what the governor has been busy doing with assorted poll takers, advisers, counselors, hangers-on, and strategists. His standard stump speech is beginning to sound like a smorgasbord, with just the right Pavlovian lines to make different segments of the electorate salivate.

The Clinton persona is definitely being put together — in much the way a patchwork quilt might be. There's a square for everybody — populist or moderate, dove or hawk. The one consistent pattern he seems determined to work into the final product is the convenient and everpopular image of the outsider. Mr. Smith Goes to Washington and all that.

But won't the other outsiders point to his decade in office, his frequent appearances in Washington, his increasing links with the same old Democratic fund-raisers and pollsters? "I don't know how I could be an insider," he protests. "I've never had a Washington job."

Wa-a-a-it a minute. Isn't this the same Bill Clinton who responded to remarks about the Stature Gap and his lack of experience in foreign affairs by saying he once worked for the Senate Foreign Relations Committee? Just what did he do for the committee and where if not in Washington?

If he was just a nineteen-year-old aide in Senator Fulbright's office back in the bell-bottom era, Mr. Clinton could probably still pass as a certified outsider. On the other hand, if that's all his connection with the Senate Foreign Relations Committee amounted to, that blows his claim to acquiring any great expertise in foreign policy there. (If it's any consolation, he'll always have the manner of an insider.)

Moral: It ain't easy to build a persona, especially from the outside in. One wishes the modern politician were more interested in being a person.

Alas, the technological demands of a campaign require that The Candidate be constructed to meet the demands of the latest marketing survey. When he talks politics, Bill Clinton sounds not so much like a person as a series of excerpts from *Time, Newsweek,* and any of the now popular books that say the Democratic Party must recapture the white working class (like E. J. Dionne's *Why Americans Hate Politics*).

Ask him a question and you can almost hear the governor's agile mind rippling through the stack of index cards that contain his standard responses. If he draws a blank, it's because some of the cards — like Foreign Policy and Defense — just haven't been filled out yet. But he's slowly completing his official, consistent persona. (It's a little eerie to ask him a question a few months apart and get the same answer word-for-word.)

His performance is not made any more palatable by those personal non-revelations about his family life that the Washington press corps and rat pack deem obligatory; his variations on that gratuitous theme, forced out of him by an increasingly nosy society, only make the ladies and gentlemen in that crowd, if any, squirm.

Let it be noted — let it be emphasized — that Mr. Clinton is not the only American pol undergoing the standard persona-lift complete with political tuck here and there; it's a widespread rite of initiation into presidential politics. It's a pity his act is so predictable, so derivative. We had hoped a candidate from Arkansas would be an original — instead of a pastiche of the latest neo-liberal fashions.

But originality means risk. It means taking a stand somebody somewhere might actually disapprove, and that has not been Bill Clinton's style since he got beat once about ten years ago and apparently resolved to please everybody in the world ever after.

The governor keeps saying he wants to wage a presidential campaign that would not embarrass the rest of us in the state. That should be the least of his concerns. He needs to wage a campaign that would distinguish himself — as a person. There still is one somewhere in all that persona, isn't there?

THE HOLLOW MAN
JULY 8, 1992

Why do Americans hate politics? The answer is that Americans don't hate politics; we just kind of despise it. In part this is a healthy reaction to decades during which politics became a substitute for religion, a secular form of salvation. Politics was supposed to have all the answers to society's problems, and, when of course it didn't, Americans tended to blame politics rather than our own failure to see its limits.

Another reason for the low estate of politics is the general quality of our politicians: superficial, photogenic, poll-driven. In short, they tend to say what they think we want to hear rather than any authentic message of their own. We deserve them.

The candidates for the Democratic nomination this year are scarcely poetic figures, yet they could have stepped out of T. S. Eliot's "The

Hollow Men." Lined up before the camera, they might repeat in chorus: "We are the hollow men the stuffed men . . . Shape without form,
Shade without colour . . . gesture without motion."

At this stage, they interest mainly the political groupies and pundits,
the CNN addicts and sidewalk pols, the professionally obsessed and
amateurishly fascinated who watch politics even in non-election years
— the way baseball fans will read Roger Angell in the dead of winter.

Of course Bill Clinton would lead this drab gray pack.

He is handsome and, more important, stylish. That is, telegenic. And
nothing counts more in this age of the visual in which words have been
reduced to mere accessories.

He is a good talker — not a great orator. He has the talker's talent for
absorbing the vague emotions of an inarticulate crowd, and turning
them into vague words. His only fault as a speaker is a tendency to go
on forever, as when nominating Michael Dukakis for president in '88,
or when demonstrating a detailed knowledge of some deservedly
obscure subject. His speeches combine fervor with imprecision. But
who notices in these undiscerning times? The object of political oratory is not precision but impression.

And if he has no vision, Bill Clinton does have a myth that he car-
ries around with him like a tirelessly polished brass tuba: Appealing
Young Governor of Small Southern State Restores American Values and
World Leadership. Oompah, Oompah. Well, it was enough to get Jimmy
Carter elected, if not enough to make him an effective president. That's
the problem with a myth. It can be so . . . mythical.

But Bill Clinton never tires of constructing his. He's still going
around the country depicting himself as an early supporter of the war in
the Persian Gulf. When the governor first fixed me with those innocent
blue-green eyes and gave me that routine in the most matter-of-fact
way, he almost made me doubt my own memory. Not till I got back to
the office and went through the clips did I find what he had told the
Associated Press at the time (January 15, 1991) — "I agree with the arguments of the people in the minority on the resolution — that we should
give sanctions more time and maybe even explore a full-scale embargo
. . . before we go to war."

When I found that quote and held it in my hands, I knew how Winston Smith in 1984 felt when he discovered the photograph proving that
the Ministry of Truth he worked for had no connection with truth. Or
maybe Jack Burden in All the King's Men when he found the yellowed

letter that revealed all, and thought: "For nothing is lost, nothing is ever lost." . . .

There are other holes in the fast developing Clinton Myth; almost any Arkansas newspaperman is familiar with them. This champion of the middle class has left Arkansas a tax structure whose principal effect is to squeeze the middle class. This advocate of civil rights has defended voting districts drawn to protect white incumbents and, after eleven years of a Clinton administration, Arkansas remains one of only two states in the Union without a civil rights law. This protector of the environment has done precious little to protect Arkansas's. This defender of the family had to be sued by advocates of children's rights before he moved to reform this state's child-welfare system. And so dismayingly on.

Bill Clinton is in a race not just against other candidates but against his own record back home. He's nimble enough, and the national press corps slow enough, for him to stay a few feet ahead of his record all the way to the Democratic nomination, and maybe the White House. They don't call him Slick Willie for nothing.

Even if some of these awkward facts do catch up with him some day, would anyone notice, or mind? . . . So accustomed have we become to the substitution of image for reality, smooth public relations for crude principle, that we expect it by now. It is the year, and maybe the era, of The Hollow Man.

Caught: The Unraveling of Slick Willie

July 12, 1992

Americans who examine a letter he wrote twenty-two years ago, Bill Clinton assures us, will find a "conflicted and thoughtful young man." Conflicted, definitely. Young, certainly. As for the thought, it was muddy in places. But we like the confused, slightly overwrought young man who wrote this letter much better than the smooth customer he turned into.

The young Clinton, bless him, didn't know enough to not put his inward doubts into writing, including a confession or two. He was still capable of feeling guilt and shame. He had not yet re-created his past to show himself in the best light at all times; he hadn't yet reduced his defense to a series of glib, interwoven formulas. He wasn't as good at changing the subject. In short, he was twenty-three years old.

This Bill Clinton of 1969 was terribly interested in explaining himself to others, and to himself, and in getting that explanation down in the hard currency of thought: words. He knew when he was lying and why. Yes, he was already something of a self-obsessed careerist, but he had only started to prettify his motives.

Contrary to an older and not necessarily wiser Bill Clinton, this latest flap in his presidential campaign is *not* about a twenty-two-year-old letter. It is about the essence of his political style, the germ of which can be found in a single sentence buried deep in the text of this document. To the colonel who he thinks has saved him from the draft, he writes: "Also, I began to think I had deceived you, not by lies — there were none — but by failing to tell you all the things I'm writing now."

Anyone who has covered Bill Clinton for a couple of decades should know that the governor is seldom if ever caught in a lie, yet he can deceive without blinking — whether he's talking about how he balanced the state budget for eleven years or how he was an early supporter of the president's as war loomed in the Persian Gulf. It's not that he lies outright; he's just selective about the truth.

Now add Bill Clinton's military record, or lack of one, to the list of topics he's discussed smoothly, but not fully. For at least thirteen years, since this issue first arose, Mr. Clinton has left the public with the impression that he finally submitted to the draft in 1969 out of a sense of duty: "I was not seeking to avoid military service by this . . . I put myself in a position to be drafted. Not very many people were doing that . . . the draft was the law and if I'd been called, I was ready to go and do the best I could."

Good applause lines, but only applause lines. This letter makes it clear that, when young Clinton opted for officers' training and later took his chances with the draft, he was violating his deepest beliefs about the war in Vietnam — namely, that it was wrong, wrong, wrong. As he put it: "After I signed the ROTC letter of intent I began to wonder whether the compromise I had made with myself was not more objectionable than the draft would have been, because I had no interest in the ROTC program in itself and all I seemed to have done was to protect myself from physical harm." The young Clinton's honesty is admirable; the older Clinton's plastic reconstruction of these events is not.

Why did Bill Clinton finally take his chances with draft? "The decision not to be a resister and the related subsequent decisions were the most difficult of my life. I decided to accept the draft in spite of my beliefs for one reason: *to maintain my political viability within the system.*" There you have it. Going to jail was for others. However fine their principles and character, and however highly he spoke of them, they didn't have the shining political promise that would have been lost if Bill Clinton had been killed in a rice paddy or branded a draft resister.

Even at twenty-three, Bill Clinton was ready to offer up principle on the altar of career — but at least then he agonized about it. In his relief and gratitude at having got out of the draft, the young letter writer may not have realized that his moral compromise would come back to haunt him just as he was reaching for the brass ring. He could not have known that some colonel would save this letter for twenty-two years before releasing it — not when a mere gubernatorial bagatelle was at stake — but when this state's golden boy would be seeking election as president of the United States and, yes, commander-in-chief of the armed forces.

CHARACTER: THE ISSUE THAT WON'T GO AWAY
OCTOBER 8, 1992

Let's talk about character. Others have mentioned it in this presidential campaign, although often without bothering to define it. Sometimes the word is used as a synonym for personal morality. Or it may be tossed into the list of presidential qualifications as if it belonged somewhere between seniority and speaking ability. In this year's campaign, character is often used to denote some kind of permanent quality, as if one acquired it early, like full height or a college diploma, and it never changed.

Character is something more, and less. The familiar figure who has led a life of probity and honor only in order to toss it all aside in one moment of passion has become a staple of literature. So has the story of the reprobate who, after failing every test, rises to the occasion and is redeemed in a single instant. Character refers not just to underlying values but to how they fare when tested, and the testing is continuous.

Character is more than principle. There is such a thing as someone rising above his principles — like Huck Finn deciding in one moment of abandon not to inform on his friend Jim. That decision meant abandoning the conventional morality that told him it was wrong to run off with someone else's property, namely, a slave.

A person of character will hold to his principles, but not necessarily. A scrupulous British liberal named Joe Burgess, who was defeated by some Cro-Magnon candidate because he wouldn't compromise here and there, made it into literature via this rebuke from George Bernard Shaw:

> When I think of my own unfortunate character, smirched with compromise, rotted with opportunism, mildewed by expediency . . . stretched out of shape with wire-pulling . . . I do think Joe might have put up with just a speck or two on those white robes of his for the sake of the millions of poor devils who cannot afford any character at all because they have no friends in Parliament. Oh, these moral dandies . . . these spiritual toffs . . . who is Joe, anyway, that he should not risk his soul occasionally like the rest of us?

A person of good character is supposed to keep his commitments — and so Jephthah in the Good Book sacrifices his daughter to honor a vow, while Father Abraham, having been told by the Lord Almighty himself to offer up his son, Isaac, is dissuaded at the last moment by the opportune appearance of an angel, a mere messenger. Which was the man of character?

The president of the United States breaks a campaign promise when he agrees to raise taxes in order to save a budget agreement. Later he will confess his breach of trust, ask forgiveness, and vow to sin no more. The governor of Arkansas breaks his promise not to run for president in order to . . . run for president. He pretends that he has been released from his vow by a series of meetings carefully concocted by his friends and supporters across the state. He admits, and perhaps sees, nothing wrong in his conduct. . . . Which candidate has character? Is the Character Issue to Bill Clinton what the Vision Thing has been to George Bush? The ability of Arkansas's governor to touch a deep wellspring of doubt in the American public is often attributed to certain long-past indiscretions — his sly misadventures with the draft, his experimenting with marijuana, and other incidents that need not be detailed. But all that might trouble only those unforgiving types who never sowed wild oats of their own.

What troubles is the long string of excuses, evasions, irrelevancies ("I didn't inhale"), and prettifications that The Candidate rolls out to explain his slips even unto the present day. It is not Bill Clinton's private actions so much as his shifting public rationalizations for them that inspire doubts about his character, and an increasingly intense search for signs of it.

A friend from Virginia put it something like this: "If I had a teenage son who, over the years, sitting at the dining room table, had told me as many different stories as Bill has about various things, I believe I'd take that boy aside and tell him, 'Son, you go on like this and nobody's going to believe a word you say. You're developin' a character problem.'"

The pols who give me the willies are those who have no doubt whatsoever about their character. They're likely to be the ones who explain that their bad checks on the House Bank were not bad checks but examples of "overdraft protection." They seem to have an excuse for everything and no qualms about anything. That kind of cocksure confidence invites scandal, the way pride does a fall.

The politicians who assure in the character department even as they amuse are those rare types like a congressman from Arkansas named Ray Thornton. Not too long ago, he apologized profusely for once having written a single uncovered check for $18 on the House Bank. One sign of character is not being too sure of one's own. The fellow who takes his own faults seriously may not need to have them pointed out by others. Then there is another sort. These easy-going types can be terribly casual about things like draft notices and bank overdrafts and conflicts of interest, so confident are they when it comes to their own character. They seem to think they don't need to go by the rules and cautions that restrain the rest of us. Theirs is a kind of self-destructive innocence. We've all known somebody like that. We don't fear them so much as fear for them. My nomination for the scariest thing Bill Clinton has yet said in this campaign is this simple sentence: "I don't have any reservations about the strength of my character."

———————

One of the more troubling things about Bill Clinton is that no one seems able to imitate him well, as if there were too little there to mimic:

THE INIMITABLE CLINTON: IT'S EERIE

FEBRUARY 8, 1993

Dana Carvey of *Saturday Night Live* and *Wayne's World* bopped in at the White House during the waning days of the last administration to do his George Bush routine and got a rave review from the outgoing (in both senses of the word) president. The comic deserved it. His George Bush is often better than George Bush's.

Art not only imitates life but can surpass it. Dana Carvey had it all down: The clipped, telegraphic prose. The unnatural, almost Nixonian, gestures that somehow seem natural for Mr. Bush. The strange, Dan Quayle crashes of this president's rhetorical flights. The stylistic combination of simple-minded preppy and corporate memo writer. Mr. Bush is, in short, highly imitable.

So are many presidents. Comics have made a career doing some of the more pronounced presidential personalities — like John Kennedy and Ronald Reagan. But don't bet on the emergence of a great Clinton imitation any time soon. Not enough idiosyncrasies there to imitate. . . .

Dana Carvey also does a good Perot. Who couldn't? Just talk like anybody from Texarkana and points South and West. To quote Carvey-as-Perot: "The deficit is like a crazy aunt down in the basement, no one even paying attention to her. An' she is just getting ornerier and stinkier. I say take her out, slap her around and hose her down. . . ."

There was no report of Dana Carvey's planning to do Bill Clinton at the White House. As for Mike Royko's rendition of the president-elect, it just doesn't sing: "Ah have cures for everything, so ah will cure you of everything. . . . Ah don't charge a fee. Ah prefer to think of it as an investment." Maybe it's the stock, too-broad Southern vowels. That's the mistake most Clinton imitators make, as if Bill Clinton were from Mississippi.

The exaggerated Southern accent might work if the next president were really from Hope rather than Hot Springs, which was a resort town with a heavy Chicago connection when Bill Clinton was growing up there — playing the sax, not the guitar. (That says a lot.) Then he was off on the Washington-Oxford-Yale circuit before his linguistic roots had a chance to sink deep, or his Southern phrasing to sprout high.

Bill Clinton's language, like his cast of mind, is more American '90s than regional any time. He is so much a part of his time — unlike George Bush's dated Yalie-isms or Ross Perot's country-western twang — that his time may not find Bill Clinton distinctive.

To Yankees, Bill Clinton sounds definitely Southern but from no place in particular in the South. To Arkansawyers, he sounds nondescript — like any other winner of a Voice of Democracy contest. His country phrases seem studied, his technotalk natural. When he does lapse into country, it seems premeditated — less country than countrified. The rhythm and enunciation of his speech can expand or contract on demand, but only slightly — and never as cunningly as his ideas and positions.

To his credit, Bill Clinton doesn't change his accent, like his ideas or phrases, depending on his audience. His voice may be hoarse on occasion but his accent is not affected. Unlike many Southerners, he does not seem to be constantly putting it on and taking it off, depending on the occasion or audience.

Words are revealing, especially when they reveal no clear basis or rooted conviction — ideological, regional, or historical. As a politician, Bill Clinton is more a technocrat, and as a technocrat, more a politician. That is, he's a centrist to the hollow core.

There's something so wholesome and South-central neutral about the Clinton accent that it's a bit eerie, as if it had been dictated by computer. He seems at home not in language or history or religion but in music — both the smooth, free-floating margaritaville variety and, more encouraging, old-time rock 'n' roll. Which is a hybrid of black and white but is all Southern.

It would be a relief and assurance if some comic could indeed do a dazzlingly funny imitation of Bill Clinton. I can hardly wait. But how exaggerate what's not there?

It is not what's present in the new president's familiar voice that may disconcert a fan of American accents, but what's absent: any distinctive character. Listening to the steady drone can give one an eerie feeling, as if the practiced phrases had been prerecorded-for-broadcast-at-a-more-convenient-time.

THE FIRST 100 CLINTONS
APRIL 30, 1993

It is an artificial construct, the First 100 Days, a case of latter-day presidents imitating FDR, or maybe of journalism imitating politics. As with almost all his appointments, Bill Clinton is late for this one, having been delayed by a filibuster against his spending plan. Nor is there a national health-care plan in sight, which may be just as well if it turns out as slapdash as the leaks indicate it will be.

Nevertheless, let it be said that Mr. Clinton has fully lived down to expectations. The ranks of the betrayed, from Haitian boat people to the American middle class, continue to grow. For me, the low point has been his acting as negotiator-in-chief of the armed forces over the issue of homosexuals in the military. He should have ordered an end to discrimination or not; instead he opened negotiations. Would it reveal any military secret to note that our commander-in-chief seems to have no sense of command?

But is there any graceful way to say I-Told-You-So? Or anything useful to be gained by saying it? Does any reader foreign or domestic need still another list of campaign promises rendered obsolete, of believers betrayed, of the new positions that continue to succeed the old, always with a slick explanation? (At least that much has remained constant.)

More interesting, surely, would be a list of those things that have fooled me about this administration, developments I failed to foresee. For example:

- The speed with which it is unraveling. Sometimes the effect has been comic, as in the mad search for an attorney general who never needed to hire a nanny. Sometimes the results have been anything but, as at the burned-over territory just outside Waco. . . . Surely this is not what Candidate Clinton meant when he promised voters "an explosive 100-day action period."

  Only the reactions of Janet Reno and Bill Clinton to the disaster at Rancho Apocalypse were predictable, with the attorney general admitting misjudgment and taking responsibility, and the president explaining, after taking cover for twenty-four hours, that responsibility really belonged to an irresponsible nut. (Come to think, maybe his explanations aren't as slick as they used to be.)

- The outburst of hope and optimism immediately after the Inaugural, especially among the young, should not have surprised, though it did. It was good while it lasted. Unfortunately, cynicism and resentment may prove all the deeper when promises are not kept. . . .

  Never underestimate the Comeback Kid, but I begin to fear for the steak dinner I have riding on Mr. Clinton's reelection. You can't fool all the people all the time, but surely Slick Willie should be doing better than this.

- One might have expected the Clinton honeymoon, both with Congress and the public, to have lasted a little longer. If the president had compromised his spending program instead of pushing Republicans to the wall, he could have claimed a great victory — however modest it really was. A $16 billion program out of a trillion-and-half budget is no New Deal. Instead, gridlock is back and the president looks ineffectual. He loudly deplores stalemated government, but doesn't seem to realize that it takes two to gridlock.

What remains consistent about the new administration is its inconsistency, its general impression of drift, rather than mastery. Worse, the choice seems deliberate. Examine just one, though symptomatic, slice of undifferentiated verbiage from the president's latest press conference. Here's how he covered a variety of issues with one quick coat of semantic fog:

> Not every one of these things can be distilled simply into politics. A lot of these things honestly involve real debates over ideas — over who's right and wrong about the world toward which we're moving — and the answers are not self-evident. One of the reasons that I wanted to run for president is I wanted to sort of open the floodgates for debating these ideas so that we could try to change in the appropriate ways.

Mr. Clinton gets an E for emptiness. Ronald Reagan this isn't, even though there was much talk about a Reagan model for the Clinton presidency: a few strong themes pushed into decisive programs early on. Problem is, Bill Clinton — intelligent and energetic policy wonk that he is — knows a lot, but what does he believe? And what he knows seems only a vague swirl, changing from day to day, minute to minute — as information will in a computerized, televised, clintonized culture.

The Hollow Man filled with electronic impulses remains as hollow. The constant search for new information, combined with an absence of beliefs, leaves a government almost wholly dependent on experts — just as the Justice Department was at Rancho Apocalypse.

Even now, a national health policy is supposed to sort of glob together once enough experts can be gathered together in a kind of critical mass. That way lies bad news.

What the clintonized culture hath wrought is summarized pithily in one of the better chapters of Jack Butler's new Arkansas novel, *Living in Little Rock With Miss Little Rock:* "People . . . understood reality as machinery rather than God's own dream of existence, intelligence as information rather than judgment. . . ."

Information, not judgment. Perhaps the reason this president keeps changing is that information, which he may confuse with truth, does. That may be why he has been transforming the bully pulpit that is the American presidency into some vague graduate seminar.

Behind the talk of action, there seems a remarkable passivity. The goal becomes How to Act in Appropriate Ways in the World Toward Which We're Moving. Rather than to act and create a world. Not Ronald Reagan but a quite different president comes to mind as a model for this administration: Jimmy Carter, who was always dithering while he waited for the picture to clear. Without judgment, it never does. There is always more information to process.

This is an administration that responds so well to information and pseudo-information, events, and polls that it may prove less a government than a mood ring. Don't expect leadership from Elastic Man so much as smooth changes in position. We may have seen only some of the first 100 Clintons.

The spotlight that was soon focused on President and Mrs. Clinton unavoidably illuminated some of the activities of the Governor and Mrs. Clinton earlier — as well as the relationship between money and power, which turned out to be as cozy in Arkansas as anywhere else:

THE CLINTON FUNDS
JULY 20, 1994

It's no secret that various Arkansas interests chipped in to forward some of Bill Clinton's favorite programs while he was governor of Arkansas — education reform, economic development, tax law, ethics legislation, his own presidential prospects. . . .

Such contributions were considered an investment not just in the governor's programs but surely in civic betterment as well. It's easy to make too much of these funds, whether their effect is to help a politician or his program or, as in this case, both.

It's also easy to make too little of them, which seemed to be the aim last week of Betsey Wright, Bill Clinton's indefatigable excuse-maker. If the funds were old news, the new news was the way they had been financed: through personal loans to Bill Clinton himself from the little ol' Bank of Cherry Valley. (Maurice Smith, owner, long-time Friend of Bill, and former highway director.)

Why wasn't the public told about this arrangement before now? "There was no vehicle for disclosing this stuff at the time," Miss Betsey explained. Gosh, why not just write a letter to the editor? Because, while the funds weren't secret, important details weren't to be publicized, either. Which indicates that the Clinton administration knew how it would look if it had come out that personal loans to the governor were being paid off by powerful interests. Who knew about the governor's involvement in raising these funds? "The people who contributed did," says Joan Roberts Watkins, one of Bill Clinton's former press aides. "But it was not a part of the public discussion. . . ." And for understandable reasons.

Was the set-up secret then? Not exactly. "If people asked," Miss Betsey explains, "we wouldn't have hidden it from them." Once again the word to describe Bill Clinton's approach to politics is: Nixonian. When the Nixon Fund was revealed in 1952, the Republican candidate for vice president never denied the existence of a political fund set up by his friends — it was perfectly legal and completely audited — but he hadn't advertised it, either.

Of course there were differences between the Nixon and Clinton funds; the Nixon Fund hadn't been financed through unsecured personal loans in his name. Were the Clinton Funds audited? Is there a complete record of their collections and disbursements anywhere?

A partial list of contributors to the Clinton Funds reads like a Who's Who of Arkansas interests:

- Frank Higginbotham of TCBY, $25,000.

- Tyson Foods, $15,000.

- Arkla Gas, $15,000.

- Arkansas Power and Light, $10,000.

- Bill Bowen, former chairman of First Commercial Bank and last chief of staff to Governor Clinton, $5,000.

- First Commercial Bank, $3,700.

- Marlin Jackson, one of Governor Clinton's banking commissioners, $3,000.

- Union Bank, $11,500.

- Worthen Bank, $2,000.

- Wal-Mart, $1,000.

And, oh yes, James McDougal, business partner with the Clintons in Whitewater, was down for $500.

At last report, the contributions to the Clinton Funds amounted to at least $220,000.

Imagine what Bill Clinton might have said if some Republican opponent had worked out a similar arrangement with a bank owned by a friend, supporter, and one of his political appointees.

No need to imagine. Here is Bill Clinton in one of his early appearances as The Comeback Kid. Gearing up for his gubernatorial bid against Frank White in 1982, a younger and oh-so-ethically sensitive Bill Clinton was lambasting then-Governor White for soliciting contributions from banks and businessmen:

> Frank White has a half million dollars in the bank from people who wanted decisions from the governor's office and paid for them. I've received a lot of calls from people who said they really had the arm put on them. A banker told me he called him and wanted a campaign contribution, and reminded him how much state money was in his bank. There was the story in the paper about the farm implement dealers anteing up because of that sales tax exemption. And everyone knows the utilities raised a lot of money for him last time, and I know for a fact that one man who

works for a utility told me that he's hitting them up again. One businessman told me he'd never seen so much muscle coming out of the governor's office for money. . . .

Exemptions to the state's tax code multiplied over the long, long Clinton tenure in Arkansas, and it would be just as unfair to assume that those who benefited by the tax breaks paid for them. Mainly because Arkansas's bigger interests would never have to pay either Frank White or Bill Clinton for favors. As one historian said of Grover Cleveland, he freely gave big business what it could not have hoped to obtain by bribery.

Then again, contributions to the Clinton Funds surely didn't hurt those who gave. It's only human to feel some sense of obligation to those who have helped us or our favorite cause, or both. Maybe that's why Fiorello La Guardia once said that the first qualification of a politician was a "monumental ingratitude." Surely no one would ever accuse Bill Clinton of being ungrateful.

In the election for governor back in 1982, another candidate expressed the belief — well, the hope — that "you should not have to be rich, or have rich friends, in order to seek public office." Needless to say, Plain Joe Purcell did not win the race for governor that year; Bill Clinton did. Lots of us miss Joe Purcell, but few ever mistook him for the most sophisticated politician in the world. Which was one of his most endearing characteristics. He was what you might call an affordable candidate. But his time had gone even by 1982.

The time when politics had little to do with money has passed, if ever there was such an idyll. Wealth and power have a way of mixing, always have. The same mechanism that was used to promote the Clinton programs — a personal bank loan — was also used for the Clinton presidential campaign. . . .

To find out who's behind a politician or his program, it's not enough to examine speeches and appointments and letterheads. In solving the mysteries of politics, forget that business about *cherchez la femme*. At the risk of being thought less than romantic, some of us would suggest: Follow the dollars.

Chapter 3

ROOTS

To understand Bill Clinton, it may help to understand where he comes from — Arkansas. Both can be mysterious entities: Bill Clinton because, behind the rich rhetoric, personal appearance, and all his highly articulate politics, there seems to be so little. Arkansas because this state of only a couple of million people contains such a diversity of types, so different and yet so similar.

Poor and populist, Arkansas also has a handful of the wealthiest families in the world, like the Stephenses of Stephens, Inc. — the biggest bond house off Wall Street — the Tysons of Tyson Foods, and the Waltons of Wal-Mart. There is no stereotyping people from Arkansas, which may explain why we go under different names — Arkansawyer for the old-time Southern planter, feed-store philosopher, or tenant farmer; Arkie for the poor but proud dirt farmer, like those who migrated to California when the Great Depression hit; and — the most popular and up-to-date, PR-conscious moniker — Arkansan, which makes us sound midwestern, urban and mod.

The fault line between the Mountain South and the Deep South runs diagonally through the middle of Arkansas from Blytheville in the Northeast to Texarkana in the Southwest. Little Rock, the state capital, sits on the cusp between the two Souths. I like to say the Old South begins at the bottom of Cantrell Hill, a point equidistant between my house in the hills and my office at the *Arkansas Democrat-Gazette* a few blocks from the river. (Southernness, in my book, is not a matter of latitude but of mean elevation above sea level. The fewer feet above sea level, the more Old South.)

Here are some impressions of Bill Clinton's native state gathered as his presidential candidacy was being debated and later as Arkansas's reputation soared and then fell with Bill Clinton's. In less festive times to come, his successor as governor, Jim Guy Tucker, would be indicted as an almost incidental target of the Whitewater investigation. That long-running spectacle turned an army of lawyers and investigators loose on the state's political establishment, which remains largely a product of a one-party past.

All this attention was definitely not sought, and many a scarred veteran of the Clinton administration, crawling back to Arkansas after meeting disgrace or worse in Washington, must have devoutly wished that Bill Clinton had never been elected president of the United States. Ditto, some fixtures of the Democratic Party in Arkansas. They found that having a native son as president meant bringing a spotlight to bear on the underside of their own small, wonderful, and once happily obscure careers.

To understand Bill Clinton's roots in Arkansas politics, it might help to look at the strained and strange relationship he had with ex-Governor Orval Faubus during the earlier years of Clinton's political career: What happened when two shrewd operators — one young and one old — set out to co-opt one another?

Result: a great show.

Bill Clinton and Orval Faubus eyed each other warily while smiling broadly at the start of Bill Clinton's first term as governor. By 1979, Orval Eugene Faubus had long been an Arkansas legend and power, having won six terms to serve the longest of any of the state's governors. Even now he represents the great watershed and earthquake of Arkansas's recent political history, which is divided into Before and After Faubus. Bill Clinton, having been elected to five terms as governor, served almost as long. (The governor's term was lengthened from two to four years in time for the election of 1986.)

No accommodation was reached between these two political phenomena, who were so different (in their age and era and style) and so much alike in their ability to win elections, work the system, and accommodate different political interests. Instead of forging an alliance with the young Clinton, Orval Faubus would wind up two years later accepting an office (director of veterans' affairs) from Frank White, the Republican candidate who defeated Bill Clinton in the gubernatorial

election of 1980. Then, in the election of 1986, the ever energetic
Faubus would challenge Bill Clinton himself, unsuccessfully.

The story of this on-again, off-again courtship-and-duel doesn't fit
neatly into the self-constructed myth of Bill Clinton's having been a
zealous advocate of civil rights in Arkansas during the Faubus Era, or
the impression that he was a consistent, anti-Faubus reformer in
Arkansas politics. It does demonstrate one of the standard operating
procedures of Bill Clinton's Machiavellian politics: Only if you can't
join 'em, beat 'em.

WHO'S THE LITTLE GUY WITH ORVAL?

JANUARY 10, 1979

It could have been worse, maybe. Richard Nixon might have shown
up. But it was awkward enough when Orval Eugene Faubus, like the
ghost of Arkansas Past, showed up at Bill Clinton's inaugural to give it
a touch of crass. Peerless Leader even gave the new governor the tradi-
tional *abrazo* that any mod Arkansas politician would now have the
prudence to stiffen against.

Mr. Faubus said he had moved away to Houston earlier (no forward-
ing address was available at the time) because he "wanted to see what
it was like to be an unknown, an ordinary citizen." Apparently he
didn't want to know badly enough to miss Bill Clinton's inaugural and
the accompanying spotlight. Peerless Leader said he showed up because
he and the new governor have been friends since Young Bill was a university student. (Mr. Clinton's reaction to that went unreported in the
Associated Press account of their encounter.)

Asked if he planned to advise the new governor, Peerless Leader had
the grace to say that, "On any particular problem that comes up that
he might ask about, I would give him the benefit of my past experience." Particularly in the realm of civil rights, no doubt. Or maybe constitutional law, public order, and good will toward men. Or casino
gambling in Hot Springs, the highway between Pine Bluff and Little
Rock, the Fair Field Price Act and other instances of philanthropy to
public utilities, secret meetings, Midnight Raises, how to finance horse
shows with public funds, how to publicize Medicare benefits from that
(monstrous) federal government just before elections, the solicitation

of funds for the erection of a private governor's mansion overlooking Huntsville, Them Lyin' Newspapers, pensions-for-pals. . . .

Wow, it all begins to come back, like a bad dream, at the spectacle of O. E. Faubus at another gubernatorial inaugural. There's even the selective history. Mr. Faubus, still in form, contributed another example of that art when he was asked to compare the state's political climate during his first term with Arkansas politics today. A lot of folks might have responded only with a sigh of relief that Faugress had come and gone, and that grass has grown over many of the old scars. Not so Orval Faubus. He responded with another self-serving reminiscence. "When I took office," he said, "the state was impoverished. There was a great need for physical facilities. It took money. Now the money is rolling in."

And it is, relatively. Despite the dearth of industrial development in this state after Arkansas became known as a haven of haters, which was perhaps the greatest injustice Orval Faubus perpetrated against an innocent people.

Watching Mr. Faubus pontificating in public once again on his political career, the possibility occurs that many in Arkansas, too, would like to know what it would be like if O. E. Faubus had always been just an unknown, ordinary citizen.

Bill Clinton also spoke.

He's Neutral on This One, Too
January 11, 1979

It would be hard to disagree with Bill Clinton's assessment the other day of Orval Eugene Faubus, whom the new governor described as a "man of significant ability." But one wishes that Mr. Faubus had used that ability in a better cause. Asked whether he meant that Peerless Leader had got a "bum rap" in history because of his leading role in the Little Rock Crisis, Governor Clinton declined to answer. (Which ought to be a practiced response on his part by now.)

The new governor is not so much a revisionist in this historical debate as an avoidist. One recalls the answer that a president of the Arkansas Bar Association gave years ago when asked what he thought of Orval Faubus's comparing the federal courts to those of Nazi Germany. Ah well, was the sum of the response, everybody's entitled to his opinion. One might have hoped for something better from this shiny new governor than that same fine impartiality between right and wrong, law and defiance, proportion and demagoguery, public service and public ambition.

Mr. Clinton's "new era" for Arkansas may begin to look suspiciously like an old one if he cannot bring himself to confront the burden of Southern history, which in this state prominently includes the leadership of Orval E. Faubus. To carry George Santayana's familiar maxim one step further, perhaps those who decline a judgment on history are also condemned to repeat it.

ONE BORN EVERY MINUTE
JUNE 12, 1979

Orval Faubus, that old super salesman, hasn't lost his touch — at least not where this still young administration is concerned. Mr. Faubus passed the word the other day that he would be willing to "let" the state's taxpayers have that hilltop mansion of his at Huntsville — the one he's been trying to peddle for some time — at "only" its appraised value. In a sense, it wouldn't be the first time Mr. Faubus has let the state's taxpayers have it.

But Bill Clinton already has dispatched the appraisers. One wonders if Governor Clinton gets the appraisers out at the request of just any citizen with property to unload, or if this kind of response is reserved for discredited ex-governors he's been playing up to.

The Faubus Mansion high atop downtown Huntsville would of course make the perfect accessory for that boarded-up fallout shelter just down the road that Mr. Faubus saddled the taxpayers with during his eternal incumbency. It's probably too much to hope that Young Will could arrange a swap-out whereby the state could get Mr. Faubus to take that old, abandoned shelter off the state's hands. At appraised value, of course. But that's unlikely with Bill Clinton doing the state's negotiating; he comes on with the air of a fellow wandering onto a used car lot suffering from a fatal attraction to chrome.

If Mr. Faubus can still get this kind of reaction from a sophisticated young governor (though not from many voters with longer memories), one wonders what Orv is doing down there in Houston when he could be back home selling this new administration on the advantages of covering the state Capitol with aluminum siding.

Ever since Bill Clinton's inaugural as governor, which could have been confused with Orval's seventh, the new governor has been busily reducing the moral distance from Orval Faubus that every post-faugressive governor from Winthrop Rockefeller to David Pryor took pains to maintain — much to the assurance of the state's taxpayers. But Young Will is not only putting together a machine that brings Faugress to mind, but playing up to its namesake. Making Peerless Leader the star of his inaugural was troubling enough. Dodging questions about Orval Faubus's place in the history of Arkansas, not to say in the history of constitutional law in this country, was disturbing enough. One hopes Mr. Clinton isn't planning to bail Mr. Faubus out with public funds, too. One had begun to hope that Arkansas had outgrown the bad old days.

Footnote: Doubtless with last weekend's rally/provocation of the Ku Klux Klan in mind, Governor Bill Clinton is reported to have sought statements from the business community pointing out that violence could hurt the state's economy. Sometimes folks who hesitate to take a moral stand may do so for economic reasons, but for one reason or another the statements were not made. The immense cost of the Little Rock Crisis of 1957 — not only moral and political but economic — seems to have faded from the public consciousness. The governor doesn't seem to have been much more successful in mobilizing the business community than the press has been in trying to get the governor to take a clear position on Orval E. Faubus's place in Arkansas history.

CUSTOM-MADE HISTORY
MARCH 29, 1986

Bill Clinton's intriguing account of why he welcomed Orval Faubus back to Arkansas politics in 1979 is another demonstration that history is the most contemporary of arts, an ever malleable medium waiting to show what the next era needs shown. Historiographers say it takes a generation for a new interpretation of the past to emerge, but Bill Clinton, being a quick study, hasn't waited that long.

Let's begin with the raw material, the very raw material: That appalling scene back in the Diamonds-and-Denim year 1979, when

Arkansas's new young governor welcomed back a discredited old one with a fanfare that would have been worthy of a conquering hero, complete with *abrazo*. The result of this tasteless display, besides insulting every reformer who ever fought to free Arkansas from Orval E. Faubus's scandal-filled reign, was to make Peerless Leader the star of still another gubernatorial inauguration — Bill Clinton's.

But that was only how it looked on the surface, according to the Bill Clinton of 1986. His real purpose back then, the governor now explains, was to get Orval Faubus to confess his sins and be reconciled. "I guess that just shows how naive I was," says Bill Clinton, "because the very next thing I heard from him was that he'd had a bill put in for the state to spend $1.1 million to buy his mansion. . . . "

This is the first time we can recall anyone's describing Bill Clinton as naive. It's not the sort of adjective that leaps to mind when asked to describe Bill Clinton, governor, congressional candidate, law professor, Rhodes Scholar, and, off and on, Slick Willie. Now if Frank White were to explain that he had brought Orval Faubus back into state government, which, alas, he did, because he was naive, that would sound plausible. But Bill Clinton is not and never has been a Gov. Goofy. His failings generally have been those of calculation, not innocence. And his description of himself as "naive" has the ring of those masterful old country politicians who used to begin their speeches, "I'm just a country boy. . . ."

Someone who hadn't realized what a young innocent Bill Clinton was in 1979 might have suspected that he was rolling out the reddest of red carpets for O. Faubus because that ambitious young governor thought he might be able to reconcile the Old Guard with his New Guard in one unbeatable machine. Happily, Mr. Clinton now has offered a quite different explanation, though it took him six years to do it. Only now does he express the appropriate shock at Mr. Faubus's wanting the state to hand over a cool million or so for his private mansion in the clouds. When that deal was first proposed, Bill Clinton seemed to entertain it seriously, or at least without calling it the outrage it was.

In 1979, the state's young governor waited until others denounced this proposition to let it fade quietly away instead of denouncing it himself the way it should have been denounced — openly, immediately, and without reservation. It was bad enough that the once Eternal Incumbent should have left the governor's office with his hand out for donations from any and all, and without releasing a comprehensive list of the donors. That gross impropriety alone would have justified his impeachment. But for the Mighty Oz to come back a decade later and try to sell the taxpayers his hilltop mansion for a million or so, well, that is to add insult to impudence.

Listen to what Bill Clinton now says about the state's buying that mansion from Mr. Faubus: "As one of his friends who's now a supporter of mine told me: 'I've already paid for that mansion once. I don't want to have to pay for it again.'" That's plain enough, but it would have been more assuring if Mr. Clinton had talked like that in 1979, instead of waiting until an election year in which Orval Faubus was running against him.

If there is one thing that holds us together in Arkansas, it's the same, almost ingrained trait that holds us back: a statewide inferiority complex rooted in a long history of poverty. It comes complete with the two classic symptoms: a deep-down doubt about ourselves, and a compensating instinct to rally 'round everything from Arkansas, including a presidential candidate:

That Complex Again: Singing The Inferiority Blues

October 8, 1991

Arkansas's oldest and biggest problem was discussed the other day in a piece by a Little Rock columnist. He blamed the state's notorious inferiority complex for any lack of enthusiasm that Bill Clinton's national ambitions may have generated back home.

And how did the columnist demonstrate that Mr. Clinton was indeed a fine candidate for president? He immediately cited the high opinion in which the governor was held by two visiting columnists, one from the *New York Times* and the other from the *Detroit News.* Hey, these guys come from the city; they wear suit coats and have clean fingernails. How dare anybody in Arkansas disagree?

Besides, said this capital-city columnist, a Clinton campaign would prove to folks across the country that Arkansas has one nice couple. Or as he put it, the governor "is an attractive and intelligent young man with an attractive and intelligent young wife who cannot help but improve the image of Arkansas where ever they go."

That's the important thing for a state riddled with a firm belief in its own inferiority, isn't it? That others think better of us. That we prove we have attractive and intelligent young couples here. (It had never occurred to us that anyone might doubt it.) Image, as we are endlessly told, is all. Perception is reality, or is it the other way around?

Anyway, it's clear that Arkansas has been an embarrassment to Little Rock's more nervous classes for some time and the Clintons are now conceived as a public relations tool. It's not exactly the best argument ever made for electing someone president of the United States.

Clearly, the only hope for a state so bereft of standards for excellence that it has had to settle for Fay Jones in architecture, Paul Klipsch in the technology of high-fidelity sound, and Brooks Robinson at third base must be a presidential campaign for PR purposes.

Why, sure. Just look at what Lyndon Johnson did for Texas's image, and Jimmy Carter for Georgia's. (Both California and New York can be grateful that Richard M. Nixon's greasy-gray aura was so deracinated that it is not readily associated with any particular part of the American Union.)

What of Bill Clinton's substantive qualifications for the presidency? They were offered in the headline over this column: "Clinton's candidacy not a joke." This is apparently what passes for high praise for a presidential candidate from Arkansas.

The Little Rock columnist does have a point about this state's chronic inferiority complex. We have yet to see a better example of it than his column.

With the nomination of Bill Clinton as the Democratic candidate for president in July of 1992, Arkansas's old conviction of its own inferiority began to give way to the obverse, an exaggerated version of homey Arkansas virtues. Suddenly we were fashionable, and Arkansas Chic was sweeping the country. As this editorial pointed out, Bill Clinton did us "semi-proud." Though grateful to him for casting Arkansas in a new and shining light, some of us still harbored fears about the impression he might yet leave of the state, and hoped the strength of character we had searched for in vain during his long tenure as governor would yet emerge in the presidential candidate:

The Imagemaker: Bill Clinton and Arkansas

July 16, 1992

"I don't think sufficient attention has been paid," an old friend told us the other day, "to Bill Clinton's service in dispelling the conventional ridicule of Arkansas as a miasmal backwater inhabited by crude and loutish ignoramuses."

Consider this editorial a small down payment on that debt and attention deficit. The governor's success and energy, youth and intelligence, are indeed coming to be associated with Arkansas, perhaps identified with the Natural State, formerly the Land of Opportunity. Other qualities of Bill Clinton's may also be associated with Arkansas before this election year is out, notably the governor's subtlety and sophistication — or are those euphemisms for slipperiness and superficiality?

One need not be taken in by our winsome governor to take pride in his accomplishment. As of last night, Bill Clinton of Hot Springs, Arkansas, is no longer the Democrats' presidential nominee presumptive but his party's standard bearer. Call it Clinton Fever, but breathes there the man, with soul so dead, who never to himself hath said, this is my own, my Native Son!

Even critics and curmudgeons get caught up in floor demonstrations from time to heart-warming time when all is forgiven and almost forgotten. There'll be plenty of occasions for ironic smiles and rueful memories after the nomination is accepted and before the standard lies are retold. Last night was a recess from our divisions. It had to be one of those rare occasions when all Arkies, as independent a bunch as ever populated a state, were one.

There would be time enough the morning after to review past promises and performances. But this one glittering night honored not only The Candidate but his long misunderstood state. It was as if only now, so long after Reconstruction, we had made it back into the American union, or at least American uniformity. Doubts were put aside, as they should be on a social occasion. It was party time.

Is this new, blown-dry Arkansas of the Clinton campaign posters a step up from the old stereotypes of hillbilly and planter? The answer — a resounding Yes! — will be obvious to old-timers who long ago grew weary and wary of jokes about A Slow Train Through Arkansas, or the novelty of an Arkie's wearing shoes. Not to mention Bob Burns, his bazooka, and the whole Lum 'n' Abner routine. Wouldn't you really rather be represented by Bill Clinton of Yale, Oxford, and modernity? Not to mention Hillary Clinton, Modern Woman.

A healthier sign than the Clintons' coming to represent Arkansas may be that so little attention has been paid to the change this represents in our icons. Does this mean Arkansas's greatest burden — the state's puzzling inferiority complex — has lightened to the extent that Arkansawyers/Arkansans now care more about what we think of ourselves than what others may think of us? That would be a refreshing change.

Take it as a sign of self-respect that so many of us are weighing Bill Clinton and the Ms. as candidate(s) for president of the United States, rather than automatically cheering for Our Candidate as one would root for the Razorbacks in a bowl game.

Bill Clinton is not the first political figure to give Arkansas an upscale appeal. There was J. William Fulbright and, before him, Joe T. Robinson. Senator Robinson, lest we forget, was his party's nominee for vice president when Al Smith headed the Democratic ticket in 1928. Considerable attention was paid that year to how his prominence was changing Arkansas's sad image. Not very much, as it turned out. Perhaps there is a message here for those who look on the Clinton campaign as great PR for Arkansas.

Lest we forget, Messrs. Robinson and Fulbright both stood for certain principles even if they were arguable ones: Senator Robinson earned a permanent footnote in American history by leading the push for Franklin Roosevelt's court-packing scheme. Senator Fulbright embodied an aristocratic assumption fashionable in the 1960s: that the role of responsible American leadership was to oversee the country's inevitable decline as gracefully and rationally as possible.

Whatever one thought of the principles espoused by Senators Robinson and Fulbright, they had some identifiable ones. What does Bill Clinton — and the new Arkansas he reflects — stand for? Good question. We certainly don't pretend to know the answer.

Why should a candidate with so many virtues — intelligence, retentiveness, friendliness, political savvy, to name only a few — pale out-

side the convention hall? Can it be because, rather than using his political career to advance certain ideas, good or bad, as both Joe T. Robinson
and J. William Fulbright did, Bill Clinton uses ideas to advance his political career?

Bill Clinton has been able to lift us up in our own estimation because
he's more a national than a regional candidate. He is proof that we can
be assimilated and proud of it. He is the very essence of Arkansan, but
a lot of us at bottom are still Arkansawyers and, worse, stubbornly and
irrationally attached to that identity for no better reason than it has . . .
character.

Character is what Bill Clinton may yet search for in this campaign if
he is wiser than his years, and character is what Arkansas may yet provide him if he will only look for it — not in the polls and crowds and
hoopla, but right here. Governor, you do us semi-proud. And hurry
back. You may have left something behind in Arkansas that you and
the country will have need of.

A President Elected and Arkansas Restored

NOVEMBER 5, 1992

So this is what History feels like: Small knots of people beginning to
form through the late afternoon, drifting down side streets, and, no
longer aimless, drawn to one place: the suddenly too small expanse in
front of the Old State House in Little Rock, Arkansas, till there forms
not a Jacksonian mob trampling the grounds of a storied capitol, but a
citizenry, triumphant *and* civil. How American. How Southern. How
Arkansan.

And this is what History sounds like — Carolyn Staley, a sweet
singer of the city, sounding out O Say Can You See as if it were an aria,
a hymn, and a marching song instead of an impossible national anthem.
The music of a different generation resounds in the night, as if it were
a bugle call announcing an arrival.

Some things don't change: The gospel voices of the Philander Smith
choir go out, out, out across the dark rolling fields of the republic to its
great and suddenly attentive cities. So an ongoing republic is born anew,
as it is every quadrennium according to unchanged constitutional

decree and ever changing popular exuberance. Only this year, the great pluralistic election-night swirl is rooted and centered in this singular place: Arkansas.

Victory speeches are no great test, even if victory is. His test behind him, and a greater one ahead, Bill Clinton could party for one night. He had earned it. What a campaigner. Now at forty-six he stands at the pinnacle of American politics, the ingenious machinery of the Electoral College having transformed a 43 percent plurality into a Decisive Mandate for change. And not even David Pryor, junior senator and senior critic of the American electoral system, is heard to murmur about its terrible, undemocratic dangers. May the winner live long and prosper, and confound his critics' every trepidation, especially ours.

Already now The Candidate becomes the president. Adulation succeeds mere support among his followers, and affection begins to erode suspicion among his critics. One can almost feel the country begin to knit. The campaign lingers on only in the winner's laundry list of topics, beginning with AIDS and proceeding alphabetically on. As always he goes on overlong, touching more bases than one thought existed, settling an occasional score, quoting himself, and striking some tinny notes as the champion of "truth" and "those who play by the rules. . . ." The boy from Hot Springs even opts for a Hollywood ending ("I still believe in a place called Hope") rather than something more authentic.

Yet the speech succeeds. And convinces. For there are hopeful signs in it, too. The now president-elect consciously borrows from the best, namely Ronald Reagan, when he proclaims A New Beginning. He remembers to praise George Bush for having served the nation, raising hopes that the transfer of power in this country still does not require a formal purge à la Russe and a new official history every time administrations change. (Although the presence on the platform of Al Gore, who only recently depicted the president as being at the core of a criminal conspiracy greater than Watergate, looms over the scene — like Torquemada at a Spanish coronation.) But all is forgiven when the gracious winner calls on us "to be Americans again" after the small bitternesses of this campaign. And the nation comes together.

The candidate who was foolishly derided because he comes from a community instead of a megaplex also makes the one defining remark of this whole, glorious night-become-day. It happens when he says: "I want to thank the people of this wonderful *small* state." How sweet the truth can be.

The talking heads in their sealed-off rooms still can't tell one Arkansas choir from another, they aren't quite sure what time zone this state is in, and they may not be able to get the name of its newspaper right, but they soon will, they soon will. Power attracts attention to all its surroundings. After all those years of being dismally Out, Arkansas is headily In. Thank you, Bill Clinton.

And finally, the Little Rock Crisis of 1957 is buried without ceremony in the only way historical identities can be changed — not by being ignored, but by being replaced. Not by being rationalized but by being redeemed. It is 1992 now, and a sea of upturned faces, diverse and united as America, full of hope and triumph, now represent us to the nation. The real Arkansas has rejoined the consciousness of the Union. We have Bill Clinton to thank for that, too.

Mr. Clinton was not everybody's candidate before election day, but now he is everybody's president to be. Let us wish him, let us wish ourselves, well. And in the unlikely event the losers in this wonderful small state still harbor the smallest bitterness, they can look on the election results Tuesday this way — the day one Arkie licked two Texans. That holds even if Ross Perot is barely a Texan, having missed the benison of being reared in Arkansas by approximately six Texarkana blocks, and even if George Bush will remain a Connecticut Yankee no matter what his mailing address.

What a night History makes. Nor does History stop the next day, when it wears a less public face — that of a weary street cleaner at six in the morning picking up discarded empties and yesterday's leaflets. And the thought occurs: how easily adulation can turn to cynicism in a media-ocracy. How quickly the same fickle crowds that reached out for a touch, a handshake, even a glance from the Conquering Hero can turn their backs at the first bump in the long road that leads from Triumph. Beyond margaritaville and the strains of Fleetwood Mac, History still stalks.

The Romans made it a practice, when a victorious general returned with his spoils, to assign a supernumerary to his chariot as it was driven through the cheering crowds. The only duty of that slight figure was to keep whispering in the hero's ear: "Fame is fleeting." George Bush would have done well to hire such an aide in the glow of Desert Storm, and such a post needs to be the first job slot filled in the coming Clinton administration.

———————

At least Bill Clinton's omnivorous eating habits remained real in the White House — and assuring. His appetite for junk food may have been the one consistent thread of his persona, and it hurt to watch the food police demand that he abandon it:

LET HIM EAT WHAT HE WANTS

JANUARY 6, 1993

Uh oh. The food police are after Bill Clinton. And he hasn't even unpacked his duds yet at the White House. Seems that more than sixty busybodies styled CHEF, or Chefs Helping to Enhance Food, have sent our president-elect a letter advising him to lay off the good stuff. Like it's any of their business. Besides, any cooks who use an acronym instead of Tabasco sauce merit suspicion.

The (mean) spirit of this letter was summarized by Alice Waters of the Chez Panisse in Berkeley, California. (Of course). It's the kind of place where health food goes for about $65 per five-course dinner. On balance, I'd take pepperoni.

"Just seeing what Clinton eats is pretty distressing," Ms. Waters told the *Washington Post*'s restaurant critic. "McDonald's and Cokes. It's a terrible image." Image is one of those hectoring terms — like Role Model — that should be banned from respectable discourse; they always spell trouble for any remaining Americans who would like to live their own lives, thank you. What does she want from the guy? He does run just about every morning, kind of. And why should *she* be distressed at what *he* eats? He isn't forcing a Quarterpounder and chocolate Frosty on her, is he? Why should she be dictating garden quiche to him?

Julia Child, who used to seem above this kind of pettiness, and whose straightforward, no-frills way in a kitchen restored one's faith in the American Way, now turns out to belong to this censorious pack. She claims the right to kibitz state dinners because, when the Clintons entertain guests at the White House, "it's our entertaining, not theirs." This would seem to be carrying the power of the public purse a bit far. Next thing, a congressional committee will be investigating the quality of the chicken-fried steak and cream gravy served. There hasn't been quite this much of a flap over a White House menu since Frank Roosevelt, as Huey Long called him, served the king and queen of England hot dogs and Ruppert's beer at Hyde Park. As if a kingdom that had survived a diet of bangers, kippers, Yorkshire pudding, and haggis would be affronted by All-American cuisine.

Even if the president's diet were a proper subject of public inquiry, what business is it of these calorie-counters and fat-weighers what Mr. Clinton orders on his late-night pizza? He isn't planning to have it with François Mitterrand and Elizabeth Two there in the White House kitchen, is he? Can't this cuisinary court-martial leave him alone just long enough to scarf down a peanut butter and banana sandwich on gummy white bread?

We all have our secret vices, and a president of the United States has enough stress without having to look over his shoulder every time he downs a longneck Bud. Appetite may be as close as this next president gets to the national mythos. Let's encourage, not suppress it. Bill Clinton and the country will need as many grand, invigorating myths as we can hold onto in the coming characterless, clintonized culture. This generation has a rendezvous with mediocrity. Must its leader's diet be lite, too?

By the time these Chefs Helping to Enhance Food and Make the President's Life Miserable have their way, he'll be eating dinner instead of supper, and fried okra will be only a happy memory. As for desserts, the poor man will be spooning up Sliced Pears with Yogurt Sauce (yum, yum) or maybe some banana-flavored air — instead of digging into a piece of lemon chess pie from Bryce's [an old-fashioned cafeteria in Texarkana]. Is this the reward of high office?

Only a sadist would dwell on the changes that the C.H.E.F. & M.P.L.M. might have in mind for Mr. Clinton's palate. Instead of corn dogs and chili pies, cucumbers with paprika and curried rice-bean salad. Instead of chili con queso with jalapeño peppers, zucchini and carrot sticks. Instead of chicken enchiladas, chicken breasts Veronique with steamed Brussels sprouts. Instead of barbecue, generic fish. Instead of sweet potato pie, an apricot ice. Instead of gusto, blah.

On this denatured diet he'll be expected to deal with the likes of Saddam Hussein, Boutros Boutros-Ghali, Slobodan Milosevic, and Bob Dole. It all sounds less like chefs enhancing food than dealing out cruel and inhuman punishment. Isn't this unconstitutional? These people would force George Bush to eat broccoli. And probably ban mushroom soup for any purpose other than mushroom soup.

A policy wonk might eat like this, but surely not a person. And a wonk is all Bill Clinton might be without his music and food. What are these interior environmentalists going to do next, take away his rock 'n' roll?

Enough. Send these chowline vigilantes back to their organic veggie dip and gram weights, tell 'em it's a free country, and let the rest of us, including the chief magistrate of the Republic, nosh in peace. Good appetite, Mr. President-elect, and please pass the cream cheese.

ROUND UP THE USUAL SUSPECT: ARKANSAS

APRIL 4, 1994

As the whitewater rises, the mind rewinds, searching for some earlier scenario that already has played itself out, and so offers the great comfort of being mercifully over. Whitewater brings back Watergate not just because of its superficial similarities, but because one knows how it came out. The suspense is exorcised, the anxiety eased. It is like watching an old B-movie for the *n*th time; one can notice the artfulness without getting caught up in how it will end.

The last time I caught Bill Clinton's act at the Governor's Mansion, it was a typical performance for the young comer but even then old trouper: long stretches of wonkhood occasionally interrupted by some really astounding, truth-defying star turn that deserved not only an Oscar but whatever they give Trapeze Artist of the Year.

The highlight, delivered in the most offhand way, was Bill Clinton's assurance, his repeated assurance, that, yes, of course, he had supported authorizing the president to use force in the Persian Gulf earlier that year. (Mr. Clinton was never one to desert his country in its hour of victory.) His manner was that of someone merely repeating a well-known fact, and ready to move on to something interesting. He almost shrugged, as if to say: How could you even question anything so obvious?

I felt like the poor lady in *Gaslight* whose husband convinces her she's imagining things, and that she has gone quite mad and started to remember events that never happened. Well, this sucker had me convinced for almost an hour — till I could get back to the office and check out the clips and my mental faculties. Yes, it was a star turn.

At one point in that meeting, the then-governor flew into one of his empty rages. And all I'd done to provoke it was to suggest in the mildest way that, by appointing his own quasi-judicial commission to investigate the business affairs of his Republican rival in the state, Sheffield Nelson, that he had invited a conflict of interest and committed the grossest abuse of power since the Faubus Years in Arkansas.

Okay, it wasn't just a suggestion, and, no, it wasn't mild. Nor is it accurate to describe one of Bill Clinton's hissy fits as a rage, mainly because there never seems any moral force, any authentic anger, behind them, but only petty irritation at how this might look, as if he were speaking from an empty core. No character, no real choler. But he does turn the prettiest shade of azalea-pink at these moments, adding a touch of color to what might otherwise be just another drab press conference. Oh, yes, he shook hands with me as I was leaving. He never misses a chance to work a crowd.

So as Great Performances go, it was a great performance. And only now, in connection with this rising tide called Whitewater, does an almost offhand remark of the then-governor's come back, reinforced by what has happened since. At one quiet point, his voice dropping to that oh-so-sincere level, he explained that one consideration would remain uppermost in his mind as he prepared to run for president of the United States: He would declare his candidacy only if he felt confident that his running for president would do nothing to hurt or embarrass Arkansas.

Even at the time, it was a revealing remark. Not about Bill Clinton so much as about the Arkansas he was appealing to: We're a little hokey in this state but, more worrisome, we seem to be always thinking about what others might think of us. How we do low-rate ourselves. And so when we produce a presidential candidate, he tells us his upmost aim will be — no, not to give Arkansas the credit, the power, and the glory — but just, please God, not to cause the state any embarrassment.

Well, Bill Clinton didn't, at least not in the PR sense his comment conveyed. On the contrary, for a while there, Arkansas was very big, as they used to say in showbiz. Now, unfortunately, Arkansas Chic is giving way to the Plains Syndrome. It happens.

The bad press that the state is getting these days is about as transient and superficial as the good press the Clintons got us earlier, but it does hurt. Mainly because we've never thought enough of ourselves. And so we tend to be overly flattered when some perfect stranger judges us the greatest thing since Southern Hospitality, and overly hurt when the next minute the selfsame jerk sounds like H. L. Mencken using Arkansas as a synonym for utter depravity.

Once upon a time that has happily passed, the roads turned to mud when you crossed into Arkansas; now the press does when you leave. Just mention Arkansas, and ordinarily sane publications turn into conspiracy mags. The editorials in the *Wall Street Journal* went over the edge a while back when they invented something called Arkansas Mores, which are supposed to be worse than anybody else's in America, because here in Arkansas we mix politics and — steel yourselves — business! Unlike, say, Washington or New York or Chicago and every other American locale. (Ol' Calvin Coolidge must have been talking about only Arkansas when he said the business of America is business.)

One bottom-feeding editorial in the *Journal* tossed off this description of Arkansas somewhere toward the end of a piece dealing with — to mention only a few of its highlights — a mugging in a Little Rock hotel, the abdication of Edward VIII, and bimbo eruptions: "The state seems to be a congenitally violent place, and full of colorful characters with stories to tell, axes to grind and secrets to protect." This shocked reaction comes from a publication whose masthead avers that it is headquartered in . . . New York City. Makes you feel a little like that cowboy in the salsa commercial being offered the real stuff direct from New York City?!

Any Arkie who would like to get away for a while need only read some of the descriptions of his state in publications like the *Journal* and the *New Republic*. He wouldn't recognize the place, or himself.

What the *Journal* has done is to confuse Arkansas Mores with Clinton Mores. They ain't the same, for which let us give thanks daily. Slick Willie — well, Slick William now that he's president of the United States — has scarcely changed since he was setting up his own kangaroo court to investigate his Republican opponent in a gubernatorial election. (One of the distinguished lawyers he recruited for that panel had the perfect credential; he described himself as a yellow-dog Democrat.)

Justice can be mighty raw sometimes; now it is Bill Clinton who finds his business affairs of years back under scrutiny. The president was complaining just the other day about being asked "to undergo this level of scrutiny about something that happened so long before . . . in the absence of any credible evidence that any violation of the law occurred." Here in Little Rock, a Republican by the name of Sheffield Nelson probably knows just how the president feels.

Of course it's unfair to equate the investigation into Whitewater with the specially appointed Public Service Commission that Bill Clinton had look into Sheffield Nelson's connection with the Arkla-Arkoma contract. The special prosecutor assigned to peer into Whitewater seems impartial, and the president has solid Democratic majorities in the House and Senate as the congressional investigation takes shape.

These two cases would be similar only if a Republican president — George Bush, say — had appointed a special tribunal consisting of rock-ribbed Republicans to dig into Bill Clinton's connection with Madison Guaranty and Whitewater Development Corporation just as the presidential campaign of 1992 was getting under way.

Soon enough Arkansas Chic gave way, as some of us had feared, to an opposite but equally exaggerated picture of the state:

WELCOME TO DARKEST ARKANSAS
OCTOBER 12, 1994

On the eve of Bill Clinton's nomination for president of the United States, an old friend mused about the effect his new national prominence was having on Arkansas, or at least Arkansas's reputation. "I don't think sufficient attention has been paid," he said, "to Bill Clinton's service in dispelling the conventional ridicule of Arkansas as a miasmal backwater inhabited by crude and loutish ignoramuses."

It was a time when Clinton Fever was mounting and Arkansas Chic was just around the promising corner. But even then, it occurred that the identification of the Natural State with a particular politician might prove a mixed blessing. What would happen when the bloom faded? We here in Arkansas are finding out, and it's not pleasant. . . .

Those naïfs who have never associated Arkansas with the Life of the Mind clearly have never heard of John Gould Fletcher, poet and rhetorician, or Richard Arnold, our own Learned Hand, let alone George Guess, better known as Sequoyah. (The great Cherokee chieftain, lawgiver and scholar may have been born in Tennessee, but passed through Arkansas via the Trail of Tears.) . . .

In the brief Clinton Glow, which was nice while it lasted, H. L. Mencken's references to Arkansas, usually with the back of his hand, soon faded from memory. At last Arkansas was In. Unfortunately, the president's popularity has faded with dismaying speed, and with it Arkansas's. Fickle thing, intellectual fashion.

In place of Arkansas Chic there now develops a sinister picture of the state that no one who actually lives here would recognize. It's the view of Arkansas presented in the *Wall Street Journal*'s editorial columns and throughout the *American Spectator*, which continues to obsess about the Land of Clinton.

It's surreal, this strange and ever darker picture of what one knows to be a bright and beautiful place, especially this time of year. (October is to Arkansas as spring is to Paris.) How describe the Arkansas depicted outside the state? Call it a portrait of a small wonderful state as seen by Salvador Dali, or maybe R. Crumb. And now even this caricature has been topped by the editor of the *London Times*, who manages to blame this president's problems on Arkansas. To quote William Rees-Mogg:

> In Washington, people gossip about some mysterious inner secret which the White House is desperate to conceal. If there is a secret, it is Arkansas itself. That small and backward state no more represents the ordinary life and government of the United States than the city of Palermo represents the ordinary life and government of Italy. What's new about drugs, sex, corruption, the red-neck mafia, money-laundering or murder in Arkansas? What's new about dogs having fleas?

Charming. Especially that hyphen in redneck, which stands out like socks on a rooster. Mr. Rees-Mogg's view of Arkansas appears unspoiled by any actual contact. To judge by his piece, his expedition to the New World got as far as the East Coast. He quotes the tabloids in New York, and speaks of vacationing in Rhode Island — much like someone writing a piece on Wales direct from Tibet. The result is an essay that would make Mr. Mencken's jaundiced view of the Natural State sound flattering.

For example, here is Rees-Mogg on money, murder, and the tonsorial arts in Arkansas:

> Arkansas politics is a very old-fashioned network; it relates to money and that money is, to some extent, penetrated by crime. There are people there for whom threats, extortion and, where necessary, murder have been part of life's business. When the Governor went to a barber shop, he could find himself sitting with a

banker on one side and a killer on the other. It is Arkansas which lies behind the Whitewater scandal. . . .

Oh, for the days when Arkansas was being described only as a miasmal backwater full of louts and ignoramuses. Now the state is routinely painted as 50,000 square miles of corruption brightened only by the occasional ax murder.

There's been a lot of this stuff going around lately, like the flu. It's usually inspired by partisan spleen, and then kept alive by "sources" who see a chance to get back at the Clintons for some slight real or imagined, and even make some money at it. Soon enough innocents like our British visitor are taken in. And now this phenomenon has a name that conjures up both its vitriol and its smoggy texture: Rees-Moggism.

How does even an outlander get such an impression of Arkansas? Well, partly from the Arkansas Defense that has been used in Whitewater, namely: This is the way everybody in a small wonderful state does business. But principally the new image of Darkest Arkansas festers on ignorance, which lends not only enchantment but license. Doesn't every vacuum of information beg to be filled with colorful anecdote and wild exaggeration?

To many Americans, let alone foreigners, Arkansas remains largely Terra Incognita. Here Be Monsters! Which means the process of substituting myth for experience can be carried on with relative impunity. Arkies should be used to it by now. For good or ill, these unknown parts have been mythologized at least since Thomas W. Jackson published *On a Slow Train Through Arkansaw* in 1903. Now, deprived of any other basis on which to form a fleeting judgment, many Americans tend to think of the state as but the extension of a president they're getting to know and loathe.

Moral: When a state is reduced to the ever changing shadow of its native son, the result may not always be a service.

Chapter 4

BILL CLINTON AT HIS BEST

Having been defeated after his first term as governor, Bill Clinton was careful to dilute the reforms of his second with a heavy dose of practical politics. There were times when the mix adds up to state-craft instead of cynicism.

ROOTING FOR BILLY
JANUARY 23, 1979

Billy Clinton is finding out how the big boys play in the legislature. First Max Howell, who's big in the state Senate, let the boy governor off the hook after ramming a particularly flagrant piece of legislation through an all too obliging General Assembly.

(Let it be noted that there were a few more screams of outrage than usual in the legislature, particularly from Preston Bynum in the House of Representatives. That's a good sign of the generation gap that seems to be developing in the General Assembly. Its younger members no longer seem eager to take orders from the Old Guard.)

In the end, Senator Howell requested that his appropriation be vetoed, giving the Young Turks a victory and the new governor a stand-off.

The next confrontation in the continuing adventures of Billy, Boy Governor, is with the banking lobby, no small adversary. First, the governor offered a quid in the form of a bill allowing banks and savings associations in the state to pay less than the going interest on federal securities when that rate exceeds 10 percent — the state's old-fashioned limit on interest.

One would think that would be sufficient generosity with the tax-payers' money to extract a quo from the bankers in the form of a bill that at last would allow the state to pick up unclaimed deposits left in banks and savings-and-loans. (And also with utilities and insurance companies.) But while perfectly happy to pay less than the prevailing rate federal securities provide, the state's banking lobby has shown no enthusiasm for this bill on unclaimed deposits. The state Senate, tradi-tionally the fortress of the special interests, passed the bill favoring the state banks but has held up the one that would favor the state.

At one point it was said Boy Governor would have to veto part of his own banking package in order to apply pressure. But now he's signed the bill allowing idle state funds to be deposited in state banks at the lower interest rate. Has he made a deal, or just thrown away his trump card? One hopes he will get his way. No governor since Winthrop Rockefeller has dared put forth this much effort to accomplish so sim-ple and long overdue a reform. (Elsewhere across the union, states have been heir to abandoned deposits for years.) The taxpayers will want to see who comes out on top in this latest match between Boy Governor and Old Experienced Lobby. We're rooting for Billy. But not betting.

Highlights and Lowlights
October 12, 1983

Bill Clinton deserves a good word, probably several, for the program he has served up to this special session of the Arkansas legislature. It is politically adroit; the compromises already have been made so that leg-islators needn't waste time whittling down some utopian dream. It deals with only one subject — education — but that is surely the single most important subject on this state's agenda. And the Clinton program deals with education comprehensively. At last count, the governor had included some fifty items in his call to the legislators — enough to cover education higher and lower, secondary and vocational, adult and child.

Doubtless some unforeseen crises will arise during the session — they almost always do — but those that could be foreseen have been. The governor's tax program may be mostly regressive (raising the state sales tax from three to four cents on the dollar), but he has made a bow in the direction of equity. He proposes a new, if not very high, severance tax on natural gas. Plus an end to the tax exemption for cable television fees and dues paid private clubs. Nor has he shut the door on repealing some of the more blatant tax exemptions for special interests — if the legislature can summon the courage he couldn't.

The governor's approach seeks to help the schools without leaving the impression that it's unspeakably idealistic. Mr. Clinton seems to have estimated the most he could get out of a very well-lobbied legislature, and asked for no more.

It was the school aid formula and its highly technical ramifications that captured the headlines last week. It may have been noted only as an afterthought that various parts of the governor's program were already being passed into law: A bill to require school districts to map out their own improvement plans for the coming six years. A bill requiring written disciplinary policies in every school district. A bill authorizing summer programs in nine different subjects for gifted and talented students. A bill to identify schools with a record of academic achievement and use them as statewide models. A bill to recognize those teachers who achieve the most. A bill to help administrators and members of local school boards get ready to meet the new, higher standards for public education that Mr. Clinton — and Mrs. Clinton — have been plugging.

All of these promising proposals, which might have created a stir if presented in isolation, whizzed past one house or the other while the state's attention was drawn to the fight between poor and wealthy school districts. Both sides were still in the opening stages of the debate, feinting and posturing. But real progress was being made elsewhere. More huffing and puffing may lie ahead before the governor's package is accepted as the practical compromise it is.

In the meantime, the governor deserves some measured praise for making progress on the sidelines. Like many of us, Bill Clinton may prefer fulsome praise. And when none is forthcoming, he is capable of providing it himself. Legislators weren't the only ones posturing at the capital last week. The governor touted his modest proposal as magical and donned a beautifully tailored hairshirt to argue for it. "It's something that's worth putting myself and whatever career I might have on the line for," he said — as if anyone but the stodgier Republicans and the more chronic aginners would deny that public education in this state needs more money.

But by the time Bill Clinton got around to presenting a tax program for the schools, even former governor Frank White — who is about as radical as Calvin Coolidge — had come out for one. Lest We Forget, the impetus for this special session came not from the Governor's Mansion but the state Supreme Court — which found the state's present system of underfinancing public education unconstitutional. Governor Clinton should have presented a program like this one during the regular session — of his first term. Proposing what has become unavoidable scarcely makes him a martyr to political idealism.

It was in education that Bill — and Hillary — Clinton made the greatest contribution to Arkansas. In 1983, the governor won his spurs:

A Star Is Born
November 15, 1983

Whatever its historic accomplishments (in education) and its historic failures (in equity) this special session of the legislature may have produced something even more important than its program for the state. Perhaps not since Winthrop Rockefeller has a governor so challenged a legislature to overcome its ingrained inertia and rise above its usual self. Tax laws and state programs can be changed every session of the legislature; the opportunity to develop a great governor doesn't occur as regularly.

This special session of the legislature seemed almost as long as a regular one. During those long weeks of long days and nights, Bill Clinton faced down one special interest after another, whether wrapped in mercantile respectability or pseudo-academic pretension. Whether it was the state Chamber of Commerce or the Arkansas Poultry Federation or the Arkansas (not so) Educational Association, the governor took them on one after the other or all at once, whatever their pleasure, like Douglas Fairbanks whirling his way through a swashbuckler.

Bill Clinton didn't have to do all that. He could have made some cosmetic compromises with the usual power blocs, proclaimed them all Great Reforms, and gone home. Then he wouldn't have antagonized corporations that net over $100,000 a year or those teachers and school administrators who disapprove of tests, at least for themselves. He could have appeased the chicken lobby, the beer-and-wine people, and the other special interests he challenged. It was as if he had set out to offend all of his old political allies except the people, as if he had decided to do right and simply trust the public. Whether that will help or hurt him politically, the governor should be able to sleep soundly of nights after this special session. And after this extraordinarily tiring Extraordinary Session of the General Assembly — the longest since they've been keeping records — he'll probably need some sleep.

No, he didn't win them all. But he tried to. He cut to the heart of issues, he compromised where he felt he had to, he fought the good fight, and he let some other folks know they had been in one. Once he threatened to kill his entire tax program, on which he had staked his all this special session, unless it was accompanied by higher standards for education. At one point or another he took on greed and apathy and ignorance and arrogance — not to mention some hurtful, gratuitous distortions directed against him, his program, and his wife. (The AEA, once such a fine organization, has seldom looked so low.) Bill Clinton has been a public servant these past five and a half weeks, and a magnificent fighter. The people ought to let him know they've noticed. He was fighting for them, and their children.

The governor's final speech to a joint session of the General Assembly wasn't a cry of victory or a complaint against defeat so much as a simple message: Wait Till Next Year. He told the legislature that his education program, which the whole state can take pride in, is "just a beginning, not an end to the work we must do." He brought up the corporate income tax that the legislators had turned down, and their failure to raise the state's abysmally low severance tax on natural gas. "I am confident," he said, "that Arkansas will not forever be the only state that gives away its natural resources." It was as if he were making a list for next time. "This is not the end of our efforts in this area," he promised. This boy may have just begun to fight. Correction: This *man* may have just begun to fight. He is keeping faith with those who elected him to this state's highest office. The decision never looked better. And neither did Arkansas's future.

The pleasing jangle that the more imaginative could hear when Bill Clinton walked away from the podium after his final words to this special session of the legislature was the sound of the spurs he had just earned.

———————

Governor Clinton's leadership in education — and his willingness to offend an occasional special interest — earned him his first endorsement from some of us skeptical of his sincerity:

For Bill Clinton at Last
May 22, 1984

This time, the fourth time Bill Clinton has run for governor, he has earned an endorsement. Mainly because during this term he stood up against a slew of interests — the Arkansas Education Association, the truck lobby, and the utilities to mention only a few — for no better reason than to advance the general welfare and assure a brighter future for this state.

This was the term Bill Clinton showed not only greater maturity but undeniable political courage. That quality may prove indispensable in a leader if Arkansas is to keep advancing. It was at the special legislative session called to set higher standards for education (and pass the taxes to pay for them) that young Mr. Clinton came of age as a leader. . . .

At his embattled best, Bill Clinton calls to mind the ambitions of Winthrop Rockefeller for this state. It was Mr. Rockefeller whose administration began this modern line of forward-looking governors in Arkansas, and it is good to see Bill Clinton joining it. Like Win Rockefeller, Governor Clinton has had to offend one entrenched interest after another:

He earned the abuse of spokesmen for the Arkansas Education Association when he insisted not only that students meet new and higher standards, and that taxpayers support education by forking over another penny on the dollar in sales tax, but that teachers be tested on their basic skills.

He warred with the truck lobby because of his insistence that those behemoths of the road pay a fair — well, a fairer — share of maintaining the state's highways.

He didn't win any popularity contests among utility executives by appointing a new, more vigilant Public Service Commission. He also made it clear that he for one would be willing to consider some dramatic alternatives — like having the state acquire Arkansas Power and Light — if that were the only way to assure the economic future of Arkansas. Right now that future is clouded by the imminent threat of a shocking surge in electric rates occasioned by the construction of Middle South's nuclear plants in Mississippi and Louisiana.

When he tried to plug some of those notorious loopholes in the state tax structure, Governor Clinton also risked offending the beer-and-wine people, the state Chamber of Commerce, the poultry association, the oil-and-gas crowd . . . and wound up many a time defending only the public interest.

This is not to say that Bill Clinton's greatest weakness — an excessive caution that in the past has obscured his promise as a leader — has vanished. His cagey silence on the Great School Consolidation Uproar in Pulaski County speaks voluminously of his talent for calculation. The spirit of Slick Willie has not been completely exorcised. The Bill Clinton who could compete with Frank White at badmouthing Cuban refugees in 1980 still lurks.

But Bill Clinton has come a long way this term. Remember that this is the same politician who once opposed Initiated Act 1, the far-seeing reform program of the Arkansas Education Association. That proposal prefigured his own approach to school consolidation and educational reform last year. This is the same governor who used to back out of the way when the trucking lobby raced its engine. And yes, this is the same governor who wouldn't associate himself publicly with a prophetic report from the Young Turks in his administration when they warned of disastrous consequences if AP&L's customers had to pay for expensive nuclear power out of a place called Grand Gulf, Mississippi.

The progress of Bill Clinton is to be celebrated, cheered, and, yes, endorsed. In addition, he continues to offer this state a remarkable intelligence, a well-stocked mind, and a seemingly inexhaustible supply of energy. . . . His appreciation for the power of idealism in government seems to grow greater as he matures.

Bill Clinton long has been one of this state's great resources. But during his second and bolder term in office, he has shown the state what such a resource might yet produce for Arkansas: A system of education that strives for excellence. A system of taxation that not only produces more for the state but aims for equity. A government that puts the public interest first, despite powerful pressures from both big businesses like AP&L and big unions like the AEA. Bill Clinton's promise as a leader is one the voters of Arkansas should seize, and hold him to.

The Pine Bluff Commercial *repeated its endorsement of Governor Clinton in November's election, in which he faced a Republican candidate so obscure his name escaped this editorial writer:*

FOR BILL CLINTON
OCTOBER 30, 1984

Bill Clinton deserves an even stronger endorsement at the polls November 6 than he got in the Democratic primary last spring. Because now his good record as governor this past term has been augmented by the poor campaign of his Republican challenger, What's-his-name from Jonesboro.

Governor Clinton remains one of the great political resources of this state, and Arkansas has begun to profit by it. What was mainly promise earlier in his career now becomes achievement. Exhibit No. 1: The most impressive package of education reforms in the state's recent history, which became law last year largely through Bill Clinton's leadership, diligence, and courage.

One might wish those reforms had come sooner, but they did come, and they came during a Clinton administration. For that, he deserves credit, appreciation, and reelection.

Largely because of Mr. (and Mrs.) Clinton, the public schools and public school teachers of Arkansas are getting the financial support they need, and at the same time the public can be assured that students, teachers, and school systems will be meeting new and higher standards. All of which bodes well for the future of this state and of its young people.

What's-his-name from Jonesboro, on the other hand, needs disciplining at the polls. If he succeeds in saving teachers from higher standards and school districts from consolidation, he may also save a lot of schoolchildren from education.

A clear and present danger is looming over Arkansas's economic future — a massive increase in electric rates to pay for out-of-state power that Arkansas doesn't want and can't use. What's-his-name would respond to the danger by firing the most pro-consumer Public Service Commission in recent times. (The commission was appointed by Bill Clinton.) In short, What's-his-name's campaign for governor has been the most forgettable Republican effort since that of Bubs Ricketts in 1962.

The choice for governor November 6 is clear: Bill Clinton has earned reelection and his Republican opponent has earned rejection.

When it was a choice between Bill Clinton and Orval Faubus for governor in 1986, it was no choice for some of us:

FOR BILL CLINTON
MAY 21, 1986

Bill Clinton's merits as a political leader can be argued interminably by political buffs, but he should be the clear, decisive, overwhelming choice of his party for governor come Tuesday because of the undeniable demerits of his opponents. They are not the sort a responsible voter could favor with an innocent protest vote, as say for Monroe Schwarzlose in years past. Both Orval E. Faubus and W. Dean Goldsby are two sad political jokes on Arkansas — one old, one new — whose election or even strong showing would say all the wrong things about the direction in which Arkansas is headed: down and out. This state deserves much better.

At one point in this ennui-filled campaign, Mr. Goldsby proposed a debate. Maybe there should have been one between him and Mr. Faubus over whose political background was most marked by scandalous administration. In terms of volume and length going back at least to 1957, Peerless Leader would, well, have no peer. But in terms of what-have-you-done-to-the-state-lately, Mr. Goldsby could point to the ignominious collapse of the government agency he directed (the Pulaski County Equal Opportunity Agency) from sheer overspending. Arkansas doesn't need either one in the Governor's Mansion.

Whether you think of Bill Clinton as Mr. Wonderful or Slick Willie (the two tend to change places from time to time), a big win for the governor Tuesday would encourage his better self. A look at his record indicates that he has done important things for education in this state, if not enough, and that he has faced down many a special interest, if not enough of them. A big win in Tuesday's Democratic primary might give this governor the courage to follow his best instincts instead of compromising with his worst. It is particularly important for this state's future that its governor be encouraged to push ahead with his ambitious plans for education and not get the message that promoting progress may be dangerous to his political health.

In summary: Bill Clinton could be criticized on any number of counts when compared with some ideal candidate, or even with a less than ideal candidate who nevertheless held out the promise of continuing this state's post-Faubus tradition of progress. But he has no such opponent in the Democratic primary Tuesday. . . .

A vote for Orval E. Faubus or for W. Dean Goldsby can only encourage the Slick Willie side of this governor's politics, the side that doesn't dare support progress openly, that counsels compromise with the mossbacks and special interests. Don't encourage Slick Willie in the Democratic primary under the illusion that a vote for the governor's opposition will improve his politics. On the contrary, it will send him the wrong signal.

Consider this endorsement a message and a plea to voters in the Democratic primary Tuesday: Don't do anything to encourage Slick Willie; vote for Bill Clinton instead.

When the legendary Orval Faubus, once the colossus of Arkansas politics, met defeat for the third time, there was hope that this once unbeatable candidate might stop haunting Arkansas politics, and it was time to rejoice in Bill Clinton's having slain the Jabberwock:

O Frabjous Day
May 28, 1986

Let word go forth that Arkansas voters for a third time have rejected the low politics of Orval E. Faubus. The state could hardly hope for better publicity this day after a long, dull, and not very elevating campaign. By dawn's early light, Orval Faubus's share of the Democratic vote was receding toward the level achieved by Monroe Schwarzlose in 1980. Once again the voters of Arkansas were putting the threat posed by the Great and Powerful Oz in proportion.

Here is still another happy ending. The figure who once dominated Arkansas politics was being dominated by it. Like Dale Bumpers and David Pryor before him, Bill Clinton has overcome the once peerless leader. His victory confirmed that this state is looking to the future, not the past. O frabjous day, callooh, callay, another beamish boy has slain the Jabberwock. It is becoming a familiar scenario, but the happy ending is no less welcome for that.

Unfortunately, Governor Clinton had to run not just against real candidates but against unrealistic expectations. While he captured the Democratic nomination for governor without a runoff, the governor did not bag as high a percentage of the vote as various pollsters and pundits had predicted, and so he was reduced in his hour of victory to explaining that the low voter turnout yesterday may have kept him from scoring as decisive a win as he had hoped for. Score one more pernicious effect of the polls upon modern politics. But let's not allow that to deprive Arkansas of a sense of celebration and forward movement this happy day after.

By November of 1986, the quality of his opponents had become the best argument for endorsements of Bill Clinton:

FOR BILL CLINTON
NOVEMBER 2, 1986

There are some close decisions and complicated issues on the ballot Tuesday, but the decision in the governor's race ought to be a breeze. We endorse Bill Clinton for reelection not solely but in large part because of the quality of his opponent. Far from measuring up to the standards the job demands, Frank White hasn't measured up to his own in this race. Big Frank is as nice a guy as ever entered Arkansas politics, but to judge by the quality of Darrell Glascock's campaign on his behalf, as governor he would be a medium disaster.

Bill Clinton can be too slick for our tastes, but, compared to Frank White's attempt to come down on both sides of every issue in his career, Governor Clinton is simple and straightforward. Perhaps more important, Bill Clinton is deeply engaged in trying to shape the future of this state while his opponent is back there picking old quarrels. In terms of who would be better for Arkansas for the four long and influential years ahead, the responsible choice has got to be Bill Clinton.

This governor can be recommended on his own merits, too. On one and perhaps the most important issue — Which candidate will do more for education? — Governor Clinton has a record that is more than defensible; it is outstanding. It is a record of vision, for the governor has looked ahead and tried to encompass all aspects of schooling in his program. It is a record of sound judgment in that it recognizes that education is the best long-term investment this state can make. It is a record of courage, in that this governor has had to offend all those interests that balked at his reforms — from the teachers' union to folks with a stake in keeping small and inadequate school districts as small and inadequate as they are.

Let it be noted that Bill Clinton is an astute politician who knew full well how offensive his improvements would be to some — and how welcome they would be, too, among those voters who still equate education with progress. Whatever the political calculations, he has not let them keep him from pushing ahead and pushing the state ahead. It wasn't popular to ask for taxes as well as higher standards, to demand more work from teachers and students, and to insist that small school districts had to consolidate if they couldn't give kids a better education. But he has done all these things. That required courage. For someone as ambitious and cautious as this governor, it required a lot of courage. He should be reelected on the strength of it. And applauded.

The rest of this governor's record is not as clear or as inspiring. Yes, there have been high points — as when he faced down the special interests to close some loopholes in the state's tax structure. But then he went along with the legislature in opening still more. Somehow necessary taxes for the highways were raised but over his formal veto. He either failed to see the hook in some legislation or lacked the courage to oppose the interests when they dreamed up mistakes like the ill-considered tax exemption for college donations and Amendment 59, the school crippler. He had the energy to pass an economic development program but not the creativity to design one that would be more than imitative of other states. But he has not been negligent in office, and he has represented Arkansas well — no small thing in a state that is only now recovering from its long association in the national mind with Orval E. Faubus, whom Frank White appointed to high office.

Frank White's record is not mixed. Would that it were. It is consistently dismal. If the state wasn't marking time when he was governor for two years, it was marching to the rear. The crowning disachievement of the White Years had to be the Creation Science Act & Farce, which cost Arkansas even more in reputation than it did in legal fees, reviving memories of the Monkey Trial and the Faubus Years. That he signed the thing without even reading all of it is an excuse, but not an acceptable one.

The clear choice Tuesday is Bill Clinton for governor — for a higher quality of education and for a higher quality of state politics.

As governor, Bill Clinton reformed the state's tax structure, if not enough for some of us:

LEDGIANA: OF TAXES AND REFORM
FEBRUARY 6, 1989

Whew. Governor Bill Clinton's conscience-salving tax reform managed to slip through the Arkansas House without a vote to spare. It needed every one of the seventy-five votes it got in order to meet the requirement laid down by the state's Constitution, whose tax provisions could have been written by Ebenezer Scrooge. (Only fair taxes need a three-quarters' vote in both houses.)

Tax reform may clear the state Senate more easily — thanks to influentials like Little Rock's Max Howell. Then the way would be open to pass the governor's unfair tax — another 1 percent sales tax — because regressive taxes require only a majority vote.

This barely approved reform will drop the 254,000 people too poor to pay federal income taxes from the state income tax, too. It will double the tax credit for child care, which would give another 75,000 taxpayers a break. It will increase the homestead exemption from $12,000 to $15,000 — which should benefit another 5,000 taxpayers. It will raise personal income taxes to a flat 7 percent on individuals and corporations making more than $100,000 a year. (This is a change from an earlier version of the bill, which started applying the flat rate to corporations at $50,000 a year.)

Governor Clinton is to be congratulated on fighting, angling, politicking, and sweating the bill into law. Here's hoping he didn't give away the treasury to get the bill passed. David Matthews, floor leader for the bill, deserves more than a good word; his efforts on behalf of simple justice were long, complicated, and tireless. . . .

If this reform can be faulted, and it can be, it is because it does not go far enough. Exempting groceries from the sales tax remains on this state's unfinished, perhaps even unstarted, agenda. Even a 2 percent increase in the sales tax with groceries exempted would probably be less regressive than a 1 percent increase on every purchase.

This reform does offset the effect of an additional 1 percent sales tax, but not that of the 4 percent now being collected. And it helps only some of the poor, not those at the bottom of the heap who don't pay any income tax even now. But that's scarcely Bill Clinton's fault. He's a politician, not a miracle worker, and it would take a miracle to soften some of the hearts at the legislature. Given the outpouring of popular support for unfair taxes in last fall's election, little more could be expected this winter.

One of the finest moments of the Clinton presidency had to be his successful fight for NAFTA, the North American Free Trade Agreement with Mexico, after having picked it apart during his presidential campaign:

NAFTA? We Hafta! Attaway, Mr. President
October 15, 1993

"And so I say to you in the face of all the pressures to do the reverse, we must compete, not retreat." — Bill Clinton

It was a delight to see the best political campaigner in the country campaigning for a program worthy of his skill — the North American Free Trade Agreement, also known as NAFTA. To the audience Bill Clinton was addressing in San Francisco, the national convention of the AFL-CIO, the trade agreement is also known as The Cockroach That's Going to Eat the American Economy.

Not since the Yellow Peril has there been anything quite like NAFTA to stir fear, which means that it also stirs just about every fear-monger in American politics — Pat Buchanan, Ralph Nader, Jesse Jackson, and the dean of them all, Ross Perot. The little Texican with the big bankroll could have just stepped out of the 1930s, where he might have outmaneuvered both Father Coughlin and Dr. Townsend for sheer populist appeal — and destructive potential. Lots of folks fight the future; few have billions to do it with.

The president challenged all this economic paranoia when he showed up to defend NAFTA at the epicenter of American opposition to free trade, Lane Kirkland's labor union of labor unions.

Let it be noted that Mr. Clinton didn't just defend the trade agreement that he had spent the presidential campaign criticizing and undermining. He went on the offensive. He sold it. He sold it the way good ol' Dr. Tichnor sold antiseptics, the way Mad Man Muntz sold used cars and Henry Ford new ones . . . in short, the way Bill Clinton sold himself in last year's presidential campaign.

It was not an easy sell. This audience had been prepped and propagandized to boo NAFTA, not cheer it. The president came on like a George Bush with personality. Indeed, this is essentially Mr. Bush's farsighted trade policy that Bill Clinton is defending, though Bill Clinton didn't dare admit it in these surroundings, and maybe not even to himself.

It's a great feeling to have Bill Clinton on the right side — and, in NAFTA's case, on the side of simple reason. Not an easy sell, simple reason. Certainly not in these nervous times. When folks are fearful, they tend to hunker down, not buy. They cheer the demagogue, not the responsible leader. Which means responsible leaders may have to borrow a trick or two from the irresponsible to win over a mercurial public.

Public opinion, that fickle collectivity, can swing from wild optimism to dread and suspicion in a matter of months, even in a matter of moments. Compare the jubilant outpouring election night in Little Rock, when one might have thought the Millennium had arrived, to this convention crowd, which was on guard from the moment Mr. Clinton approached the podium.

It wasn't enough for the president just to point out that NAFTA should result in a net gain in American jobs; that it would create a three-country, $650 billion market of 370 million people for American products; and that it would make this country more competitive everywhere else by putting together the Canadian, American, and Mexican economies. The president had to do more than accent the positive; he had to raise some counter-fears. He did. And they are legitimate fears: Without NAFTA, this country's economy will grow more inbred, isolated, protectionist, and soon enough weaker. North America must unite if it is to meet the challenge of Japan and its economic partners in Asia.

Mr. Clinton played on his themes like Toscanini leading a symphony orchestra: Without NAFTA, the United States may lose an estimated 200,000 jobs in higher-paying, export-producing jobs over the next couple of years. If the president didn't win over his audience, he may have got some of his listeners to think — always a major accomplishment for the forces of simple reason.

Not just at San Francisco but in Washington and around the country, the president begins to lead this fight to move a hemisphere into the twenty-first century, and it's a heartening sight. The Perotistas are being countered by a president selling hope and confidence.

Bill Clinton put it like this at the White House not long ago: "In a fundamental sense, this debate about NAFTA is a debate about whether we will enhance change and create the jobs of tomorrow, or try to resist these changes, hoping we can preserve the economic structures of yesterday."

The president's performance has elicited a rave review even from Bob Dole, who is nobody's Democrat. To quote the Republican leader in the Senate after he heard Bill Clinton make the case for NAFTA, "President Clinton hit it out of the ballpark." What a nice change from the Kansan's usually ham-on-wry style. And the president had earned the accolade.

Don't tell anybody, especially that union audience, but Mr. Clinton's side agreements represent only window dressing. His new commissions on labor and the environment cannot issue binding orders or supersede this country's laws, federal or state.

But do tell good union people and anybody else who will listen that NAFTA is not going to give cheaper Mexican labor an unfair advantage. It is actually cheaper to produce many exports (automobiles, for example) in the United States than in Mexico. Parts, shipping, inventory costs, and other factors are so much more economical here.

Labor represents only 8 percent of the cost of making a car in this country, and only 15 percent of the production cost of all American manufacturing. Maybe that's because American workers are seven times as productive as their Mexican counterparts.

And where salesmanship is concerned, it would be harder to imagine anybody more productive at it just now than Bill Clinton.

AFTAH NAFTA: TIME TO PROMOTE THE PRESIDENT

DECEMBER 6, 1993

Bill Clinton defined his own moment the other day. The regulars on what the *New Republic* calls the Clinton Suck-up Watch must have decided the phrase Defining Moment is now as passé as George Bush. So the president was left to trot out the cliché himself. "Tonight's vote," he declared without fear of contradiction or originality, "is a defining moment for our nation."

However hackneyed his words, Mr. Clinton had a right to crow, having just led the Republicans in the House of Representatives to victory over his own party on NAFTA. In terms of free trade, the North American Free Trade Agreement was the defining issue of this congressional session.

Most free traders are Republicans nowadays, and NAFTA got the vote of 132 Republicans in the House and only 102 Democrats, though there's no telling how many Democrats would have come through if the president had really needed them.

The final tally demonstrates that the president is either a great bipartisan leader or a great leader of the opposition. It scarcely matters. He won, even if the NAFTA that Bill Clinton managed to pass isn't quite the free-trade agreement that he inherited from George Bush, who signed it in 1992, or the dream envisioned by Ronald Reagan, who proposed it in 1979. But NAFTA wouldn't bear the Clinton imprint if its essentials hadn't been vaguely compromised. And it was Bill Clinton — not Ronald Reagan or George Bush — who got it passed.

The vote on the trade agreement represents an unalloyed triumph for Bill Daley, who ran the boiler-room operation for NAFTA in the proud tradition of his father, the late great Richard J. Daley of Chicago. Hizzoner would have been proud. His youngest son's mastery of old-style politics impressed; this Daley can round up congressmen quicker'n an old-time cowboy could a herd of steers. Woodrow C. Call of *Lonesome Dove* had nothing on William M. Daley of Chicago, Ill.

The poobahs of organized labor may still be muttering, but ever more quietly. "I can't help but think that this NAFTA issue has damaged the prospects" for the Clintons' health plan, Lane Kirkland of the AFL-CIO claimed immediately after the vote — a comment as sound as much of his opposition to NAFTA. The administration's victory in this fight can only strengthen it for future and, unfortunately, less worthy battles. No doubt Mr. Kirkland will be at Bill Clinton's side again in many a bad cause. In these intramural fights, amnesia is often the better part of valor.

Bill Becker, the AFL-CIO's man in Arkansas, used to mutter imprecations against Bill Clinton, too, but went along quietly in the end. What was the alternative? The already fading unpleasantness over NAFTA will be forgotten, much like Lani Guinier, the middle-class tax cut, and Bill Clinton's using a little public money to break a strike back when he was governor of Arkansas. . . . The Bill Beckers of the world don't stay mad long, maybe because they figure they can't afford to. In some ways, that's a pity. It would make politicians more accountable.

All this having been duly noted in the court of editorial opinion, let it also be said that, if Bill Daley is a heckuva political organizer, he had a great cause to organize — free trade — and a president who never quits. Not since Lyndon Johnson has the White House been occupied by a more unceasing lobbyist, salesman, negotiator, and arm-twister. This president can call congressmen in his sleep and theirs. If he starts late, he never stops. Bill Clinton would make the Energizer Bunny look like a short-timer.

In the late-starting but fast-finishing fight for NAFTA, Bill Clinton showed all the political skills he had honed in Arkansas. Except he demonstrated them on a nationwide scale.

Considering the national stage on which Bill Clinton now employs his unmatched talent for campaigning, it may be time to retire the diminutive nickname Slick Willie for the alter ego that still lurks in the darker corners of 1600 Pennsylvania Avenue. . . .

In honor of this victory for free trade, and considering the dignity of the office this native son of Arkansas now holds, something more exalted is called for in the way of a sobriquet. It should be something more decorous, something that approaches the sweep of his politics/negotiation/salesmanship. Mr. Clinton has earned a promotion. Yes, from now on it might be more fitting to refer to the forty-second president of the United States as Slick William.

It should be noted that President Clinton had some expert help in rounding up votes for NAFTA. A familiar name unleashed some memories in an editorial writer who spent a year with the old Chicago Daily News:

ANOTHER TIME, ANOTHER DALEY
DECEMBER 8, 1993

The White House was on the phone. I knew better than that. Buildings don't make phone calls, people do. Who exactly is it, I wanted to know. Somebody named Daley, they said, and I hopped. Instinctively. In a way I never do for Mack McLarty. My year-to-a-day in Chicagoland back in the '60s had left me with a reflexive response: If a Daley calls, answer!

The unmistakable voice of a Daley over the phone brought it all back: State Street, That Great Street. Chi-*ca*-go, Chi-*ca*-go, That Toddlin' Town. The raspy tones of Hoagy Carmichael sure beat Muzak. South Side, West Side. Independence Boulevard. Maxwell Street, where you could always get a bargain. And the best pastrami and halvah in the world, no matter what New Yorkers say. Jack Ruby's old stomping grounds.

No, there was nothing Second City about Maxwell Street — or Jefferson Street, in its heyday the world capital of second-hand shoes. That's where my Zayde Chaim (Grandpa Charlie in the vernacular) got his start. Comiskey Park, home of the White Sox. Ravinia Park, summer home to the stars. Union Station. Boilermakers . . .

And, inevitably, life at the late *Daily News*. And death, which was the regular fate of my editorial submissions at the hands of an editor with the touch of a butcher. On the upscale editorial page, we were decorous anti-Daley Republicans every day of the year except election day, when the paper knew what was good for it. Mayor Daley even had the support of David M. Kennedy, chairman of Continental Illinois Bank and Trust before he stepped down to become Richard Nixon's secretary of the Treasury.

It all came back: the way the wind whistled under the El tracks and everywhere else. I thought of my old green plaid overcoat, which had been just perfect for the weather — in Pine Bluff, Arkansas. Now, sitting in a warm, comfortable office in Little Rock, waiting to take a call from a Daley, I suddenly felt a chill.

The voice on the other end was definitely that of a Chicago Daley, but it was not The Voice, the gravelly foghorn that could direct Chicago's unruly City Council through every hoop in sight and quite a few that weren't. This Daley's tone was more cultivated (what a loss!) and lacked his father's bulldog bravura, but it was just as direct, informal, and authoritative.

"Bill Daley, NAFTA Special Counsel," the caller announced, and I hastened to explain that the paper already had come out for the North American Free Trade Agreement, lest he get the impression that we might give a Daley any trouble. Bill Daley was on and off the line in what seemed like seconds, his manner quick but unhurried. Doubtless he had a lot of other calls to make. After learning Mayor Daley's boy was on the case, I never had a doubt that NAFTA would get the votes it needed in Congress. In the fight over NAFTA, he didn't leave a string unpulled.

Bill Daley's kind of political talent must be in the blood, or maybe it was a product of early training on the South Side, specifically at 3536 South Lowe in Bridgeport.

One regrets only that Daley the Youngest lacks his father's genius for malapropism, though that term scarcely does justice to Hizzoner's unforgettable way with the language. My favorite piece of Daleyana was uttered when the press insisted on reporting the less than gentle behavior of Chicago's Finest during the chaotic Democratic convention of 1968:

"Gentlemen, get this thing straight, once and for all," Hizzoner told those inky wretches. "The policeman isn't there to create disorder, the policeman is there to preserve disorder!"

There is a wealth of Daleyisms for the connoisseur to choose from:

"I resent the insinuendoes."

"That isn't even true enough to answer."

"They have vilified me, they have crucified me, yes, they have even criticized me."

"It is amazing what they will be able to do once they get the atom harassed."

And enough other gems to make even Casey Stengel look like an amateur at the malaprop. Particularly endearing was Hizzoner's reliance on baseball metaphors, and even the occasional understatement. He could combine them with rare, not to say egregious, skill. For example, in 1968 he disavowed any kingmaking ambitions in the 1968 presidential race with the unlikely assertion: "I don't hear much about what is going on around the country. I'm strictly a local boy serving the great City of Chicago. . . ." That's the city slicker's version of the populist pol's "I'm just a little ol' country boy. . . ." On hearing any such phrase, be sure to check and see if your wallet is still there.

Soon after, in the heat of all the presidential maneuvering that year, Bobby Kennedy let it slip that "Daley means the ball game." Asked about it, the mayor just looked blank-faced and explained: "He means I'm a great White Sox fan."

If ol' Yogi Berra was the master of malapropism in sports, Mayor Daley I was its exemplar in politics. His eldest son, also named Mayor Daley now, shows signs of promise along these lines.

Alas, Bill Daley doesn't seem to have inherited the family talent for non-words, neo-words, and close-but-no-cigar words, like "insinuendoes."

Bill Daley has, however, displayed the same fine Irish hand for politics — for which two presidents (Clinton and Salinas) can be grateful, along with free-traders everywhere.

That the Chicagoan got NAFTA passed only after a late start impresses all the more. (Clinton Standard Time is usually behind the rest of the country's by an hour and a half, and sometimes by weeks.) Despite the delay, Bill Daley got NAFTA okayed with a workmanlike lack of mystique, and then — even more impressive — he went home.

A Carville or Stephanopoulous he isn't, nor does the youngest Daley need to be. When it comes to the big time, he grew up in it; he needn't jostle for perks and a rep. And a good thing, too, because on his arrival in Big Rock, D.C., he was mainly condescended to.

Bill Daley left Washington just as the undisguised flattery started rolling in, including the stale presidential variety. ("Two months ago, this was Mission Impossible. There's only one person for Mission Impossible — Bill Daley!" — Bill Clinton. Cheeze, as any real Chicagoan would say, where does he get this stuff, out of a tube of grease?)

Having arrived and departed without any of the usual fuss and folderol, as undaunted by predictions of defeat as he was unfazed by victory, unburdened by a political philosophy and other impedimenta, Bill Daley is now out of Big Rock and back in real life. He did only two things while he was there: See NAFTA through and demonstrate that what New Democrats need is more old Democrats like him.

It may take a while, and many a twist and turn, but this president can act like one if you're willing to wait. See Haiti, occupation of, in 1994:

BILL CLINTON DOES THE RIGHT THING
SEPTEMBER 23, 1994

Whether or not the president had the constitutional authority to order an invasion of Haiti, he was certainly wise to seek approval for such an action. Any president will need all the support he can garner when American lives are on the line.

Bill Clinton is not the first president to order troops into Haiti, nor would he be the first to find congressional support for military action growing tenuous at the first sign of trouble.

Remember how J. William Fulbright, champion of the Tonkin Resolution, became its chief critic once the war in Vietnam bogged down? Or how Dale Bumpers, who took Mr. Fulbright's place in the United States Senate, could scarcely deliver a speech in the days before George Bush's invasion of Kuwait without evoking the image of body bags? And how Senator Bumpers then grew supportive when the war in the Persian Gulf went according to plan?

For that matter, remember how a presidential hopeful named Bill Clinton waffled shamelessly on the war in the Persian Gulf, then claimed to have supported the president after it was safely won?

Moral: Succeed in accomplishing the nation's objectives, Mr. President, and Congress will follow the American public in applauding your wisdom. But fail, and even the minimal support for an invasion of Haiti would have disappeared. At least since Tom Paine's day, there has been no shortage of sunshine soldiers. But no one is going to desert you in your hour of victory. The great test of a leader is whether he can rally his country in a cause that may not be popular but is necessary. It took a while, but it was good to see Bill Clinton take his case directly to the American people. It was time the people were addressed, not just polled.

What was the president's case for an invasion? Those who wanted to be assured that American interests were at stake before going to war got the usual list of objectives: "to stop the brutal atrocities that threaten tens of thousands of Haitians; to secure our borders and preserve stability in our hemisphere; and to promote democracy and uphold the reliability of our commitment around the world."

If the president's language about securing our borders needed any explanation, it was not a reference to any threat of imminent invasion by Haiti's Ton-Ton Macoutes, but to the danger of being swamped by Haitian refugees as they fled their oppressors in great numbers.

Those who demanded authority in international law for an invasion of Haiti could find it aplenty in the resolutions of the Organization of American States and the United Nations. Haiti's dictators had toyed endlessly with both organizations, as well as with this country's State Department, but they had refused to step down until it became clear that this president meant business and learned that the paratroops were on the way.

Jean-Bertrand Aristide, Haiti's legitimate president, is no great bargain himself, but he did win a free election. And once the junta realized the Americans were coming with or without its permission, it crumbled. Which figures: Wouldn't anybody prefer a cushy exile [in] some place like the Spanish Riviera to Manuel Noriega's fate? Haiti's Raoul Cedras showed better judgment than Panama's caudillo did.

In the end, after all the legalisms had been recited and the arguments from Realpolitik debated, the question of whether to undertake an invasion of Haiti did not depend on arguments from self-interest. The issue was simpler and more profound: Should America be true not only to her international commitments, but to her best self? Would we stand by and watch while a poor and pitiable people only a few miles offshore were denied their unalienable rights in the cruelest fashion? Or would we be a good neighbor?

In the end, what was at issue here was as simple and hard and impossible to deny as duty. When a neighbor's house is on fire, do Americans just sit by and watch? We had to act — not in order to make friends or further any material interest. On the contrary, the United States will doubtless be denounced soon enough by the very people whose rights we have upheld. America had to undertake this mission not because it will profit us, but because it is the decent thing to do.

One more word: Some of us have wondered if Bill Clinton would ever take any action that might not be popular simply because it is right. Now we have our answer. Even though the polls said the overwhelming majority of the American people opposed an invasion of

Haiti, this president and commander-in-chief acted like one. I for one am proud of him.

It can't have been easy for Bill Clinton, and it is not likely to get any easier. The continuing vivisection of Bosnia, to cite another example of a world in chaos, awaits a similar show of American leadership and international cooperation. And if even Haiti can have a free and lawful government, how much longer will Fidel Castro be allowed to keep neighboring Cuba in thrall?

In keeping America's word, and, more important, in remaining true to what America means in the world, this president has shown what determination in a just cause can accomplish for both peace and freedom. Here's hoping he impressed that lesson on himself, too.

THE BEST KIND OF VICTORY IN HAITI

SEPTEMBER 25, 1994

As I was writing Saturday, before peace suddenly erupted in Haiti, "maybe if the junta realizes America has a president who means what he says, no invasion will be necessary. The junta may crumble when it realizes it cannot bluff any longer."

By Sunday night, with all signals Go and the 82nd Airborne on its way, the president and commander-in-chief could begin his broadcast: "My fellow Americans, I want to announce that the dictators of Haiti have agreed to step down voluntarily."

Life-saving thing, credibility. Or as the first president and commander-in-chief put it in the first State of the Union message: "To be prepared for war is one of the most effectual means of preserving the peace."

It may have taken awhile for General Washington's sage counsel to sink in with this administration, but it begins to — with salutary results. At last, Raoul Cedras and disconcerted company began to suspect over the weekend that the Clinton administration might really mean what it had been saying for a year.

The "credible and imminent threat of a multinational force," to borrow a phrase from the current president, can wonderfully concentrate the attention of the Raoul Cedrases of the world. Force they understand. Maybe not democracy or justice or the rule of law, but force, yes.

Should the credible and imminent threat of force disappear, the junta's suddenly pacific mood will surely disappear, too. Nothing invites treachery like weakness. Which is why Sunday's agreement, and Washington's interpretation of it as a schedule for surrender, must be enforced scrupulously. Happily, American forces will be on the scene to do just that, and then, let's hope, clear out as soon as possible.

This time let's not stay for twenty years and wind up keeping Haiti's books. A good fire department doesn't settle down in the living room and put its feet up on the furniture after the fire has been put out. This country can't help being the Colossus of the North; let's try to be a good neighbor as well.

Haiti's generals seem to have learned their lesson, but the lesson will need to stay learned. Or as Colin Powell said at the White House — and how well the setting suited him! — this is only Day One of the settlement in Haiti. Having established their beachhead peacefully, American troops will be on hand and in a commanding position to see that Haiti's dictators don't renege on another agreement. . . .

It is possible that, with the coming of peace, even reconciliation may one day come to hate-filled Haiti. The past must be unearthed, and Haiti's courts will have to deal with it, but don't let it poison the future by setting off a wave of persecution-in-reverse. Let the deadly cycle end.

Bill Clinton was right Monday when he brushed aside the oh-so-important issue of whether Raoul Cedras and his co-caudillos would be allowed to remain on the island. Or as General Powell said of the whole question of exile and revenge, "Let that flow out." General Grant once put it even more clearly: "Let us have peace."

As for Jimmy Carter, this time he deserves kudos for his role as a free-lance diplomat (Have Foreign Policy, Will Travel), and the result is far happier than the opportunity he gave North Korea's regime to go on practicing nuclear blackmail. Maybe the secret of Mr. Carter's success is never to send him anywhere unaccompanied by Gen. Colin Powell, U.S. Army, and Sen. Sam Nunn, U.S. Congress. It is no secret that General Powell has a rapport with the Haitians, and particularly with their military, that made him especially effective in these dicey circumstances.

The use of this crisis for political advantage has been as low as was to be expected. Dick Cheney, a Republican presidential hopeful, did surprise when he accused the president of "being moved by domestic political pressure" more than strategic concerns even as the polls showed most Americans opposed to an invasion.

Some of us had assumed, wrongly, that Mr. Cheney was above that kind of slur, and certainly above equating the national interest with what the public opinion polls say at any given moment. When the country's secretary of defense was named Cheney, its president didn't have an easy time rallying the American people for a great effort to liberate another small country, either, but that doesn't mean the war in the Persian Gulf was not in the national interest.

Yes, this kind of thing is to be expected. It hasn't been too long since a presidential hopeful named Clinton waffled shamelessly on the war against Iraq, waiting till it was safely won before claiming he had been for it all along. It occurs at such times that American foreign policy will never be effective till it is bipartisan.

In the days ahead, as the politicians politick and Haiti's departing dictators dicker, let's not forget that this was a victory, and learn from it. It has lessons not only for Haiti's leaders, but for this country's. Imagine what might have been avoided in Bosnia with a credible display of American leadership and international force, and the effect such a demonstration might have had on a world slipping into chaos. Peace has its victories just as war does. This is one of them. And though it is harder to learn from victory than from defeat, let's try.

The administration acted like a good neighbor when Mexico stumbled into financial trouble:

BILL CLINTON TO THE RESCUE
FEBRUARY 6, 1995

Poor Mexico, they say: So far from God, so close to the United States. And forever caught up in the wake of this Colossus of the North.

This time the peso was whipsawed by Mexico's own ruling politicians, who waited too long to devalue it lest their reelection be endangered, and by investors north of the border who went from greedy enthusiasm for Mexican stocks and bonds to sheer panic when things started to get shaky.

This "bold new" Congress didn't help; it turned fearful and indecisive when the moment of truth came, and the president asked it to co-sign a $40 billion bailout for a neighbor with problems.

On the other side of the aisle, Newt Gingrich and Bob Dole both favored this deal, understanding the importance of Mexico to this country's own markets. When a good customer with vast resources but short of ready cash needs a loan, the wise merchant does what he can to help. But the president was unable to bring his own party along, any more than Messrs. Gingrich and Dole could deliver Republican support once the Democrats held back.

Here was a golden opportunity to take advantage of a neighbor in trouble, and for a while it looked as though every Honorable was going to stake out his own favorite pound of flesh to claim in return for supporting this loan. Some congressmen wanted a better extradition treaty while others demanded that Mexico keep its people at home. (Why not? East Germany used to.) Others wanted Mexico to pass new drug laws, or labor regulations, or environmental rules . . . it was a wonder nobody demanded that the Mexicans put up a few of their national monuments as collateral.

In this new isolationist era, showing some international responsibility can give a party a bad name. And so while all the responsible leaders might have favored the deal, each found some reason not to support it in practice.

It was one of those moments in history when the Congress of the United States looked just the way it does in those lurid caricatures of Western imperialists in high hats with dollars signs on their vests. Our distinguished congresspersons are not a pretty sight when caught between fear (of their own constituents) and greed (for whatever the Mexicans had left to lose). Here was an issue made for the Pat Buchanans and Ross Perots to exploit, and they surely will.

In this swirling vacuum, the Clinton administration found it easier to organize the world's financial community than to deal with the Beltway bunch. Washington's formal help was cut back to a $20 billion mix of loans and guarantees over the next three to five years; the International Monetary Fund and the Bank for International Settlements agreed to lend Mexico $17.8 billion; and no congressional approval was needed. Good thing it wasn't, because it wasn't coming.

The United States remains heavily involved in the Mexican crisis, but Congress slips off the hook with an audible sigh of relief. Foreign aid has become about as popular as leisure suits these days; nobody wants to be associated with it.

Even with these loans, the Mexican recovery will be fragile. Those who wanted to send a message — by letting its people suffer and punishing investment there — have forgotten that the message already has been sent in the most powerful way. The collapse of the peso and of Mexican securities will not soon be forgotten. Mexico is not getting off lightly; it's just being saved.

The United States and the international community need to tie some tough conditions to their aid and insist that the Mexicans make some basic economic reforms to prevent a repeat of this roller-coaster effect. But let's confine the treatment to the illness, not prescribe pain in general. And let's forget political demands that will only offend, and should offend, a proud people and a good customer.

In this crisis for Mexico — which soon enough would have been a crisis for American exporters and investors — Bill Clinton proved himself a resourceful and decisive executive while Congress dithered. In short, he acted like a president. And he deserves credit for it. He's come a ways since the presidential campaign of 1992, when he was exploiting Americans' suspicions about NAFTA and the whole idea of free trade with Mexico.

Now others will try to turn those same, festering suspicions against the president, but he will have the consolation of having done the right thing for both Mexico and the United States. One of the great advantages of acting like a good neighbor is that it raises the tone of the whole neighborhood.

Chapter 5

In Charge?

B ill Clinton's style of executive and legislative leadership is simple enough: compromise and protracted negotiation. The negotiations may not lead anywhere even if they seem to go on forever, but solving a problem or meeting a challenge is scarcely the major aim of this style of leadership. Rather, the objective becomes to leave all the participants with the impression that Bill Clinton has protected their interests. That impression may prove short-lived once the inevitable clinton clauses surface in the small print, but by then The Great Negotiator will have flitted off to complicate another subject.

This style of leadership, not easily differentiated from temporizing, became familiar to the country during the year-long impasse over changing the American health-care system. Even when he starts off with a bang, Bill Clinton is likely to end with a whimper, which will usually be described as a great victory, although for what or whom is not always clear. The pattern goes back at least to Bill Clinton's first term as governor:

RETURN OF YOUNG SMOOTHIE
JUNE 27, 1979

Bill Clinton has come back from vacation just in time to mess things up. Now he's flirting with the idea of calling the legislature into special session to do the truckers' bidding, namely raise the maximum weight limit on Arkansas highways to a crushing 80,000 pounds. As if the legislature hadn't accommodated enough special interests during the regular session.

The fuel crunch and truckers' strike is the occasion for the governor's making the sounds of an imminent cave-in to another special interest. Of course he's made no definite commitment; he seldom does at this tentative stage of the game. Note his kind words for the pensions-for-pols deal when it first came up at this year's session of the General Assembly, and then his furious backpedal when all clamor broke loose. Or how he didn't take a position in favor of retaining the state's regressive sales tax on groceries last year so much as sidle into it. The level of public outrage hasn't reached the point where he has been forced to abandon completely the hope of finding some state agency, any state agency, to take that swank eyrie at Huntsville off Orval Faubus's hands, but already Young Will begins to let that (bad) idea die. This governor seems to react not to issues but pressures. . . .

For now, Mr. Clinton is as usual drifting with the most voluble pressure group in this matter, the truckers. Like water, his political ambition tends to seek its own level. Not unless some countervailing pressure is applied — from the Highway Commission, or motorists, or taxpayers, or consumers in general — can this governor be expected to do anything but drift with the current. One felt safer with him out on vacation.

Increasingly, Bill Clinton comes across as a politician without hard-and-fast stands on important issues — like truck weight limits — and only squishy principles if any underneath. In a way, he's the perfect politician for this rudderless time, when a lot of folks may just want to get through the current crisis, smoothly and articulately, without having to face it. Which may explain why the crises keep coming.

Not that Mr. Clinton is taking a clear stand on behalf of the truckers, either. Getting Bill Clinton to commit himself at this stage of discourse is like trying to pin down a politically talented amoeba.

NOT SO SPECIAL SESSION
APRIL 23, 1980

Special sessions of the Arkansas legislature, at least in post-Faubus times, aren't as scary as the regular version, what with the legislators being reined in by a governor's call. Which may explain why last week's went smoothly enough, reaching a compromise between the public and public utilities on the length of time that the state's ironically entitled Public Service Commission may sit on rate cases.

The governor limited his objectives at this session to some of the most pressing of the state's problems, which was probably prudent considering the caliber of the legislature, and Bill Clinton seemed content enough with what he got. He was heard to say that he was "very pleased" with getting twelve of his thirteen proposals past the Ledge.

Unfortunately, that thirteenth was of great importance; it would have guaranteed the public schools $21 million of the tax windfall the governor has engineered by switching from quarterly to monthly collections. There would also have been $2.6 million more for cities and almost $2 million more for counties. That money is going to be needed more than ever as the federal government gets serious about balancing its budget and cuts its grants to local governments. . . .

Governor Clinton's box score of twelve out of thirteen doesn't stand up so well when one considers just what was lost in the Senate. That however, can scarcely be blamed on the governor, who doubtless did his best but got outmaneuvered by some of the state's most experienced maneuverers. The Arkansas legislature has struck again, this time at local government and public schools, leaving behind mainly a case for a two-party legislature. Or at least one that a progressive governor can work with more effectively. Bill Clinton, like any politician, will be tempted to make the very best of this special session's record, but there wasn't much special about it. He made some modest requests and, thanks to the state Senate, didn't get all of those. In view of the legislature's performance, it becomes clearer why knowledgeable leaders lower their expectations when they must depend on the legislature to fulfill them.

These are shaping up as times of great challenge but mediocre performance in state government. One is used to so much worse from the legislature that the temptation is to celebrate any session that is safely, if inadequately, concluded. The great, hoped-for revolution in state politics will surely come when people expect so much more of the legislature that they will rise up in outrage instead of breathe a sigh of relief at the conclusion of a mediocre session. For the moment, the state may be grateful for almost anything short of disaster. Like Bill Clinton, most Arkansans may ask little of their legislature and settle for less than that.

More Mush from the Wimp

MARCH 12, 1983

At least when Frank White abandoned all responsibility for a high-way program, it was as open as any abdication since Edward VIII's. Governor White simply let it be known that whatever deal the truckers and the Highway Department could strike would be just swell with him. The governor was reduced to a bystander. He seemed prepared to take whatever the bureaucracy and the interests could dish up between them, mainly potholes. The result of such non-leadership was a non-program. And highways that continued to crumble.

As befits a Rhodes Scholar, Bill Clinton has taken a much more subtle approach, but the end result may not be much different. He began by pledging formal allegiance to the Highway Commission's $26 million tax package, but only after giving the truckers the leverage they needed to oppose it — the new eighty-thousand-pound weight limit. That made the governor's allegiance to higher truck taxes only formal. And he caved in like an Arkansas secondary road when the Highway Commission's bill stalled in the House. That's when he hitched a ride on the truckers' light, not to say flimsy, vehicle.

The tax program that went through the House like an eighteen-wheeler past a stop sign should bring in either $15 million a year (according to the truckers) or $9.5 million (according to the Highway Department). In either case, that's scarcely enough to pay for the monumental damage being done by the new eighty-thousand-pound loads now allowed on the state's highways. . . .

To judge the gap between the amount the Highway Department needs to maintain decent roads, and how much the truckers and state representatives plan to raise, note this estimate from David Solomon, chairman of the Highway Commission. He says the state needs $380 million a year to build and maintain roads, but is collecting only $256 million. Some $15 million in new taxes will scarcely fill the gap. As for the new federal highway taxes being turned back to Arkansas, Mr. Solomon notes that those are reserved mainly for interstate and primary highways, leaving the state's secondary roads to deteriorate even further. At this rate, the Clinton administration could mark a crucial turning point in the state's history — when Arkansas was allowed to slip back into the mud.

But now the governor has switched sides again and joined forces with the Highway Commission behind a weight-distance tax that is supposed to bring in about $21 million a year. "I'm not flip-flopping," Mr. Clinton insisted while flip-flopping. As the truckers' bill and the Highway Department's were pitted against each other, the governor commented: "Now it's a race to the wire to see which passes first." As if he were just there to watch.

It was Frank White's neutrality all over again, but this time with rationalizations added. "That's been my strategy all along," explained Slick Willie sagely, "to try to get them so close together that we'd pass something." This governor may have abdicated too, but he wasn't about to admit it. According to the authorized gubernatorial version, Mr. Clinton now has these competing interests — the Highway Department and the truckers — just where he wants them. No need to consider the possibility that they might have him just where they want him.

It's enough to remind one of that leader in the French Revolution who was desperate to know where the mob had gone. "I must know," he cried, "for I am its leader." Bill Clinton would never be so crass. He just wants to see where the lobbies are going. He needs to know because he's their buddy.

RELAX — FOR A WHILE
MARCH 22, 1983

The state can sleep better of nights; the legislature has adjourned. It not only has decamped but has taken with it those who seemed to do most of the governing this past session — the lobbyists. The special interests long have been influential at the legislature, but at this session it was deemed a rare victory when the governor and legislators could exert a little influence over the special interests. No matter what the subject — truck weights or school consolidation, day-care centers or tobacco licenses — the final law seemed more a product of the lobbies than the lawmakers. After edging closer to that goal for years, Arkansas at last seems to have achieved government of the lobbies, by the lobbies, and for the lobbies.

[Citizens] concerned with protecting the public interest soon learned that the most effective technique was to enlist a lobby or two on their side. There is nothing like self-interest to supply the final push for the disinterested public good. That's how, against all the seeming odds, the state was finally able to assess a minimal tax on those trucks that have been doing maximal damage to the roads: The highway contractors and railroad lobby were enlisted to offset the trucking and poultry interests. It takes one to beat one.

It was as if the governor and legislature had delegated their powers of persuasion to the special interests, who were left to check and balance each other. Bill Clinton presided over the whole Roman circus with fine impartiality, giving each lobby separate but equal support, even if that meant switching sides in midsession. Only the public interest went unsupported.

There was an exception to the governor's rule of impartial support for all private interests: the utilities. He consistently opposed them, or rather they consistently opposed his attempts to regulate them. It was a fight Bill Clinton couldn't lose. If he had won in the legislature, it would have been a case of David slaying the Goliath of Arkansas politics. If he lost, which for the most part he did, he would emerge with a hot issue and convenient scapegoat for 1984 — specifically, the same theme he ran on in 1982, the sins of the utilities.

One observer of Arkansas politics just arrived from Texas found the goings-on at Little Rock tame compared to those in Austin, where he claimed the lobbyists even had their own dormitory at the Capitol. That isn't necessary in these parts because (a) Arkansas lobbyists never sleep, and (b) Arkansas legislators themselves double as lobbyists, or vice versa. That eliminates the middle man and assures direct representation — for the interests. Direct lobbocracy has many such advantages over the representative kind.

What may have been missing most at this legislative session was gubernatorial leadership. Bill Clinton seemed to put it in storage as soon as he heard about the shortfall in state revenues. After that, he offered a lot of gubernatorial followship as the problem was delegated to the competing lobbies.

The White and Clinton administrations may mark a watershed in Arkansas politics. The disinterested devotion to the public interest associated with the post-Faubus period, and particularly with Winthrop Rockefeller, seems to have dwindled steadily over the years. Dale Bumpers and David Pryor both demonstrated their independence of the interests. But under Governors White and Clinton, that independence seems to have all but disappeared. Governor Clinton, a.k.a. Slick Willie, consistently puts an idealistic gloss on his surrender to various lobbies, but his basic relationship with them does not seem much different from Frank White's.

Once the interests' business was done, the legislature adjourned, leaving much of the state's undone. As for the important business of the state, it was treated with a lick and a promise, if that. Education was probably the most prominent casualty of this session of the Ledge, which did little or nothing to consolidate the schools or create an adequate system of higher education. Such urgent business was left for later, if ever. Some school districts may or may not be consolidated by 1987, depending on a committee not yet appointed. The state is as far away from a first-class university system as it ever was, if not further. That modest weight-distance tax is not likely to offset the growing pressures on Arkansas's crumbling roads, let alone add new four-lane highways — like the one Pine Bluff long has needed to the south and east. Only the prisons' needs have been met for the time being, and perhaps only for the time being. That figures. A society that will not spend on education or on the sinews of economic development, like adequate highways, will likely find itself spending more on prisons. Meantime, the legislators occupied themselves with pressing matters like . . . the Suffer Little Children bill to exempt church day-care centers from state supervision.

After all the talk about repealing this state's multitudinous tax exemptions in order to raise much-needed revenue, this legislature succeeded in enacting more. In the process, the governor and legislature agreed not to raise the state's most notoriously low severance tax, the one on natural gas. The odds in favor of a general tax hike increase with every new loophole voted for the special interests. So it may not be long before a special session of the legislature meets to require all the taxpayers to make up for favors granted at this session, probably through another raise in the sales tax. . . .

Arkansas may be able to turn its back now that the legislature is adjourned, but not for long. So relax and Be Prepared.

Bringing Up the Rear
July 18, 1983

Bill Clinton must have dropped a seventh or eighth shoe by now when it comes to calling a special session of the legislature. The latest, broadest hint came in a talk with about 150 of his political supporters, who got the impression that the governor plans not just one but two special sessions. The first would address the problems of education. The second would deal with the truckers' problems with the new ton-mile tax. At least Mr. Clinton did not put the truckers first this time.

A couple of those who attended the meeting said the governor was "fairly definite" about his plans, which is a nice change. One source said Mr. Clinton had told the gathering that he had no option but to call a special session for education — except to defy the state Supreme Court and its ruling against the present, unequal treatment of school districts in Arkansas. Thank goodness for the Arkansas Supreme Court. Without it, there's no telling how long the governor would have been able to ignore the needs of education in this state.

Politics still seems uppermost in Slick Willie's calculations. He is said to have asked the crowd to help build support for a 1 percent increase in the state sales tax, which would be used to improve education. But he himself isn't ready to go public.

When it comes to acknowledging openly the need to raise money for the state's schools, young Fearless Leader still lags behind the teachers, the press, legislative leaders, his wife's commission on educational standards, his political supporters at this meeting, maybe the people in general, and even Frank White.

Ever since he got beat by Frank White back in 1980, Mr. Clinton has been super-cautious about expressing progressive ideas, particularly if they involve taxes. He's now coming to the rescue of the state's public schools at the speed of molasses — cold molasses.

To make certain that no one would confuse this governor with a leader, his staff director — Betsey Wright — insisted that this gathering of his political friends was but "another in a series of ongoing meetings the governor has held with various groups to discuss the state's problems and the alternatives for dealing with them. He did *not* announce a special session." The emphasis is Betsey Wright's. As becomes usual in this administration, the emphasis is on what the governor is *not* prepared to do to meet the state's needs.

Years after the need for a better way to finance Arkansas schools became undeniable, months after a regular session of the legislature should have dealt with the challenge, and weeks after the state Supreme Court's ruling left him no practical alternative to a tax raise, Bill Clinton still dallies and confers. The one accusation nobody is going to pin on this governor is leadership.

The Sage Puts It Plain
June 3, 1985

William F. Foster, the state representative and sage of England, Arkansas, once again has taken the lead in trying to save Arkansas's highway system. Somebody needs to, since the governor has offered a vacuum of leadership on this issue. After Bill Clinton vetoed the highway bill at the last session of the legislature, Representative Foster led the fight for the bill — and the additional four-cent-a-gallon tax on gasoline to fund it.

That tax was designed to benefit primarily rural roads, like those in Mr. Foster's home county of Lonoke, but it would also provide crucial matching funds for a western bypass around Pine Bluff and a decent four-lane between Alma and Fayetteville in Northwest Arkansas. Leading the charge for better roads in the legislature took concern, vision, and responsibility. It also took guts, since it meant supporting higher taxes: Four cents a gallon on gasoline, two cents a gallon on diesel fuel. Together with Pine Bluff's Knox Nelson, the Sage of England got the bill — and the roads — approved, while Bill Clinton mainly ducked.

Asked to sign a petition to refer this new tax (and the new roads) to a popular vote, Governor Clinton went along quietly, signing his name to the petition. But Mr. Foster has stepped into the vacuum of leadership again and explained why he couldn't sign such a petition. His words won't be confused with a slick out; they're the clear, direct words of a leader. It "would be hypocritical on my part to sponsor and work as hard as I did to get the gas tax and (then) sign the petition," he told a reporter, point-blank. No shilly-shallying, no vague talk about what a fine highway bill this was on the one hand, and how he didn't think the Highway Commission had really sold it to the public on the other, and on the third. . . . That's the sort of thing the Sage of England leaves to Bill Clinton, who may be the only politician in the state — with the possible exception of David Pryor — who can keep *both* ears to the ground. Slick Willie is definitely back and not doing the state's roads a bit of good. But Bill Foster is doing more than a bit; he's demonstrating how a leader of this state should act.

The Sage of England put it plain: "It's my responsibility when they elect me not to do the popular thing, but to do the right thing. . . ." That ought to be engraved somewhere, maybe in the House chamber, or maybe in the governor's office, preferably both. That is the voice of leadership.

The governor's weaving course on this highway bill is particularly disappointing after his gallant, and successful, effort to save the new, higher standards for public education in this state. His administration is proud of those standards and should be. But even on the education issue, the governor did not act till long after it became clear that the public schools in this state needed both new revenues and new standards. First Hillary Clinton and her committee were dispatched to prepare the ground for reform through a series of town meetings all over the state. Only then, having secured his political base, did the governor lead. It's a pity Mrs. Clinton couldn't have mentioned highways while she was at it, and made it safe for the governor to come out for progress in general, not just in the schools.

The highway program finally made it past the legislature, with no public help from the governor and considerable hindrance. But now it's threatened by these petitions for a referendum, one of which bears Bill Clinton's signature. Arkansas has had governors before who didn't do much to get it out of the mud, but did you ever think you'd see a governor who would sign on *against* highways? One would like to think that Hillary Clinton would never sign such a petition, any more than Bill Foster would. They're leaders.

Short but Bittersweet
June 23, 1985

Governor Bill Clinton and his key legislative aides get an A for organization and efficiency at the special session of the state legislature just concluded, and they get something else for principled leadership.

The governor set out to put a Band-Aid on some of the gaping wounds inflicted by the regular session of the legislature earlier this year, and succeeded at that (too) modest aim. Now that the Ledge has gone home, the state can breathe only a little easier. Happily, it was not another long, bitter session. It was short and bittersweet.

The governor and his aides did a good, swift job at what they set out to do, but they set out to do so little. Instead of repealing a disastrous tax credit for colleges and universities that was wrong in its economics, its constitutional law, and its ethics, Governor Clinton proposed simply to whittle down a bad bill by two-thirds. Which means the state still has one-third of the thing lurking on the books, inviting litigation, raising church-state issues, and draining resources from the state treasury.

Instead of repealing a clearly unconstitutional law that kept the state of Arkansas in the business of sponsoring prayer in the public schools, the governor had the legislature omit the word *prayer* but keep the concept. Surely only a justice on the Supreme Court of the United States might fail to see what was going on; any layman who followed the legislature had to know better. The legislature was out to save this prayer period in the schools without saying so.

Of course it would be a rare governor who would come right out and ask legislators to do the honest, forthright thing on this issue; he would doubtless be an ex-governor by the time the know-nothings got through branding him as anti-God because he wanted to separate church and state. This little change in the law was just the usual politician's compromise, and another example of what happens when the state starts laying its hands on that which is considered holy. It profanes it. And when caught by the courts, government may not lay off, but just get sneakier. As in House Bill 2, it doesn't mention *prayer,* but it's one more attempt by the state to meddle with it. . . .

SALES TAX A-COMIN'
MARCH 30, 1987

The people of Arkansas not being a corporation, they can expect no special tax exemption from the state legislature. An increase in the general sales tax looms larger after the state Senate refused to plug a variety of loopholes that now disfigure the state's sales tax, which doesn't apply to lawyers' fees, country club dues, and so on. . . .

Governor Clinton, who has been for and against a sales tax this session, now has proposed one. At first he was talking about excluding necessities like food and utilities from the tax: "There are two things I won't support. I won't support quitting and going home now, because we don't have enough money to fund the school standards. I won't support a one-cent, across-the-board increase in the sales tax because it's regressive, it's unfair, and it raises more money than we need. In between that, I am open to all options if they will fund the school standards in a way that will not overly burden the working people of the state." What he decided to propose was a quarter-of-a-percent sales tax that's regressive, unfair, and will overly burden the working people of the state. Though perhaps it's not as regressive and unfair as letting the legislature kill the new school standards. It shouldn't be long, assuming a sales tax passes, before the governor hails it as a triumph of idealism. Politicians, especially ambitious ones, are like that; they can make a victory out of a sow's ear. . . .

A Botched Session
April 6, 1987

There have been worse sessions of the Arkansas legislature than this last one but few so raggedy. It seemed to go on forever, beginning in uncertainty and ending the same way, especially for the schools. Bill Clinton didn't have his program organized at the start, and the legislature was its usual, disorganized self at the end. Even with strong, decisive, well-organized leadership from the Governor's Mansion, the Ledge isn't easy to lead. See the experience of reform governors from Winthrop Rockefeller to David Pryor. But without that kind of leadership, the General Assembly can become a general morass, as it did this session.

The governor has to hold on to the plow if the work done is to be straight and true, but Bill Clinton was distracted by national policies (welfare reform) as the session was preparing to get under way, and by presidential politics as it was ending. Despite his promise to steer clear of the national whirligig until the General Assembly had adjourned, Mr. Clinton was dining with president-maker Norman Lear and associates out in L.A. the weekend before the final gavel. In between, it was seldom clear whether he favored or didn't favor a sales tax. In the session's final days, he compromised his one, central, and until last week unwavering pledge: that the new school standards would not be lowered. Now he says they won't be lowered "dramatically." . . .

Among the other casualties of the session was the stand-by legislation that Bill Clinton promised to push in order to protect consumers of electrical power in Arkansas. It was virtually ignored — not just by the legislators but by the governor. It was a grand session for Middle South Utilities, known as Arkansas Power and Light in these confines, but not for its customers. The danger of AIDS was discussed at some length and with considerable heat, but it was never really addressed. English was declared the state's official language, but the legislature decided that didn't mean college professors had to be proficient in it.

Anybody who thought the four-year term for governor was going to reform Arkansas politics now has definitive refutation of that dubious claim in this long, botched session of the legislature. After a session like this one, it's understandable why Bill Clinton might want to take refuge in a presidential campaign. If he ever masters the Ledge, Congress ought to be a cinch.

Stalled on the Highway
September 14, 1987

At least since he was upset by Frank White in 1980, Governor Bill Clinton's *modus operandi* in Arkansas politics has been a simple one: Don't offend a single voter. The Clinton Method brings to mind a semi-apocryphal story that has been making the rounds of the *Commercial*'s newsroom since the paper's circulation broke 20,000. On that auspicious day decades back when the *Commercial* went out to 20,001 readers, a veteran editor is supposed to have told an apprentice editorial writer: "Don't offend a single reader!"

That approach makes a better story than it does policy. Even if successful, a determination not to risk losing a single reader would scarcely serve the interests of the other 20,000. The same principle applies to politics. A governor who never offended anybody might never do anything. Bill Clinton has done lots, but the pace can be agonizing — and there is so much more to be done. What needs to be done *now* — it probably should have been done yesterday — is to resolve the crisis building over the state's highways. The weight-distance tax, passed in 1983 to offset the damage done by higher weight limits, now has run into problems in the courts. The money collected under the tax should be going into maintaining the state's highways. But it is being held in escrow. Arkansas needs to devise a new, clearly constitutional tax soon.

Instead, Governor Clinton has been trying to devise a tax both the Highway Department and the trucking industry can agree on, doubtless preparatory to squaring the circle. The trucking lobby has never liked tying road taxes to weight and distance; it would prefer putting a tax on diesel fuel and raising truck registration fees. That way, lighter cars and trucks would share the responsibility for the damage that the behemoths do.

The weight-distance tax meant some $33 million a year more for Arkansas highways before it developed constitutional problems. At last report, the trucking lobby was willing to go to $15 million a year. The proper response to that kind of generosity, and responsibility, should be No Deal. The full $33 million should be assured or the weight limit should be reduced to the old 73,280-pound limit. There should be no compromise on that simple matter of justice and practicality. Naturally, Governor Clinton says he will continue to try for a compromise.

The spectacle of a commander-in-chief negotiating with his own generals remains the clearest illustration of this chief executive's tendency to negotiate rather than execute policy:

OUR NEGOTIATOR-IN-CHIEF
MARCH 31, 1993

Mark it Top Secret. It's not the kind of thing you'd want the enemy to get wind of, but our commander-in-chief seems bereft of any sense of command. Instead of doing a Harry Truman — that is, issuing an order to end discrimination in the armed services and letting the generals worry about how best to carry it out — Bill Clinton has approached the sensitive issue on homosexuals in the military with all the savvy and authority of the greenest recruit.

The new president's first step was — no, not to issue an executive order lifting the ban against homosexuals in the military — but to open negotiations. With just about everybody. With the chairman of the Joint Chiefs of Staff. With the secretary of defense. With the chairman of the Senate Armed Services Committee. With the man-on-the-street. Probably with the lampposts if he could have.

And the net result of all his negotiations to date is that he has succeeded in antagonizing both sides and thoroughly muddying the whole issue. . . .

On this subject, as on so many, the commander-in-chief sounds more like a negotiator-in-chief. Was this a presidential press conference or *Let's Make a Deal?* The new president took an already tangled question and proceeded to tie it and himself in verbal knots. Asked if he was planning to restrict homosexuals to certain assignments, he responded by walking directly into the trap: "I wouldn't rule that out, depending on what the grounds and arguments were."

One would think someone like Colin Powell, chairman of the Joint Chiefs, would have briefed the president on the poor results the last time the military tried to segregate a minority, in that case a racial one.

But the president plunged into the question with his usual boyish enthusiasm for subjects he had learned a lot about but hasn't the slightest feel for. (Military affairs is the leading example of such a topic, followed closely by history in general. That figures. Unfortunately for the species, the two tend to overlap.)

A lawyer to the hollow core, Mr. Clinton proceeded to deliver a strange, rambling defense of restricting the assignments given homosexuals in the service. "Well, I don't want to get into a constitutional debate," he began, preparatory to getting into one.

Then he was off and stumbling: "But if you can discriminate against people in terms of if they get into the service or not, based on not what they are but what they say they are, then I would think you could make appropriate distinctions on duty assignments once they're in. I — the courts have historically given quite wide berth to the military to make judgments of that kind. . . ."

One scarcely knows where to begin unraveling all that, and it is probably better not to try. In only a few words, the president managed to simultaneously raise and sidestep any number of legal and ethical questions in his short but serpentine brief for segregation-by-sexual-orientation. On increasing occasion, Bill Clinton combines Dwight Eisenhower's singular syntax, or lack thereof, and Richard Nixon's sound of sincerity.

All in all, it was not a pleasant thing to watch — a bit like seeing some raw cannoneer smoothly, confidently slide a round into the breech of a howitzer and draw back a mashed thumb.

But this president is apparently prepared to argue and negotiate and compromise almost anything, especially his promises. After his performance last week, some homosexual groups sounded as outraged and appalled as those on the other side of this issue. Before this extended embarrassment is over, perhaps some grand national consensus can be reached, namely, that neither side can trust this guy. Who said Bill Clinton wasn't going to unite us?

The president's man in PR, George Stephanopoulos, was equally vague, coming down foursquare on both sides of the issue. "The presumption is against discrimination of any kind," he assured the press, "but you have to balance it against the need to maintain military order and cohesion." Or in English: Everything about this issue is up for negotiation.

This may be an effective approach for a salesman or a politician to take, but not a commander. Nothing may inspire disorder more than being intimidated by the possibility of it. The troopers, like some other species are said to do, can smell fear.

The most unconvincing statement of the press conference had to be Mr. Clinton's protesting (too much) that he was perfectly comfortable as a military leader. "No, no, I don't have a problem being commanderin-chief," he said.

The assertion had the same empty ring as Richard Nixon's denial at another press conference: "I am not a crook."

No wonder they snicker when the new commander-in-chief visits an aircraft carrier, or returns a salute with only a quizzical look — as if he'd never seen that particular gesture before, but is willing to tolerate it if that's one of the military's quaint customs.

Why, sure, Bill Clinton is comfortable being commander-in-chief, and George Bush likes nothing better than to get out on the dance floor and do the twist.

What's needed here is a little on-the-job training. Unfortunately, our cadet-in-chief turned down the opportunity to get four years of beforethe-job training years ago. It's never too late. Somebody needs to get this president enrolled in ROTC even if he has to go nights. This is getting embarrassing.

———————

One of the reasons Bill Clinton is called the Comeback Kid is that he so often has something to come back from. For this presidency, the new wore off in the spring of 1993 with a now legendary haircut at LAX. The whole week seemed an abject lesson in how not to administer a presidency, let alone the country:

Warren G. Clinton's Week
May 24, 1993

Clinton-watchers should have expected the sort of snafu-filled week that fell on Bill Clinton's well-coiffed head last week. It was but a national magnification of the hands-off management that the president specialized in while still governor of Arkansas.

The Clinton management style, or lack thereof, explained the excruciatingly long tenure here in Arkansas of one Fahmy Malak, the state medical examiner who delivered a number of judgments that belong in *Ripley's Believe It or Not*. Mr. Clinton also left behind some long-running messes in the state's Medicaid program before going off to straighten out the whole country's health care.

Expected or not, it still was not a pleasant thing to watch as the Clinton administration went from incompetence to farce and back again all in about twenty-four hours. Which hurt more, the presidential haircut that tied up air traffic for hundreds of miles around, or the peremptory purge of the entire, seven-member White House travel staff? The staff was promptly replaced by a Little Rock travel agency, which was promptly replaced itself. To top it off, the president's third cousin wound up in charge of White House travel. Farce followed farce. It was as if an occult hand was at work, or maybe a screenwriter for one of Mel Brooks's slapstick comedies.

Now it is reported that Harry Thomason, the impresario of the Clinton inauguration, [was in league] with the travel executive who criticized the travel staff in a memo faxed to the White House shortly before the ax fell. This despite earlier assurances from the administration that Mr. Thomason had no stake in changing the president's travel arrangements.

With friends like that, the president needs no political embarrassments. One couldn't help but think of poor Warren Harding walking the White House floor nights as the scandals of his administration began to break, and telling Kansas editor William Allen White that it wasn't his enemies a president has to worry about but his friends, his blankety-blank friends.

Happily, neither Hairport nor the travel snafu ranks with Teapot Dome. Nor has Bill Clinton ever been the type to be paralyzed by guilt. Whatever happens, he will always have a smooth explanation for it. If he paces the floor over some embarrassment, it's only to figure out how to get out of it and on top again. And he's exceptionally good at it.

Think of how many times the pundits ruled Bill Clinton out of last year's presidential race. Neither rain nor sleet nor Gennifer Flowers nor his dalliance with the draft could keep this candidate him from his presidential rounds. The Comeback Kid, he proclaimed himself in New

Hampshire. There was an inexplicable buoyancy about the Clinton campaign, as if it thrived on scandals that would have sunk any candidate with a capacity for shame. Where is that unsinkable optimism now, when the president — and the country — could use a little of it?

Instead, a familiar miasma seems to be settling over this administration, like malaise on Jimmy Carter. Or the little black cloud that used to follow Joe Btfsplk everywhere he went in Al Capp's Dogpatch. If Bill Clinton were a ball club, his manager would be looking for a new job about now.

The most worrisome part of last week's presidential misadventures wasn't any particular misstep — they weren't so much important as amusing — so much as the general impression they conveyed in their tragi-comic totality. A wholly irrational yet distinct feeling grows that things at the White House aren't going to get much better, and that the world will be lucky if they don't get much worse. . . . The same old can't-win-for-losing atmosphere that settled over the Bush White House in its last days begins to creep up on the Clinton administration in its first.

This sort of thing just can't go on. Or can it? It's definitely time for a new rabbit's foot. Or at least a new press spokesman.

It's eerie, and unsettling. Let's hope last week was just an aberration. Unfortunately, it felt like a trend. This was supposed to be a presidential honeymoon; it's turning into a wake. There is a tide in presidential leadership, and for the moment the Comeback Kid seems stuck in the shallows. Surely no one would have anticipated that, when the Conquering Hero returned to New Hampshire last week, he would be greeted by a sign reading: "Nice haircut, Bubba."

During the presidential campaign, Bill Clinton seemed protected by some lucky star that warded off all his good-ol'-boy carelessnesses about details like character and principle. Suddenly it's gone. Surely even his harshest critics have to feel a little sorry for the guy just now. Neither his success nor his remarkable ability to turn failure around, or at least hide it, has prepared this president for a run of bad luck.

Son of Malaise: The Clinton Crack-up Continues

June 9, 1993

How could Bill Clinton, or whoever is in charge of this administration, if anyone is, have mishandled the nomination or non-nomination of Lani Guinier any more thoroughly?

Beats me. If there is a mistake, a miscue, an embarrassment, a sloppiness, a contradiction in matters great or small, in theory or technique, in principle or practice, in personal loyalty or political science that the Clintonoids missed in *l'affaire* Guinier, what possibly could it have been? Who else could have been offended, what other groups alienated, what other standards ignored?

Every mistake that could have been made, and perhaps a few one had thought couldn't be, have been. From curious start to unsatisfying finish, this administration has managed to bring off another elaborate botch, sending Lani Guinier to join Zoe Baird and Kimba Wood in the lengthening line-up of might-have-beens.

As another Clinton nominee bites the dust, the ordinary incompetencies of a new administration become something else — not just a momentary trend but a habit. This administration seems not only on the defense but continually defensive. Seeping into the news at every turn is the all-too-familiar feel of Carteresque malaise. Once again a failing — and flailing — administration founders.

The good ship Clinton was scarcely out of port Inaugural Day before it began springing leaks. The worst of it is the air of inevitability that begins to set in, as if this crash were just one more in a long line that is only beginning. It is not a pleasant thought, but it becomes inescapable. How much longer, O Lord?

Just to begin with, how did this person get nominated to head the civil rights division of the Justice Department? On the basis of personal friendship with the president, combined with his only superficial impression of her views? (One begins to wonder what other kind of impression Bill Clinton is capable of.) What happened to the great Vetting Process that is supposed to stop embarrassments before they happen?

It turns out that Lani Guinier had made a number of more-than-indiscreet proposals that cannot help but embarrass. And they were all preserved in print, thanks to various academic journals. Professor Guinier's suggestions went beyond the usual counter-gerrymandering designed to give black candidates a fair chance at election. They aimed to assure legislative *outcomes* rather than simply to balance electoral chances.

For example, the professor took the old idea of cumulative voting out of the poli-sci texts and gave it a racial if not racist cast: According to her proposal, voters could be allowed to cast several votes for one candidate in legislative races, doubtless in the expectation that black voters would cast all theirs for one black candidate, assuring his election, while the white vote would be split.

It gets worse. Going beyond the customary two-thirds' requirement to pass important legislation, Professor Guinier suggested requiring super-majorities that would oblige legislatures to satisfy a minority of black legislators in order to pass laws. She dubbed this bad idea "proportionate interest representation."

John C. Calhoun had a better name for it. The old defier from South Carolina spoke of the need for a "concurrent majority" rather than a numerical one. His aim: to give slave states a veto over national legislation that might affect their supposed interests. Bad ideas don't die; they just get revived by separate but equally fervid ideologues. Lani Guinier came across as the John C. Calhoun of today's politically correct class.

Worst of all, and deeply offensive, was her blacker-than-thou rhetoric. In the *Michigan Law Review*, she wrote of those representatives who are "authentic" blacks as opposed to those who aren't. Presumably illuminati like herself would decide which are which. Those who didn't measure up to her standards of blackness would be guilty of "false consciousness." (That's intellectual for being an Uncle Tom.)

Republicans need not apply for admission to the professor's cozy club, to judge by her comment in an article for the *Virginia Law Review*: "Identifying 'black representatives' raises several questions. For example, would descriptively black representatives who were also Republicans qualify as black representatives?" Which rules out Frederick Douglass. And most black leaders of the first Reconstruction. Not to mention more contemporary figures like Ed Brooke, the Massachusetts senator.

Lani Guinier's litmus test for blackness brings to mind the segs of the '50s who called anybody who disagreed with them a traitor to the race. Doesn't anybody in this administration read a nominee's writings before, rather than after, they come back to embarrass her? Or weigh those views after they've been brought to the administration's atten-tion? Remember when Bill Clinton was campaigning against "brain-dead" politics?

In these last few days, as a pitiless president left his latest, hapless nominee to twist in the wind, it wasn't clear whether Lani Guinier was defending her controversial views or disavowing them, mainly because she was doing both simultaneously and fervently. It was a spectacle, but not an edifying one.

At one point Lani Guinier came perilously close to saying that what a nominee believes shouldn't count, dismissing her own ideas as "polit-ical theory that has no place in the public policy framework." So much for ideas having consequences. Or as she explained: "Most important, I think, is not what I wrote but who I am." (Not bad. Editorial writers might find that line useful after having perpetrated some particularly offensive piece of prose.)

At other times, Ms. Guinier tried to palm off her worst ideas as the work of others. It would all have been funny if this had been a work of fiction rather than a presidential nomination.

As forcefully as one might disagree with the professor, it is also hard not to feel outraged and appalled — and insulted on her behalf — at the shoddy way the lady has been treated by this administration. All of these dubious and worse opinions of Lani Guinier's represent but snip-pets culled from reams of her writing, or rather verbiage. (The quality of her prose alone should have sufficed to disqualify her for any position requiring a minimal clarity of thought.) Yet she will have no chance to justify her views or even minimalize them.

Compare the plight of the professor to the experience of Clarence Thomas, who got a chance to defend his name and face his accusers. The result was one of the more exhilarating moments in modern Amer-ican political history: A nominee told off the bumblers on the Senate Judiciary Committee rather than cower in approved fashion. You didn't have to want Mr. Justice Thomas on the Supreme Court of the United States to admire the way he confronted those yahoos. Lani Guinier will never have that opportunity.

It may be hard to imagine how Professor Guinier can defend some of the things she's written, but she won't even get the chance — because her "friend" Bill Clinton, either too lazy to read her writings or too poorly informed to know about them, now has thrown her into his growing pile of discards.

The president explained that to stick with this nomination would be "divisive." As if abandoning it has not been.

This president still doesn't get it: A principled defeat can be far better than one more mealy-mouthed compromise. Ronald Reagan could exercise more leadership by losing a nomination in Congress (Judge Robert Bork's) than Bill Clinton has shown by edging away from his nominee.

Mr. Clinton's tendency to please everybody reflects his own absence of any clear political principle for which he would go down fighting. Another name for this lack of spirit, this hollowness at the core of belief, is malaise.

It was generally agreed at the beginning of 1993 and the Clinton administration that the American health-care system needed reforming. After endless changes, complications, negotiations, and general folderol, the failure of the Clinton plan to make it through Congress had to be the most disappointing failure of his administration. Whatever this extended debate said about the state of American health care, it spoke worlds about the limits of Bill Clinton as an executive who could envision a reform and carry it out:

A Vision without a Road Map — Or a Price Tag

September 27, 1993

Politically, it was one of Bill Clinton's more effective speeches. But medically, economically, and administratively, his proposal may prove something less. Only the bare outlines of the president's health-care plan are now visible, obscured by shining hope and only misty information. Did you hear a single mention, guesstimate, or hint from the president of how much universal health coverage would cost? I didn't. The figure being tossed around elsewhere, like an anvil, is $700 billion over the next five years.

As always with a Clinton program, everything is subject to change. Also to negotiation, influence, delays, and last-minute shifts. Just like the president's speeches and schedule.

Even if most of the pieces are still missing, Bill — and Hillary! — Clinton deserve credit for putting health care where it belongs: at the top of the national agenda. Mr. Clinton was at his most eloquent and convincing when he said the nation's health-care system, or partial system, was "badly broken, and it is time to fix it."

Surely no one would disagree who has had the slightest contact with that system — its paperwork, its waste, its confusions and uncertainties, its immense bureaucracy and irritating complications, and its growing, devastating impact on the nation's economy. The problem, like the system itself, is vast and not easy to grasp, let alone correct.

It was clear from the president's usual longish speech that he couldn't decide what points to stress about his not quite formed plan. Security? Simplicity? Savings? Choice? Quality? Responsibility? He compromised by stressing them all:

Security. The fear of being left without health coverage hovers over the land. It keeps many Americans locked in jobs they despise or have grown out of and erodes both the national economy and the national spirit. The president hit upon the perfect symbol to assure support for his plan — a simple, portable national health card that would cover all. Like a Social Security card. But would it work as well? Would this new health security card cover all costs, or only some? Would it allow free choice of physicians and treatment, or only some choice?

Social Security has become a byword for, yes, social security. But that system need transfer only money, not deliver services. What's more, even after the new health system is in place, it will still be linked to one's job. Doesn't that mean health plans could change with every change or loss of employment? The devil turns out to be in the usual details.

Simplicity. The president promised one single, standard health insurance form. It's about time. But with all the new bureaucracies the president is proposing, and their different links to different forms of insurance — private and public, new insurance-buying pools, and old government programs — how can such complicated arrangements be reduced to a single form? It all sounds too good to be true, and may be.

How are new bureaucracies going to cut down on bureaucracy? At this point, the president's approach sounds like a Vance-Owen plan for health care, imposing new complications on top of old. How, by complicating the system further, will it make the paperwork simpler?

The president displayed the new health security card with some pride and to great effect. Some of us would have been more impressed if he had waved that single form he spoke of.

Savings. Savings there will have to be, and in vast amounts, if the American health-care system is going to deliver more services without enacting more broad-based taxes. Surely this will prove the most dubious of the president's promises as the debate stretches out over the coming months.

How calculate savings when there is no indication, at least to the public, that this administration has calculated the costs of this program? When experts are surveyed about the Clinton plan, the same phrases keep popping up in connection with its finances: "fantasy . . . not credible . . . difficult . . . wildly optimistic . . . reaching a long way. . . ."

The country's health care is to be left to "managed competition." Instead of a policy, Americans are handed a conundrum, an oxymoron, a prime example of the clintonspeak that already has clouded too many issues in this still young but slick administration. Its approach to language does not augur well for its precision in medicine or finance. The president spoke of controlling the rate at which insurance premiums rise. It will not be easy to control prices without controlling costs, treatment, and . . .

Choice. It would be nice to give every patient a choice of physician and treatment regardless of how much or how little health insurance he buys. That is also impossible in a world of finite resources. Yet that's what the president seemed to be promising. That all too familiar escape hatch, the clinton clause, hasn't been detected yet in the murky text. When it is, the familiar disillusion will set in, and hope will turn to cynicism. It would be better if Mr. Clinton promised less and delivered more.

Here's the plan's basic premise: An administration that couldn't get the text of the right speech on the president's TelePrompTer at the outset of this speech is going to manage all aspects of competition in the country's sprawling health industry. Interesting.

Once again government, not the individual, is going to be relied on, this time to shape the cost and quality of American health care. Gifted campaigner that he is, the president somehow made that prospect sound attractive. It's as if he had found the secret of appealing to our vast distrust of ourselves.

Quality. More government control is going to assure it, says the president. Doubtless government can assure quality in some ways. It can also suppress quality — by managing competition, and by removing incentives for invention and innovation.

Looking on benignly from the gallery was the new surgeon general, Joycelyn Elders, who preferred quantity to quality when it came to distributing condoms in Arkansas. Not exactly an advertisement for quality control.

Responsibility. Agreed. All should be more responsible. Not just businesses that may now have to bear new and maybe unbearable taxes, but a president in his words. Let's trust that these presidential promises are based on fact, solid figures, and sound business practices. But let's remember to cut the cards.

Given the gaps and waste in the country's health care, and the grave threat they represent not only to the economy but to countless patients, the president is being responsible when he demands change. The great danger is that this president will not demand enough change, that he is only papering over an inadequate system with new layers of bureaucracy and taxation — instead of empowering the individual.

The notion that Bill Clinton is some kind of dangerous radical sounds even less credible after his stirring but vague presentation. Instead of making a clean break with a broken system, this president may be only extending it. By temporizing and compromising, he may miss a historic opportunity for real change. When it comes to health care, he may prove less a dangerous radical than a dangerous moderate.

Too Much Plan, Not Enough Health

November 1, 1993

The grand unveiling this week of the Clinton administration's already much exposed health plan offered few if any surprises. The best part: At last the American people would get universal health coverage — Hoorah and About Time! — and a little peace of mind, if not enough.

The president and Mrs. Clinton are to be commended for understanding the need to insure all Americans, rather than leave anybody to the tender (and expensive) mercies of hospital emergency rooms. Nobody, including the hospitals, wants that.

"A comprehensive package of health-care benefits that are always there," the president promises, and one that "can never be taken away — that is the bill I want to sign." It's a worthy, if modest, goal. And the president's determination to pursue it is cheering.

But after a guarantee of universal coverage, and the talk of a single form for all health insurance, sprawl takes over. The possibilities for confusion, as in an old Abbott-and-Costello routine, keep multiplying till all hope of finding out who's on first has disappeared among the sections, subsections, and cross sections.

Have you seen Dick Armey's schematic drawing of the Clinton health plan? It looks like a flow chart for a bowl full of jelly.

Congressman Armey may be the most incisive critic of the plan, but the president himself has backed away from what should have been, and was, his basic goal: to separate health insurance from employment.

The absence of a meaningful cap on malpractice awards under this plan, glaring as that omission may be, is only a minor oversight compared to the administration's having lost sight of making the individual, not his job, the focus of insurance reform.

A basic package of benefits is still available under this plan for folks without or between jobs, but for most Americans health insurance will still be tied to their jobs, and their health plan may still change with their work. There is no logical reason it should, any more than Americans should have different Social Security plans depending on where they work.

To quote one student of health plans, Yale's Michael Graetz, "it is simply bizarre to link the right to health-care coverage to employment" and then "fill in gaps for those who work for small businesses or are unemployed and retired. . . ."

But history can be bizarre. The link between health insurance and employment was forged almost accidentally during the Second World War, when both companies and unions realized they could get around wage-and-price controls by giving workers health-care benefits instead of raises, which had to be limited in the war years. Later, untaxed health benefits offered a way around payroll taxes. And so health care became an aspect of employment.

Just as one intervention in the economy leads to another, each way around government controls leads to another, and new complexities complicate old ones, until you get something like this horse-choker of a health plan.

That's not the worst of it. Arguably, all these complexities might be worth the trouble if they solved the problem, but somewhere along the tangled line, the problem was forgotten: how to free health insurance from employment. It's as linked as it ever was, maybe more so, because now even more complex arrangements and subsidies and tax breaks depend on the connection between job and health insurance.

This administration may have missed the chance of a lifetime. This is a time when every poll indicates that American public opinion is ready for radical — that is, root — changes in the way health care is insured and assured. So this administration has huffed and puffed and consulted and finally unveiled . . . a papered-over, even more bureaucratized extension of the same old patchwork system.

There was a better way to go: Have all Americans pick a health plan and pay for it with their own tax-free dollars. As for those who can't afford health insurance, have government buy them a package of basic benefits.

This route was dismissed early and often by this administration, which never gave it a fair hearing. It was too simple, I suppose. Too direct and competitive and efficient. And it would have given the individual the power to choose health plans — rather than a collection of public bureaucracies and private corporations. If there is one guiding principle — or rather assumption — in this Age of Clinton, it is that Government Knows Best.

To call the cost estimates that come with the Clinton plan utterly unreliable is to give them entirely too much credence. Forget that another slew of campaign promises can now be forgotten. (No new taxes to finance health care, no cuts in Medicare or Medicaid.) It is sufficiently worrisome to note that few who have studied the administration's estimates of its costs for this plan have been able to figure out where they come from — perhaps from some dreamland in which competition is managed, choices dictated, and bureaucracies simplify a system rather than complicate it.

There is no way this plan or any other is going to limit costs without limiting choice. Even the plan's supporters will acknowledge as much in honest moments. The Clinton plan tilts heavily toward the collectivized practice of medicine, though it was changed at the last moment to allow any patient to pick a doctor of his own if he really insists, and if he can find a way to do it despite all the red tape.

With the formal presentation of the Clinton plan, the negotiations don't end but only begin. Those familiar with the Clintons' method of operation can now expect to see the loudest wheels greased as each interest, pressure group, and bureau makes its demands, perhaps for good reason.

Any resemblance between the plan unveiled this week and the final Health Security Act that will be adopted, as one surely will be, may be purely a coincidence — as the writers of other fictions warn their readers.

The complexities have only begun to multiply, though what was needed most was simplicity — a new deal instead of one more reshuffle.

This administration continues to be fortunate in the quality of its opposition. Phil Gramm, senator and simplifier from Texas, already has decried the Clinton plan as "socialized medicine." Senator Gramm could have stepped out of a Republican presidential campaign — from the 1940s.

Socialism, I always thought, was government ownership of the major components of an economy, like health insurance. This plan proposes to have the government not own but regulate, restrict, hamstring, and generally nag at every stage of health care, its delivery and financing. This isn't socialism so much as a kind of bumbling, inefficient, nanny-knowns-best fascism. Another NRA out of the '30s. Maybe we could revive the Blue Eagle.

In the course of delivering his plan of plans and show of shows, Bill Clinton warned that "the present system we have is the most complex, the most bureaucratic, the most mind-boggling system imposed on any people on the face of the Earth." Just wait till you see what his plan brings forth. My advice: stay well.

---

*A year after the Man from Hope won the presidential campaign he
had so long planned, it was still an open question what he proposed to
do with it. But some distinguishing marks of his executive style,
already familiar to Clinton-watchers in Arkansas, had emerged:*

What Is Clintonism? After a Year, the Answer Is Still Partly Cloudy

November 3, 1993

It has been a year now since Bill Clinton claimed victory before the
cheering throng at the Old State House in Little Rock. What a night of
hope and triumph. It was the climax of a long presidential election in
which his hometown paper could not endorse him. ("Not for Bill Clinton: A Non-endorsement for President" — *Arkansas Democrat-
Gazette,* October 28, 1992.)

We just had too many doubts, among them:

"As for who Bill Clinton might be, what he stands for, what principles and policies he represents . . . none of that is as clear as his political pizzazz. Is he going to bring us together or set class against class?
Tackle the deficit, embark on more spending programs, either or both?"

One would think that, a year later, after the presidential transition
and well into this first year of the Age of Clinton, some answers would
be looming out of the fog. Maybe like an iceberg headed for the *Titan-
ic,* but at least clear.

Not so.

Bill Clinton continues to communicate like a gusher in every direction. Or maybe a mist. He still lapses into clintonspeak at critical
moments, and covers more bases than exist. Now he's got David Gergen to help him, which is a big improvement over George Stephanopoulos, who was too much like his boss to assure.

Is this president going to bring us together or set class against class?
Why not both? He still seems able to inspire great numbers of the
young, which is a good sign in a president. But he doesn't hesitate to
offer up a scapegoat at the first sign of trouble — and maybe before.

The president's list of people to blame may change from time to time
— the rich, Republicans, pharmaceutical and insurance companies, doctors, white voters. . . . The other day, Mr. Clinton played the race card

in a campaign speech for New York's embattled Democratic mayor, saying he didn't want to accuse those supporting the Republican candidate of "overt racism." Presumably they're guilty of the covert kind. Occasionally even a friend like Lani Guinier will be sacrificed to appease the gathering mob. It seems to work. The Clinton coalition still holds.

"Would he continue this country's involvement in the world," we wondered a year ago, "or shrink back from free trade and the defense of free institutions?"

The answer to that question appears as clear as the now clintonized NAFTA agreement with Mexico. Typically, Article III of the newly negotiated side agreement begins: "Recognizing the right of each party to establish its own levels of domestic environmental protection . . .," and it concludes that each country "shall ensure that its laws and regulations provide for high levels of environmental protection and shall strive to continue to improve those laws. . . ."

And so meaninglessly on. (The Great Fellini, late the world's master at portraying life as an empty circus, could have written the screenplay for Year One of Clintonism.) If this side agreement to NAFTA doesn't mean much, that may be its purpose. Window dressing is not supposed to mean, just attract. The non-language may be intended, like so much of the Clinton program, just to be there — as evidence that this administration has improved on the last one's work. Don't ask precisely how. Press spokesmen come and go, but Slick Willie still lurks in the background, distributing murk, fashioning escape clauses, making excuses in the guise of analyses, and — his specialty — unpromising promises.

Abroad, there is some constancy but not enough. This administration's continued support for Boris Yeltsin in Russia, though hesitant at times, indicates that the White House can follow at least one unambiguous policy — if it inherits one.

In Haiti and Somalia, this new and very green bunch has managed to get sucked into on-again, off-again commitments. Mr. Clinton is proving about as effective and decisive a commander-in-chief as one might have expected from his military record. To borrow a Thatcherism, for Bill Clinton now is always the time to go wobbly. [The Clinton administration would eventually act in Haiti and disengage from Somalia.]

There seems no consistency, let alone vision, in Our Wavering Leader's approach to much of the world. The horrors in what was once

Yugoslavia no longer horrify; America grows accustomed to its new moral isolationism. At a time when leadership is wanted, this president offers calculation. And often not very realistic calculation.

Under new management, the White House seems prepared to advance only if there is no opposition, and to retreat at the slightest whiff of resistance. Result: The administration hovers, temporizes, backs, and fills. And not just in foreign policy. The budget, defense spending, the super-collider, plans for campaign reform, the decisions of the commander-in-chief . . . all seem determined by the flux of events, by pressures and counterpressures rather than any clear policy.

This administration's approach to any issue begins to fall into a standard pattern: A jab, a weave, a feint, and then retreat. In this not so brave or new world, America's president emerges as a kind of champion of drift.

Mr. Clinton tends to meet any opposition three-quarters of the way, so that what is originally proposed — whether a health plan or equal treatment for homosexuals in the military — may be scarcely recognizable by the time it becomes hazy law. See the NAFTA side agreements for a working model of the Clinton touch, and smudge.

There seems no reason to amend the *Democrat-Gazette's* now-yellowed editorial last year on Bill Clinton's leadership: "He has mastered the art of equivocation." Nor is it necessary to change what concerned us most about him: "It is not the compromises he has made that trouble so much as the unavoidable suspicion that he has no great principles to compromise."

And yet if the administration has no great principles, it does have a preference, an approach, an assumption, and it is one not so different from the policy he practiced on occasion in Arkansas: Gather together selected experts and interests, and let them work out the problem.

Clintonism is not a belief in principles so much as in armchair experts, who surely know better than the free market, or field commanders, or anything else outside themselves, including mere reality. The select will know the right price for medical care, or what not to do in the Balkans, and even how to run the White House travel office.

Clintonism at its root seems a preference for theory over experience, for expertise over practice. Yet it is not a strong preference; the president will waver and compromise and change course at the first sign, the first hint, of opposition. Not since Arthur Miller's Willy Loman has a salesman wanted so much to be well liked.

One of the nice things about the presidential campaign's being over is that one no longer hears the phrase "Defining Moment." What was the Defining Moment, if any, of this first year of the Age of Clinton?

Maybe it was the narrow passage of the president's much compromised budget, which is not so different in essence from the tax-and-spend compromise that George Bush fell for in 1990. In terms of domestic policy, can this be a second Bush administration under an assumed name?

The other candidates for Defining Moment are scarier: Les Aspin's amateurish but bloody adventure in Somalia. The cave-in on rights for homosexuals in the military. And, most horrific, the burning of the Branch Davidian compound outside Waco — a fiery example of how those without a sense of direction of their own can abdicate in favor of expertise, and swallow a theory that is presented as the only rational thing to do.

Just why that fateful assault was allowed has yet to be explained by an attorney general who remains incommunicado on the subject. Maybe it was a lack of patience. Patience is a kind of faith, and the administration wasn't prepared to exercise it any longer. The country's new leadership was no more prepared to trust time than it is experience. And so it acted, and the result was disaster.

Perhaps it is no coincidence that the only issue on which this administration has not equivocated is abortion. To treat this moral issue as a moral issue would show some recognition of the limits on man's power to shape himself, or to destroy himself. The icon at the center of the Age of Clinton is not reason so much as a boundless rationality, a confidence that some expert somewhere knows best. But it is a confidence always conditioned by the one unbending requirement that a young but precocious Bill Clinton adopted and named with such forethought long ago: Political Viability.

THE CLINTON ADMINISTRATION AS A MUSICAL

JANUARY 26, 1994

What a roller-coaster year it has been for the Clintons and the country; sometimes America isn't so much a society as a wild ride at a fun park. The system is so forgiving (thank you, Founding Fathers) that what might spur revolutions and blood feuds elsewhere turns out to be fare for musical comedy.

I'm still waiting for an American version of *Evita* based on Miss Hillary's life story. Barbra Streisand will sing the title role ("Hillary!"), and there'll be parts for John Candy as Bill Clinton and Tom Bosley as Mack McLarty. Mister Rogers will be Al Gore, danced in the style of Jack Haley as The Tin Man.

And, oh yes, Luciano Pavarotti will sing tenor in the role of C. Everett Koop. What a show. Music by Andrew Lloyd Webber, of course, and lyrics by Tim Rice. I can hear the hit song now, "Don't Cry for Me, Wabbaseka" [Wabbaseka is a small Arkansas town].

And just think of the possibilities for annual sequels, one for every year of the Clinton administration. It could be an eight-year run. (I've got a couple of steak dinners riding on the Clintons' reelection.)

The basic plot for every show will be familiar to anyone who watched the long try-out in Arkansas. The sets may be different now that performances have shifted to Big Rock, a.k.a. Washington, D.C. And the cast may change from time to time, but the script remains basically the same:

Overture. The music should be light, dreamy, country. A mix of Willie Nelson and Beach Boys. Nothing too serious.

Act I, Scene I: Glorious Promises. (Lots of brass, some marvelous tap dancing around any real changes or great accomplishments. No need to go into details like Whitewater, a number that will be saved for next year's "The Clinton Follies.")

Act II, Scene 1: Explanation of why Glorious Promises (a) can't be kept and (b) were never actually made. The rap number ("Clinton Clauses") will become a favorite of law school skits. Then, as a kind of upbeat consolation prize, the audience gets:

Act II, Scene 2: The Proposal. Enter Miss Hillary, the power in front of the throne, leading phalanx of old pols, certified experts, Great Thinkers, campaign aides transformed into cabinet secretaries, and a cast of thousands whose names are never revealed despite a court order. The Proposal, a vague admix of Sixties reformism and Nineties technocracy, sets the stage for . . .

Act II, Scene 3: Alarums and excursions, not to say Pandemonium! as public gets wind of what could be in the complicated works. Fierce reactions from opposition, public, and Daniel Patrick Moynihan, played by Irish tenor. The president, an animated caricature modeled on Plastic Man of comic-book fame, is shown entertaining third and fourth thoughts about The Proposal down to the curtain, penciling in changes like a nervous bettor at the last minute. All of which inevitably leads to . . .

Act III: Compromise, of course. Any resemblance between the original Proposal and the final form of a bill ends with the title. This is longest act of show, requiring as it does endless zigzags, switchbacks, and 180-degree turns, most of which are strenuously denied. Members of Congress like this part of the performance best because it's when they get their favorite piece of pork approved in return for their support. Curtains close as pols retire behind scenes to horsetrade. Audience drifts off, then suddenly is awakened by trumpet call (Ta-Da!) announcing . . .

The Finale: After much suspense, most of it drummed up, it's the usual Happy Ending by a nose, probably Al Gore's as he casts the deciding vote in the Senate.

Curtain calls, bows, and hosannas — all well rehearsed — before tedium returns. Cast proclaims victory, media analyze, public mills around.

In the role of critics, the political reflexives of left and right then produce their predictable reactions while anyone with a taste for serious intellectual challenge turns to the sports pages.

It becomes clear that what matters most in the show is not victory but its proclamation, not change but the appearance thereof. The object of all this foofaraw is not to exercise power but to hold office — to pass bills, not necessarily to make a difference. Nothing succeeds in the Nineties like the *appearance* of success.

Only a small claque of critics outside the inner circle grows querulous and confused as the musical is performed again and again to rave reviews. It is clear to these doubters that nothing much has happened, and that basic issues have been dodged rather than addressed, but those who say so are dismissed as soreheads. The semi-perceptive cognoscenti do not see that the play's the thing to divert the attention of the king, which in this country is popular opinion.

Meanwhile, in the back streets and dark alleys outside the theater, another and darker world keeps intruding. Its shadows have names — Sarajevo, Pyongyang, Teheran, Baghdad, Zhirinovsky . . . and others waiting to form. The price of global stability is eternal vigilance, and it's sobering to note how fast the world can disintegrate once an American president stops paying attention, or tries to paper over obvious threats with wordy formulations.

But all that somber stuff can be put on hold till after the entertainment, just as the Twenties put everything off till the Thirties, and the Hardings and Coolidges left the results of their neglect for Herbert Hoover to deal with. For now the show must go on. How about Don Knotts as Warren Christopher? Then there's "Donna Shalala" — what a title for a rock number.

THE PHILOSOPHY BEHIND A HEALTH-CARE SYSTEM

JUNE 10, 1994

. . . Even if I knew all about the mechanics of the Clinton plan — a feat only Hillary Clinton or a computer might master — it's clear that every article, clause, and subsection is subject to negotiation.

At last report, the health alliances that are said to be the key to the whole plan were less than healthy, and might even be expiring. What was once the president's Absolute Dead-Certain Minimum Demand — universal coverage — may become universal access. What a difference a word can make. Employer mandates could become individual mandates. In short, the health plan is sick.

But the euphemisms will stay in place: Price controls, for example, are never mentioned; instead the plan seeks cost containment. In short, nothing about this plan may be what it seems, and, if it is, it may change.

Years ago, a letter writer who had some problems complained to the *Pine Bluff Commercial*, "It gets boring not having peace of mind all the time." Think about it. With the Clinton administration, it gets boring having change all the time.

Nevertheless, one can spot three principal approaches in the Clinton health plan that aren't going to change:

1. Political viability. Note that any and all difficulties arising from this health plan would be handled by somebody outside the administration — a national health board, the health alliances, the states, any surviving insurance companies — anybody but the administration itself.

Unlike national health care in other countries, this plan represents a diffusion rather than concentration of political responsibility. That way, the administration can take all the credit for the plan and none of the blame for its problems. The underlying principle is simple: If nobody in the federal government is in charge, nobody in the federal government can be blamed.

Contrary to the president's critics, this plan isn't socialist. It's not clear enough to be socialist or anything else. It's less a plan at this stage than a patchwork cloud.

2. Egalitarianism. Note the plan's emphasis on turning out general practitioners rather than specialists. The system is skewed against specialization and excellence in general, which almost by definition is rare and therefore unacceptably elitist.

The proposed limits on medical fees inevitably will amount to a system of rationing, since everyone theoretically pays the same, and, just as inevitably, will look for ways around the limits. Which is why the plan outlaws "graft" and "bribery" to obtain medical services. Only if payment for health care were limited by law would paying for it become "graft" and "bribery."

In the Soviet Union of unhappy memory, patients resorted to influence and under-the-table payments to get better care. The chief target of government planning the world over remains the same: the free market.

3. Technocracy. Medicine, too, now becomes a system of interchangeable parts to be created, regulated, and compensated through some sort of assembly line. With or without government intervention, art becomes science, which becomes technology, which becomes bureaucracy, which becomes slipshod, which becomes neglect.

Despite what its critics say, the Clinton plan is as American as efficiency experts and time-motion studies. There's a lot of W. Edwards Deming in this plan. His influence in American society is much more evident than his name. He's the latest management guru to be canonized in an American line that goes back to Henry Ford, Frederick Taylor, and Eli Whitney.

Wherever production consists of much consultation, quality control with the emphasis on control, and group rather than individual responsibility, W. Edwards Deming is present. It is no coincidence that the Japanese should have discovered him. Now one can spot his ideas in everything from plans for public housing to Outcome-Based Education. This administration didn't introduce systematization and depersonalization into medicine or the rest of American life; it's just trying to codify and police those trends.

The specific clauses of the Clinton plan may change, but these general approaches — political viability, egalitarianism, and technocracy — won't. They're too close to the vague essence of whatever Clintonism is. And whatever the spirit of the nineties will be. . . .

LIKE MAKING SAUSAGES
JUNE 11, 1994

President Bill Clinton's proposal for health care is now undergoing the usual metamorphosis that Governor Bill Clinton's reforms went through in Arkansas: After a lot of grand proposing, what emerges is an innocuous compromise that reforms little, but represents a consensus of the most powerful interests involved.

It happened here in Arkansas time and again, whether the subject was the environment, civil rights, tax reform, school consolidation, or you-name-it. To quote one Clinton-watcher who has watched this process too many times, "He'll start almost any well-intentioned program, then go off and leave it to twist in the wind." Result: Still another murky retreat will be hailed as still another grand advance.

The health-care recipe that the president originally proposed was the product of Ira Magaziner and a thousand other chefs brought in to spoil the broth. The result was a complicated, unworkable, and unpassable Rube Goldberg scheme that both the public and the politicians began to see through in increasing numbers as the debate over it lengthened.

Now this original design has been not just whittled away here and there, but drawn and quartered by the Senate Finance Committee and other kibitzers.

Universal coverage — the one requisite for a national health-care system that the president said he would never give up — now has been abandoned, delayed, evaded, forgotten, or made optional. To employ a phrase the Brits use for buying something on the lay-away plan, it's been put on the never-never.

The 1 percent payroll tax that was going to finance universal coverage is losing its appeal, if it ever had much. In its place the Senate Finance Committee suggests taxing the more expensive insurance plans. Government rather than private insurers would be expected to cover those now uninsured. Forget that the president said his objective was to guarantee *private* insurance for all Americans.

Price controls and rationing — always called Cost Containment — were going to be imposed on health care, but that goal is fading faster than the Cheshire cat, leaving not even a grin behind. And a good thing, too. It has dawned that discouraging the best in any field is no way to improve service for all. The Clinton plan would have stifled not just specialization but progress, which is usually what happens when the dynamics of the free market are ignored.

The requirement that employers pay 80 percent of their workers' insurance costs won't be found in the final report of the Senate Finance Committee on the health-care bill. Nor will the 1 percent tax on larger companies' payrolls. Instead, higher premiums and copayments for Medicare — collected on a graduated scale — would be used to cover the uninsured.

Those compulsory Health Alliances the Clintons proposed, the ones that were going to cover most Americans and "manage" competition, have largely disappeared from the final reports of these congressional committees.

And so Congress proceeds to do a little patchwork here and there rather than make any essential change in the country's current health-care "system," which ought to be called TOPSY because it just growed.

The scope and quality of Americans' health insurance will continue to depend largely on their jobs rather than their own choices. A confusing, multitiered system of health care doubtless will remain in wobbly place, with millions still dependent on Medicaid and their nearest emergency room for health care. . . .

Chapter 6

RHETORIC

In a more advanced time, namely the Dark Ages, rhetoric was recognized by scholars following in Dante's footsteps as a species of poetry. Giambattista Vico called rhetoric a kind of philosophy, too, because he believed it should reach, reflect, and reveal the forces that bind a community together, and do so with all the power of the original insight — with the same sense of discovery and realization.

How far rhetoric has come in our time might be judged by noting that now rhetoric is defined simply as skill at speech, although a common secondary definition (according to my *Webster's New World*) is "artificial eloquence; language that is showy and elaborate but empty of clear ideas or sincere emotion."

Whatever rhetoric has become, it remains a revealing guide to a leader's style and thought, sometimes despite the leader. Read the more wooden speeches of Richard Nixon, if you're sufficiently hardy. Words still tell, often embarrassingly so. Here are some reactions to various rhetorical performances by Bill Clinton through the years, beginning with his first inaugural as Arkansas's governor:

THE CLINTON STYLE
JANUARY 12, 1979

It was an excellent inaugural speech for a new governor of Boys State. It had that strident sing-song that has come to be identified with American political rhetoric since John F. Kennedy. The speech was a Kennedyesque performance from the time the shiny new governor doffed his overcoat to deliver it in freezing weather. One recalls that

Jack Kennedy made it a practice to demonstrate his Massachusetts machismo by refusing to wear a topcoat when introducing the members of his new cabinet in the December snows, as if to indicate that what this country needed was a good presidential cold.

Full of sound and tedium, Bill Clinton's First Inaugural managed to squeeze a remarkable number of repetitions into its mercifully brief compass. There were no fewer than six paragraphs beginning with For-as-long-as-I-can-remember, including one or two that the public might be forgiven for doubting, such as "For as long as I can remember, I have rued the waste, and lack of order and discipline that are too often in evidence in government operations. . . ." Surely Young Will can remember something before that. This sort of inauguralspeak sounds better than it reads, particularly if the audience is occupied stamping its feet to keep warm.

The speech had its glimmers of hope — for quality education and economic development — but they were doused immediately by accompanying qualifications, as if the text had been written by Teddy Kennedy and immediately edited by a good bond lawyer. Behind every spark of light loomed the currently fashionable revolution of lowered expectations: "We live in a world in which limited resources, limited knowledge and limited wisdom must grapple with problems of staggering complexity and confront strong sources of power, wealth, conflict, and even destruction, over which we have no control and little influence."

American politicians begin to learn from American coaches that one way to make an impressive showing is to emphasize all the obstacles ahead. The American Dream becomes the cagey American balance sheet, heavy on liabilities and excuses. The caveats that used to appear in the small print of political promises now are writ large, and every ray of hope offered comes with an escape clause. Young leaders begin to sound like old critics explaining how little, really, can be done. Statehouses grow crammed with junior Walter Lippmanns and the spirit of Franklin Roosevelt would be regarded today as incorrigibly optimistic and much too, well, American. Young America begins to sound a bit like Old Europe; they say Jimmy Carter has struck up a great *rapport* with Valéry Giscard d'Estaing.

At least one legislator, and maybe only one, was willing to cut through the inaugural mush. "He'd better come up with something real quick," said Donald L. Corbin of Lewisville after hearing the speech.

"He's been attorney general for two years. I don't know what his program is." It would be a comfort to learn that Bill Clinton knows. His response to the Highway Commission's bold new program is, needless to say, no response. It occurs to one that his administration could prove as vapid as his campaign.

The new governor got a stranglehold on the obvious early in his inaugural speech: "Sometimes all the available choices will be less than fully acceptable. Sometimes there will be more than one good choice. Sometimes, we hope, the best choice will present itself plainly. Regardless, the decisions will have to be made." Those who followed his campaign may wonder about that last. By the end of his speech, Bill Clinton was rivaling the legendary Clarence Manion. "The future," Mr. Clinton said, "lies brightly before us." Lest anyone think it lay behind us. His original, it's-lonely-at-the-top theme had given way to a stirring vapidity.

The new governor credited "a friend of mine from Washington" with the observation that the crowd at his inaugural evinced two qualities not found in other places — pride and hope. But the whole speech had an imported sound, as though it had been written far away from the grit and gumption and good humor of daily life in Arkansas, and those qualities were being admired through the wrong end of a telescope, and reduced in scale even while being inflated in words. It would have made a good coronation speech, delivered by someone prepared to reign rather than govern and lead. For a governor, it was a poor speech but pretentious. Like a starry-eyed high school debater's idea of real class.

What else could Bill Clinton have said? He could have taken a specific line, or voiced something visionary, or just said something wrongheaded enough to set off some sparks of thought. Or he could have said that the time has come when the standard for being a good governor of this state ought to be something higher and more distinctive than just not being Orval Faubus, happy as that circumstance is. The chain of reform governors since Peerless Leader have all shared that welcome distinction, and crucial as it was, perhaps the time has come to raise a new standard. . . .

This state cries out for a new standard, for sustenance, and in his inaugural address Bill Clinton gives it some highly polished stones.

Two years later, in 1981, a defeated Governor Clinton would relinquish the governor's office to Republican Frank White with an address to the legislature that sounded more like So Long than Farewell:

His So Long Address
January 14, 1981

Bill Clinton's Farewell Address was much like his administration — an uneven performance that began with great promise and ended a small fizzle. The young governor could rightly take credit for some accomplishments; his highway and health programs in particular required courage. But the only time the legislature broke into applause was when Mr. Clinton claimed credit for having followed the "proper course" in handling the influx of Cuban refugees to the state this year.

The Ledge's sense of timing remains as perfect as ever. For Mr. Clinton's painting himself as the hero of the Cuban Refugee Crisis says less about the history of that episode than about the highly selective memory of politicians about a crisis after it is past. Yes, Bill Clinton may have been about the only Big Name in the state who showed some grace under pressure when the Cubans first began arriving. But he crumpled at the first sounds of the approaching general election. Before it was over, he was leading the chorus of howls against the refugees, saying that to send more of them to Fort Chaffee was a "terrible idea," a "bad mistake" that would "cause a great deal of trauma." At one point, he did a credible imitation of Orval E. Faubus, threatening (briefly) to stick to his guns "even if they bring the whole United States Army down here." But this week, Mr. Clinton claimed to have saved the state from a disaster; he did not dwell on how his own words and actions might have led to one.

That Bill Clinton should now adopt the role of political martyr for having expressed less than ennobling sentiments only a few months back demonstrates again how malleable history can be in the hands of those who played a part in it. One can understand why a departing governor would not care to go into detail about the shoddy compromises, the secret meetings, the various scandals of his administration. Such discretion is accepted as a normal part of Farewell Addresses. But why he should choose to focus attention on perhaps the least becoming part of his record, and with such evident sincerity, remains a mystery — and a tribute to the endless capacity of some politicians for self-deception.

In general, Mr. Clinton's Farewell suffered from too clear a focus on his own fortunes, which were supposed to be emblematic of the Republic's. As when the young governor measured the success of the American system by his own: "It is a great testimony to our system of government that someone like me could become governor at my age from a family of modest means." Here he was, just another barefoot Yale graduate and Rhodes Scholar. Beneath such a modest speech, and not very far beneath, there can readily be discerned the steady throb of the all-absorbing I, I, I, I. . . .

Mr. Clinton might make a note for his comeback: the great American leaders seldom focused on themselves, except perhaps in memoirs or when pushed by eager reporters. In their state addresses, they concentrated on this nation and its people, the greatness of the ideas bequeathed them and the challenges facing them. The emphasis in a state paper on one's own accomplishments despite humble originals is more characteristic of a Richard Nixon than a Lincoln.

But Bill Clinton does not appear to take himself lightly, as the people of Arkansas begin to perceive. Still, he is young and there is plenty of time to learn such wisdom. One looks forward to seeing him return to the arena older but wiser; he might prove a formidable figure then. One hesitates to speak too literally of his Farewell Address; perhaps it might better be called his So Long Address.

The opportunity to give the nominating speech for Michael Dukakis at the Democratic national convention in the summer of 1988, when the Massachusetts governor was riding high in the polls, was supposed to give Bill Clinton national exposure. Unfortunately, it did. Through a combination of mix-ups and misjudgments, the speech ran too long, and it would haunt the long-winded young comer from Arkansas for some time afterward. My first reaction underestimated the extent of the rhetorical catastrophe:

BILL CLINTON'S FIFTEEN MINUTES
JULY 21, 1988

It was a nice speech, certainly nicer than the unruly crowd, the pressures of time and television on the speaker, and the national impatience with any thought that cannot be compressed into a thirty-second sound bite for teevee and radio. Last night Bill Clinton got the fifteen minutes of fame that Andy Warhol said everyone would. What Mr. Warhol didn't say was that it would be fifteen sporadically interrupted minutes before a milling throng that had no emotional direction to go but down after Jesse Jackson had brought it to the mountaintop the night before. Talk about a hard act to follow; Bill Clinton drew an impossible one.

Governor Clinton went to Atlanta to nominate his friend Mike Dukakis for president of the United States and began by telling his audience that he would concentrate on the candidate's character, record, and vision. Well, two out of three ain't bad:

- His friend, he said, was a man who "wakes up in the same world every day." Stability and moderation — just what a party and a country could use after a date with Jesse Jackson the night before.

- Governor Clinton outlined the Dukakis record in Massachusetts, including a defeat after one term — a maturing experience that could be appreciated by Bill Clinton, youngest ex-governor in American history. Defeat is a great teacher, and those who have gone through its school come to respect their classmates.

  A nominating speech may say more about the speaker than about the candidate being nominated: The union leader who nominated Jesse Jackson, for example, never captured the rhythm of "Hold *on* to the plow!" No matter how many times he repeated the phrase, he never put the emphasis on the right word; it was clear he was a stranger in a strange language. Bill Clinton did better; he knew what to say and even what not to say about the Dukakis record in Massachusetts. No need to go into detail about budget deficits and tax increases.

- It was only the third and last component — vision — that remained unclear in Bill Clinton's tribute to his friend. Alas, where there is no vision, presidential hopes perish. It is the job of a nominating speaker at a great national convention to find an accolade for the candidate that may stick during the campaign. Bill Clinton tried on a couple for size: Marathon Man (not bad) and Apostle of Hope (not good). Neither measures up to Franklin Roosevelt's dubbing Al Smith "The Happy Warrior." The trick may be for the speaker to describe himself rather than the candidate; a politician may never be so sincere and enthusiastic as when extolling his own virtues.

In place of vision, this speaker offered modspeak, futurism, even statistics. Such an approach may impress those who think *Future Shock* is a great book instead of a narrow extrapolation. Mike Dukakis's friend seemed to have forgotten the difference between projection and prophecy. His words kept giving way to numbers, neither very convincing. Only when he lapsed into a single and singular biblical citation did the life of the speech return, but it could not be sustained on a diet consisting largely of technotalk.

When he could be heard above the restive crowd, the governor of Arkansas seemed to be saying that the future belonged to those who could master innovation, planning, day care, welfare reform, and technological breakthroughs. Give the American people a choice between those futurist icons and Republican exhortations about freedom, character, family, enterprise . . . and it will be no contest in November. Even this Democratic crowd seemed to be drifting away, anxious to forget about the engineerspeak in favor of a favorite tribal rite: a demonstration on the convention floor. It occurs that Bill Clinton may have read too many books about the future and not enough about the past.

Governor Clinton came closest to capturing the fickle attention of a national audience when he expatiated on education, perhaps the most popular of America's civil religions. It's a faith he clearly shares with his countrymen. But the governor soon made it clear that he was a *young* father when he confidently proclaimed that "children will perform at the level of our expectations . . ." No, they won't. Sometimes they will exceed it. Children are people, too, and so you can't always be sure, even in this technolatrous age, just what they'll do. Some of us find that assuring.

If the next generation of politicians should have learned anything from Ronald Reagan, it is that the American people demand some great vision of their standard bearer, even if it's a vision as unlikely eight years ago as record employment, low inflation, a years-long economic boom, a real arms agreement, a rebirth of American confidence, and even lower gasoline prices. You can't beat a vision with sociologese, even the brand called futurism. Nothing may make sadder or even sillier reading than the futurism of the past.

It was a nice speech the governor made last night, but the overriding impression it left was: Don't count George Bush out yet. As they say, you can't beat something with nothing. You may not even be able to beat nothing with nothing.

Bill Clinton had the toughest job at the Democratic National Convention: He had to make Michael Dukakis sound exciting.

It's Okay Now: The Validation of Bill Clinton

July 31, 1988

Arkansas can relax; our governor has been received by Johnny Carson on late-night television and treated civilly, so he must be a worthwhile person and this state a nice place after all. Television can destroy but it also validates. Weeping may tarry for a week after prime-time but joy cometh on the late-night talk show.

Johnny Carson's introduction of his guest from Arkansas bore more than a slight resemblance to Bill Clinton's unfortunate nomination of Michael Dukakis at Atlanta, demonstrating that satire can flourish on television despite the writers' strike, or maybe because of it. Bill Clinton showed himself good at polite conversation, properly self-deprecating, and not bad on the sax. None of which was in doubt but all of which apparently had to be demonstrated.

For a week now the governor has been talking as though he had something to prove (he didn't), and Thursday night he proved it, whatever it was. Let's hope he feels better and has achieved what the psychologists call closure. Maybe now the state can get on with business.

The effect of television on American politics was clearest when Mr. Carson exchanged notes with his fellow performer on tough audiences they had known. It is hard to imagine a governor meriting this kind of intimacy with a national arbiter of taste like Johnny Carson if he stood for only a policy or an idea instead of a moment in entertainment. American politics has always been part showbiz, but only in these televised times does it seem to have become a wholly owned subsidiary, the way Arkansas Power and Light belongs to Middle South.

Thursday night's was one of the better Carson shows: While the two entertainers traded notes and jokes, Joe Cocker — a serious artist —

contributed simple dignity to the proceedings. . . . We liked the film of
the three-year-old pilot the best.

---

*Attending a birthday party in Pine Bluff for an old friend (and avid
Clintonphile) I noted that the governor stayed long and, what I
thought was remarkable at the time, discussed nothing but politics
hour after hour. Not football or art or the economy or the weather, but
only politics. Politics is not just the man's vocation and avocation, I
thought, but his obsession.*

*At one point the governor took me aside for what seemed an eter-
nity and explained every misstep Michael Dukakis had made in his
presidential campaign, and how he would have handled the issues
much better, even delivering the punch lines he would have used when
challenged by George Bush in the presidential debates. I didn't doubt
him; his lines did sound superior to poor Michael Dukakis's. At the
time, I dismissed his comments as the usual Wednesday-morning
quarterbacking on a presidential election; I should have known he
wasn't looking back to 1988 so much as ahead to 1992.*

*At some part in our lopsided conversation — I mainly listened — I
told the governor of my admiration for Adlai Stevenson's eloquence
(no need to go into detail and mention that I liked Ike's politics at the
same time) and said that I'd send him a book of Stevenson's campaign
speeches back in 1952. What I thought was most absent in the governor's oratorical performances was the sense of vision. I still do, and this
list of Adlai Stevenson's strengths as a speaker still provides a guide to
what may be most absent in any speech by Bill Clinton.*

*Even as an ardent young Republican who liked Ike in 1952, I
thought Stevenson's a model of political rhetoric. My naïveté in sending them to a politician with such a different style and fate says more
about my innocence than my generosity. I should have known by
1990, amid the first rumors of a Clinton presidential campaign in '92,
that these forty-year-old speeches would scarcely influence an always
upwardly mobile American like Bill Clinton. Adlai Stevenson, after
all, lost.*

The Dying Art of Oratory
August 26, 1990

Governor Bill Clinton
Little Rock, Arkansas

Dear Governor,

Here's that book I promised you a couple of years ago: *Major Campaign Speeches of Adlai Stevenson — 1952.* You doubtless have forgotten by now, but I said I'd get you a copy. It must have been just before the presidential election of 1988 — when you were telling me how Michael Dukakis might still be able to pull it out if he would only say this, or do that, or concentrate on the right states. His problem seemed bigger to me, and part of an even bigger one in American politics and culture: the death of oratory.

With the notable exception of his acceptance speech at Atlanta, Michael Dukakis was unable to articulate his vision of America. Somebody should have slipped him a copy of Learned Hand's eulogy to Mr. Justice Brandeis with these words underlined: "A great people does not go to its leaders for incantations or liturgies . . . it goes to them to peer into the recesses of its own soul, to lay bare its deepest desires; it goes to them as it goes to its poets and its seers." We yearn for poetry; Michael Dukakis gave us prose. We ask for prophecy; he gave us tedium.

The governor from Arkansas who introduced the Democratic nominee had something of the same problem. Your speech that dreadful night turned out to be symptomatic of the Democratic campaign. Surely it would have worked if delivered to a living room full of potential contributors to the Democratic campaign; it was warm, personal, homey, if long. It just didn't offer vision.

Where there is no great vision, the people will settle for a second-rate one. What the Dukakis campaign and all its whiz kids never grasped about the "issues" that George Bush exploited — the Pledge of Allegiance, prison furloughs, the L-word, the American Civil Liberties Union — is that it is pointless to debate or even disprove each and every accusation in a campaign. That is to let the opposition set the level of public discourse. It didn't matter what True Facts, dictionary definitions, and clever ripostes the Democrats could supply. George Bush's issues and non-issues were mainly useful in transmitting his vision of

America. A vision cannot be refuted but only bettered. And that better vision never materialized. Michael Dukakis debated: he failed to dream.

His failure is the failure of American rhetoric today. Maybe it has something to do with the substitution of television for radio, the emphasis on campaign spots rather than fireside chats. Only nominating conventions and State of the Union addresses still showcase oratory. Alas, the object of both is increasingly to reflect public opinion rather than lead it. Ronald Reagan, perhaps because of his acting skills, was superb at reflecting American hopes and fears; Franklin Roosevelt understood both well enough to rise above them, channeling hope and fear into a new vision.

The last great rhetorician to run for president was Adlai Stevenson in 1952, as this book illustrates. I can't think of a better gift — not even oodles of campaign dollars — for a politician who has expressed an interest in running for that office down the road. One after another, these speeches demonstrate qualities painfully missing from today's oratory, which comes closer to sloganeering. What makes Adlai Stevenson's speeches of 1952 a treasure and education?

Brevity.

Clarity.

His understanding of his audience, the occasion, and the purpose of each address. (If you will forgive my presumption, this was the aspect of oratory most noticeably absent from your last presentation to a national nomination convention.)

Wit.

Good Humor.

Simplicity of language. The mark of a great leader is that he is able to transmit complex ideas in terms simple enough to be understood. Now we seem to have a great many leaders who can transmit the simplest ideas in the most complicated fashion.

Nobility, and the generous assumption that one's listeners will share that characteristic. Adlai Stevenson did not pander to his audience, and that came as a refreshing surprise.

These old speeches reveal the candidate's personality — that, too, is an object of political oratory in an election year — but without overworking personal anecdotes or descending to sentimentality.

Adlai Stevenson didn't win the presidential election of 1952; he found himself campaigning against one of the most popular candidates of the century and, as is now increasingly recognized, a leader who would prove one of the more successful of American presidents. But Governor Stevenson did leave behind a rhetorical legacy that still elevates. In his talk before the American Legion at the beginning of that campaign, he may have delivered the best definition yet of the peculiar nature of American patriotism:

"When an American says that he loves his country, he means not only that he loves the New England hills, the prairies glistening in the sun, the wide and rising plains, the great mountains, and the sea. He means that he loves an inner air, an inner light in which freedom lives and in which a man can draw the breath of self-respect."

Those words are brief, clear, simple, thoughtful, knowledgeable, noble — understanding and understandable. They never fail to enlighten and elevate, inform and unify. That is what vision will do.

If Adlai Stevenson's rhetorical gifts were not enough to win in 1952, let it be noted that, when he adopted a more "practical" line in 1956, and began to deliver speeches nobody would bother to collect, he lost by an even bigger margin. In 1952, he had dared to think — and he got his listeners to think. That is no small achievement. It may be a greater one than being elected president of the United States.

To write, they say, one should read the best. They're right. To speak, one should listen to the best. I'm happy to send you a collection of the best.

Rhetorically,

Paul

BILL CLINTON DEFINES HIMSELF
July 22, 1992

It was a moment of triumph and of testing for Bill Clinton last week when the time came for his acceptance speech. Only hours before, Ross Perot had dropped out of a presidential race he had never formally entered. Now the Democratic presidential nominee was due to accept his prize amidst Perotless circumstances quite different from those that had prevailed when he won the nomination.

Bill Clinton's record contains more political victories than moral revelations. The American people were waiting for The Candidate to define himself. Here was a grand opportunity to do just that. Did he meet that test? Did he tell the voters who he was and what he stood for?

The Candidate relied mainly on his imagemakers, specifically those who made the film that introduced him to the convention and, more importantly, to the American public. His acceptance speech only augmented the movie. It came as a kind of prolonged anticlimax.

One of the striking things about the Democratic National Convention of 1992 was the sea of upturned faces staring at the huge, magnified vision of The Candidate on the outsize screen above them. Meanwhile, maybe twenty feet away, the candidate himself, dwarfed by his own image, orated unnoticed by much of his adoring audience. In mod society, film validates. So why pay any attention to the person?

Just as the image overwhelmed the reality, so did sentimentality overwhelm biography. The clichés, the heart-warming family stories, the whole family-album presentation left little or no room for the mundane compromises, the less than noble detours, the humanity that fills ordinary lives. This was the adoring nineteenth-century political biography delivered by late-twentieth century video.

For some reason — maybe because the candidate comes from Arkansas, a plain-spoken state — one had hoped for something different and simpler. Instead, as everywhere else in mod America, the imagery overwhelmed the person, and the filtered history softened the prosaic record of another pol on the make.

The acceptance speech itself was mawkish enough to have been delivered by a Republican. Not a heartstring went untouched. A politician whose career is rounded with broken promises and suspect compromises praised those who "play by the rules." A governor who has made his own squalid compromises with special interests, especially where taxes and the environment are concerned, attacked the "forces of greed and defenders of the status quo. . . ."

Bill Clinton, who has made Arkansas's tax structure the most regressive the state has known in modern times, kept speaking of his devotion to the middle class. He boasted of having balanced the state's budget year after year. No need to go into detail: He had no choice. A balanced budget is required by state law. He did manage to increase the state's debt, however, by getting bond issues passed for construction projects.

Preachment after preachment contradicted his practices in Arkansas — whether the subject was taxes, the environment, or child welfare. A governor whose administration had to be sued before it would do the decent thing by wards of the state spoke movingly of children and families. He promised a New Covenant, never having done notably well at carrying out the old. I found myself envying the great throng in Madison Square Garden their exuberance, and innocence.

Was the speech a success? Did it meet the political test? Yes, but only if one knew nothing of his record in Arkansas. Then it seemed only a polished exercise in cynicism.

An appreciation of another good, if too long, specimen of Bill Clinton's oratory:

More Than Words Can Tell
January 31, 1994

This president rates an A for oratory. What a great speech he gave Tuesday night, and not just because he was lucky enough to draw wry Bob Dole as the perfect foil in style and tone to deliver the opposition's rebuttal. Bill Clinton is definitely the most improved rhetorician in America since 1988, when he spoke approximately forever at Atlanta in the year of the Dukakis Debacle.

How Republicans must miss tone-deaf Democratic leaders. Instead, they must deal with a president who, despite a deceptive stumble now and then, can be a PR man's dream. Who would not applaud many of the sentiments and insights the president reeled off in this year's State of the Union message? Just listen:

"We must set tough, world-class academic and occupational standards for all of our children. . . . We must also revolutionize our welfare system. It doesn't work. It defies our values as a nation. If we value work, we cannot justify a system that makes welfare more attractive than work. . . .

"For thirty years, family life in America has been breaking down. . . .

"As we demand tougher penalties for those who choose violence, let us also remember how we came to this sad point. In America's toughest neighborhoods, meanest streets, and poorest rural areas, we have seen a stunning breakdown of community, family, and work — the heart and soul of civilized society. . . .

"Let's be honest. Our problems go beyond the reach of any government program. They are rooted in the loss of values, the disappearance

of work, and the breakdown of our families and our communities. . . .
The American people must want to change within. . . ."

Glory be! Here's a politician who talks as if he understands that our
problems are not basically political! Cheers and hosannas. You can't
hardly beat that kind of speech. Why, it could have been given by Dan
Quayle back in '92.

Sure, it might have been denounced as divisive, holier-then-thou, and
anti-Murphy Brown, but its time has come. And this president is a master of timing. When it comes to public speaking or any other political
technique, Mr. Clinton is highly educable and self-corrective. He is a
whiz at dealing with the surface of things.

Let's hope the president gets so much support in Congress — in
reforming welfare and fighting crime and returning to first things in our
civil discourse — that he'll accomplish even more than he may have
proposed. . . .

Much of this address could have been written by William Kristol,
Dan Quayle's ace adviser. (It was often said of Vice President Quayle
that he had the best mind in Washington, namely Bill Kristol's.) Dog-
gone if the culture wars, this terrible *Kulturkampf* that is supposed to
be tearing apart the American consensus, may end up a united front. At
least rhetorically. . . .

(Come to think, did the president ever once mention abortion, or did
he manage to glide by the one issue that goes to the root of the country's
moral drift and disregard for life, and that, no matter how long it is
ignored or dismissed or shushed, keeps coming back? Just the way those
danged abolitionists kept bringing up slavery after the Dred Scott decision was supposed to have taken care of it. Why is that, do you suppose?)

Once again the American genius for co-option asserts itself as Bill
Clinton speaks of values, of community and work, and, yes, of ending
the welfare system *as we know it.* (There's always a clinton clause.)

What's got into Bill Clinton? How did he come to discover crime, the
illfare system, the dissolution of the American family? Easy. One need
only look at the polls to discover this president's next, highly effective
pitch. As soon as crime became the No. 1 concern of Americans in the
polls, it became the headliner in Mr. Clinton's State of the Union
address.

A prediction: Whatever the Focus Groups are focusing on this same
time next year will be emphasized in the 1995 State of the Union mes-

sage. We have had poll-driven, poll-sensitive, poll-driven presidencies before, but this may be the first one that is polls-only. Which explains the widespread feeling among Americans that this president doesn't have a core of values at his political center so much as a reflecting mirror.

Let's not dwell on the scant attention the president understandably paid to his foreign policy. It is impolite to stare at failure. And it is painful. For a president's failure is America's failure, and should shame us all. Let us pass over the president's talk of having "reaffirmed America's leadership, America's engagement" in the world.

Can one look anywhere in the world — Bosnia, Somalia, Haiti, Russia, China, Korea, or at the faces of great men like Lech Walesa and Vaclav Havel as their pleas for an alliance were shunted aside — without seeing a spirit of retreat and vacillation? That this new non-policy always comes wrapped in doublespeak does not make it any less shameful. It has come to this: Even the French now want a more active defense of Bosnia than this American administration.

It has taken this new crew only a year to return America to the empty and dangerous isolationism of the 1930s. The plea of Elie Weisel at the dedication of the new Holocaust Museum still resounds in the air — Do something, Mr. President! — but in an amazingly short time, a holocaust has come to be something to be commemorated, not prevented.

What has been done to the country's military by this commander-in-chief isn't easy to examine, either. Remember Mogadishu. (Les Aspin didn't resign as secretary of defense because he was such a great success.)

A note on presidential language: As the problems with the administration's health-care proposal become more and more evident — problems involving limited choices, price controls, rationing, a new and stultifying bureaucracy, and managed shortages — the president told Congress:

"If you send me legislation that does not guarantee every American private health insurance that can never be taken away, you will force me to take this pen, veto the legislation, and we'll come right back here and start over again."

That might not be a bad idea, but don't get your hopes up. Those fluent in Clintonspeak will get the message: The president is ready to compromise everything about his health-care bill except its title. So next year, he can claim another legislative victory. The current, unsatisfactory system is about to be patched up, rather than reformed.

But it was a great speech. Not that the president hasn't made some great speeches before — about political asylum for Haiti's boat people, equal rights for homosexuals in the military, the need to defend human rights and oppose aggression abroad, how to close the revolving door between lobbies and government, campaign reform. . . .

This president gives a fine speech. He just has a problem acting on it.

WHO'S BASHING WHOM? OR: RHETORIC IN A CLINTONIZED CULTURE

APRIL 22, 1994

"Let's argue about what should or shouldn't be done," the president said Friday at one of his forums on health care, "and not talk about other people's motives."

Hear, hear.

What a pleasure to hear Bill Clinton take the high road on this issue, if only for a moment. Because almost in the next breath the president had become the partisan again and was saying he was sick "of all this hot-air rhetoric and these paid television ads and all these hit jobs from people who are making a killing from the insurance business. . . ."

There is an almost athletic agility to this president's rhetorical moods. He'd make a quick-change artist look kind of slow. No sooner does he ask the country to swear off questioning other people's motives than his irrepressible alter ego, Slick Willie, is back at it. If it's not the pharmaceutical manufacturers or the doctors who are to blame for the high cost of health care, it's the insurance industry or some other scapegoat-of-the-day.

A robust exchange of opinion remains the hallmark of a democratic society, and there's nothing wrong with continuing that great tradition. But there is something wrong, and unrealistic, with expecting only the opposition to forgo it.

By now Mr. Clinton has established a tradition of appealing to his opponents to fight by Marquess of Queensberry rules while he's using brass knuckles. And he is always shocked — shocked! — when they land a telling blow. Our president has exceptionally high standards in the conduct of rhetoric, but only for others.

Who doesn't? Maybe this dual standard will be the hallmark of the '90s, this genuinely phony decade. For in this era of bad feelings, any guilt for our own words and actions can be absolved by reflecting endlessly on the purity of our own motives and the impurity of others'.

Is that why We, who are pure of heart if a bit ambitious, needn't worry about certain proprieties while They, those greedy so-and-sos, are guilty of high crimes and misdemeanors when caught trying the same tricks?

Can this be why, when some lower-down in the Nixon administration threatened to sic the FBI on a political suspect, it was part of an evil conspiracy, but when one of the Clinton Crowd does it, it's just an innocent slip, a mistake rather than a crime? . . .

But isn't the double standard an acceptable part of politics? For the most part, such rhetoric doesn't rise to the level of criminal activity. Why not just let it pass unnoted? Does anybody take it seriously any more when either Bill Clinton or Bob Dole, Dee Dee Myers or Alfonse D'Amato, indulges in these little games? What harm is done?

Dr. Johnson, as usual, has the answer. Wondering why a contemporary poet would give himself a different birthplace, Samuel Johnson spoke of those minor "falsehoods of convenience and vanity, falsehoods from which no evil immediately ensues except the general degradation of human testimony. . . ."

The general degradation of human testimony. There you have the cumulative effect of all the little clinton clauses and Hillary Humbugs any rhetorician is tempted to use to make the worse case look the better. Gilbert, he of Gilbert-and-Sullivan, called it the "merely corroborative detail intended to give artistic verisimilitude to an otherwise bald and unconvincing narrative." For example, the one about Hillary Clinton's making a killing in commodities because she read the *Wall Street Journal,* or the one about how she once got a margin call . . . all inoperative now, but still revealing.

Oh, how often the rhetorician is tempted to use one of those little flourishes that aren't quite true but sound it, as editorial writers well know. And how often the president uses only one of those. It's as if he had forgotten there is an entirely different kind of rhetoric, one that does not mislead or degrade others, but elevates all.

Political rhetoric is always going to be political rhetoric, that is, words employed for a political purpose. All such words that deal in power are going to be sullied; nobody ever came away from exercising power with entirely clean hands. That is the nature of power. But necessary as political rhetoric is, there ought to be a rule against the kind of rhetoric that is more duplicitous than it needs to be. Great rhetoric should shed some light as well as heat, and raise the level of discussion rather than direct it to one's own narrow ends.

"Truth and politics are on rather bad terms with each other," Hannah Arendt once noted. "No one, as far as I know, has ever counted truth among the political virtues. . . . Seen from the viewpoint of politics, truth has a despotic character. It is therefore hated by tyrants, who rightly fear the competition of a coercive force they cannot monopolize, and it enjoys a rather precarious status in the eyes of governments that rest on consent and abhor coercion."

There is truth, and there is political truth. They will never be the same, but they needn't be completely unrelated, either. They can even be mutually supportive, as demonstrated by an occasional Pericles or Burke, Lincoln or Churchill.

What happens when political rhetoric becomes only political? And what happens when it rises above the political? The quality of human testimony is affected, for a society tends to take its cue from its leaders. One thinks of the Socialist Realism that marked official Soviet discourse, corrupting everything it touched. It was offset by *Samizdat*, the underground literature of the time, which included Solzhenitsyn's prose and the early Yevtushenko's poetry. ("Lord, let me be a poet,/Let me not deceive people.") Then think of someone publishing a book entitled *The Wit and Wisdom of Bill Clinton* as a model for young people. Rhetoric is more than rhetoric; it is an influence.

And since Bill Clinton *is* president, head of state as well as party leader, he now sets the style for the general trustworthiness of human testimony — just as did Harry Truman and Dwight Eisenhower and Richard Nixon and Jimmy Carter and Ronald Reagan in their time. Our presidents say something about us, and particularly about what we are becoming.

What we are becoming, to judge by the ill temper of contemporary rhetoric and the general decline of civility, is a people who specialize in double bookkeeping — one standard for ourselves, a different and higher one for others. The president has been a pioneer in this kind of creative accounting for rhetoric, and by now seems to know no other.

For example: By now almost every business or profession has been bashed by one of the co-presidents Clinton, with the notable exception of commodities traders and malpractice lawyers.

On being bashed in turn, Mr. Clinton's counterpunches now come in a standard one-two-three pattern: First, denial. Second, self-pity and an appeal for a higher level of discourse. And third, another round of bashing his critics.

This is not to say the president isn't capable of changing. Ever since Madison Guaranty began making the news again, Mr. Clinton has stopped badmouthing those terrible crooks and rip-off artists in the savings-and-loan industry. Who says he can't stay on the high road where some things are concerned?

Our president long since ceased to surprise, but he continues to amaze. And to set the political fashion, which is going to look mighty strange — like bell-bottoms and wild ties — if restraint and good taste ever return.

Rite of Passage: The State of The President
January 30, 1995

Times Square all lit up, G. K. Chesterton once observed, would be a magnificent sight if only one could not read. Just so the annual State of the Union address delivered in the well of the Republic, amid the full panoply of freedom and all the regalia of authority, would be an impressive occasion if only one could not hear.

Under the stream of words — sometimes majestic and flowing, sometimes cramped and muddy — one can't miss another sound, that of the never-ceasing wheels of political calculation grinding away. Not only on the president's part but in the minds of listeners, courtiers, and instant critics. Mr. Clinton deserves to be judged on what he said, not on the basis of motives others ascribe to him. Unfortunately, deconstruction has become a habit of political commentary. And not a good one.

It was a good enough speech, but there was so-o-o much of it. Even if it had been chocolate mousse, one can swallow only so much at a setting, and this address was more like an endless strudel. An imposition of this length on even a patient public approaches rudeness, or at least raises the suspicion that the president of the United States has nothing in particular to say, and so must say everything.

Every president should have available the full armamentarium of oratorical appeals, but was it necessary to employ every one of them in a single speech? The Republican parts of this marathon were quite good, though they seemed to lack a certain inner conviction. The Democratic parts were offered almost under the table, like goods that had been declared contraband after the last election.

The president advanced carefully but usually deftly, like a chameleon on a checkerboard. He began extraordinarily well, perhaps because the audience was still fresh. Some of us sensed a new humility and maturity in his tone — unless he's snookered us again. "I am frank to say," said Bill Clinton, "I have made my mistakes." This new talent for understatement was matched by a call to put aside "partisanship, pettiness, and pride." What a refreshing idea.

It was hard to believe that this was the same brash young man who in 1992 regularly referred to his presidential opponent as "Old Bush," relished describing the opposition as "brain-dead" (how that description resonates in 1995!), and exulted in an independent counsel's endless, all-expense-paid campaign of legal libels against a former president and leading members of his cabinet.

Tuesday night, a more tempered Bill Clinton made a point of paying tribute to Ronald Reagan as well as Harry Truman. Being the subject of an independent counsel's investigation may have afforded Mr. Clinton a different and higher perspective on politics. Surely there's nothing like being the object of Rush Limbaugh's attention to make one realize the need for a new birth of civility in American discourse.

Mr. Clinton seems to have taken some good advice, and remembered that the president of the Republic is more than a party leader or even a chief executive, but the head of state — a representative of all of us. He even cited de Tocqueville on the American talent for doing things on our own through voluntary associations, demonstrating that Newt Gingrich isn't the only one with good taste in political literature.

One had almost forgotten over the past couple of years what a learner Bill Clinton can be. Now he was preaching to a Republican choir on the need to balance the budget and reduce the national debt. One thing Mr. Clinton always did learn from, and have the greatest respect for, was the latest election results.

After a great wind-up, the president delivered a wobbly pitch. His long list of My Great Achievements had the brittle, hurried, and not very convincing sound of the Old Clinton. One could picture millions of eyes from coast to coast glazing over. But the man is not without shame. Not once in this entire, one-hour-and-twenty-minute trek into deepest verbosity did the president of the United States utter the word Bosnia. Light lie the ashes of American idealism.

For that matter, the president gave the subject of foreign affairs in general only a lick and not much promise. To a republic whose fate has depended on foreign alliances and competent diplomacy since before its birth, the rest of the world appeared only as an afterthought in this address. Consider it the president's bow to the country's isolationist psyche, or a tactful air-brushing of his own record in foreign affairs, or maybe both.

Lest we forget, the president did act in Haiti — finally! — and it turned out to be his finest moment. Once again the armed forces of the United States came through, although it cannot be said that its commander-in-chief over the past two years has come through with the kind of support those forces deserve.

The president endorsed — finally! — the good work of Barbara Jordan's commission of immigration. [Later the president would back away from its principal recommendation: a computerized listing of American workers.] She suggested months ago that the country establish a computer bank to identify citizens and aliens in the work force in order to combat illegal immigration. (Any phrase like National Identity Number was prudently avoided. This frontier society still has its taboos, and any reforms that require identifications — like Social Security — dare not be too explicit about their workings.)

One reason immigration gets a bad rap is the reluctance of government to guard against the illegal kind. Amid the fears stirred by lax enforcement and porous borders, Americans begin to lose sight of the importance — no, the essential contribution — of immigration to the always developing American character, and future.

If government will just do its job, the American people can be trusted to keep things in perspective. But nothing breeds hysteria like an administration that cannot act, or even recognize, a problem obvious to everybody else. . . .

In case anyone needed reminding that Bill Clinton the ever New Democrat is also Bill Clinton the same old Democrat, the president balanced his proposal to do something about illegal immigration with an old, tried-and-failed economic remedy: Raise the minimum wage. That's one way to fight inflation: Reduce employment.

Happily, the proposed new programs were reduced to details in this State of the Union address. Instead, Mr. Clinton concentrated on the spirit of the country and on the values that need concentrating on if they are going to endure — faith, courage, decency.

At one high point, the president expressed his respect for the entertainment industry's right to express its baser self, but added that he would not be silent when that right was abused. In that case, the country should be hearing from him almost constantly. In this ever more pop culture, the only alternative to work becomes mindless entertainment instead of renewal.

After the president's talkathon, the crisp Republican response from Christine Todd Whitman in Trenton, New Jersey, came like a welcome assurance that politics is not all words. ("Before I begin," said Governor Whitman "let me assure you, I am not going to ask for equal time.") The only eloquent aspect of her mercifully brief presentation, and the only one needed, was the setting: the small-r republican simplicity of the old New Jersey statehouse. The scene was enough to make her point about the seismic shift that is occurring in American politics. Power is beginning to flow back to the states and the people. Would you have believed it? It's like seeing water flow uphill.

Mrs. Whitman invited the president to "join us as we change America." That was kind of the lady, but she didn't need to issue an invitation. It was clear from this State of the Union address — which said a lot more about the state of Bill Clinton — that the president was already rushing to get in front of the parade. In more ways than one, he's going in the right direction.

Chapter 7

AND THE MEDIA

These snapshots of Bill Clinton and the press show a politician who talks a great game of openness but doesn't always practice it. Bill Clinton fit into the culture of the national press well in 1992; there was no generation gap between him and the young comers at the *New York Times* and the *Washington Post*. But he can still fly into a hissy fit when questions prove entirely too direct. In fact, he's been doing it for some time now:

THE FLAMING ARROW
FEBRUARY 5, 1979

Having paid his respects to the principles of the Freedom of Information Act at a meeting of the state's editors, Bill Clinton proceeded to hold a private, unannounced breakfast with members of the legislature's Joint Budgeting Committee. The scene was the Flaming Arrow Club, a members-only sanctum at the Quapaw Towers in Little Rock.

When that came out, Boy Governor said he was unaware that legislative rules require standing committees to meet in public and to give at least two days' advance notice when they do. The usual explanation in these matters was proferred by Max Howell, the great patronage dispenser in the state Senate. That was no meeting, "It was just an informal breakfast."

Senator Howell said he couldn't remember how many legislators attended the breakfast. Neither could Senator Knox Nelson of Pine Bluff. But wherever two or three are gathered in the public's name or business, it ought to occur to the gatherers to at least let the public know about it.

Senator Nelson added that legislative committees need to conduct some business out of the hearing of reporters. Does that mean this wasn't just an informal breakfast? According to Governor Clinton, who deserves marks for candor after the fact, the gathering discussed keeping appropriations within the state's projected revenues. He acknowledged that those in attendance also discussed his office budget. The latter subject should have made a nice counterpoint to the first in view of the estimated 20 percent expansion of the governor's office under Young Will. Even his assistants seem to have assistants. Perhaps one of the crowd in the governor's office could be asked to keep Young Will better apprised of rules mandating public hearings and public notice of them.

The Clinton administration is still young, and one hopes the major result of the Affair of the Flaming Arrow will be to raise the new governor's consciousness about the importance of conducting the public's business in public. It's a principle that should not be confined to nice talks to editors.

MEMO TO THE GOVERNOR (FROM THE GOVERNOR)
SEPTEMBER 27, 1985

It was only last July that Governor Bill Clinton dispatched a memorandum to every agency, board, commission, and institution of higher education in the state requesting that they carefully evaluate their actions to make certain they were complying with Arkansas's Freedom of Information Act.

Maybe he should have sent a copy to himself and his staff.

Because this week it turned out that one of the governor's aides, Sam Bratton, had attended a closed session of the state Board of Higher Education. That would seem to be an obvious violation of the law, which restricts closed sessions to only certain, limited matters concerning personnel. The only officials who may attend those meetings by law are (a) members of the public board, (b) the chief administrator of the public agency concerned, (c) the supervisor of the employee being discussed, and (d) the employee. Sam Bratton is (e) none of those.

Mr. Bratton is the governor's liaison with the Board of Higher Education, and there is no provision for letting gubernatorial aides into meetings closed to the public.

Joan Roberts, the governor's press secretary, "explained" that the board and the governor appoint the director of higher education jointly, and that's why Mr. Bratton was present. That may be why the administration *wanted* him present, but there is no special privilege for gubernatorial aides mentioned in the Freedom of Information Act, nor should there be in a government of law. Even more disturbing, Ms. Roberts volunteered that the matter "has been handled that way previously. . . ." Uh oh. It's evidently happened before.

It didn't take Attorney General Steve Clark long to say that Mr. Bratton's presence at such a closed session violated the law. It's not exactly a difficult question. What was evident to the attorney general should also have been clear to the governor, his staff, and the state board involved.

Bill Clinton, Joan Roberts, Sam Bratton, and the Board of Higher Education need to read Mr. Clinton's memo from last July — and abide by it this time. As a spokesman for the Clinton administration noted back then, "It's very important that it be followed to the letter." And in spirit. Even — especially — by the governor and his staff. They're supposed to be upholding the law, not chipping away at it.

THE ARROGANCE OF SOMETHING
NOVEMBER 8, 1986

It wasn't exactly the arrogance of power; it was more like the arrogance of a four-year term. The morning after Bill Clinton was granted that historic distinction by the voters, his staff reacted by importing another out-of-state innovation: the Photo Opportunity. While the governor was willing to be interviewed for national television, the Arkansas press would be allowed to take his picture but not trouble the victor with questions.

We understand this arrangement has become standard PR for presidents, royalty, and governors of the larger states. But like four-year terms, it may take some getting used to in Arkansas. And some of us don't intend to get used to it. This new uppitiness sounds less like progress than the predictable result of a politician's getting 64 percent of the vote in a statewide election: immediately his britches get two sizes too small.

Once the governor's attention was got, he decided to talk to the Arkansas press, not just NBC. What he said was less important than his considered decision to say it to the home folks. He may be the Mario

Cuomo of the South to the national media, but back home he had some explaining to do. This may have been the briefest honeymoon a landslide winner ever had with the state press. It's just as well; there is something unnatural in politicians and press getting too close. The people may be squeezed out.

Nobody ought to blame the governor, at least not entirely, for this snafu. His staff can share the credit. But the real culprit is that four-year term and its illusion of unaccountability. Imagine what would have happened if Amendment 66 had passed and even justices of the peace had got four-year terms. Would they have started scheduling Photo Opportunities, too? The state may yet find out. This may not be the last time county officials try for four-year terms. Maybe, like four-year terms for governors, this bad idea will keep showing up on the ballot till it's adopted, too. That's how a small, once populist state becomes the Land of (Photo) Opportunity.

WIDE-OPEN SECRECY: SLICK WILLIE STRIKES AGAIN

OCTOBER 22, 1990

Bill Clinton can sound mighty progressive when he's addressing a newspaper crowd. This governor has presided over more erosions of the Freedom of Information Act than any other, but last week he assured the Arkansas Press Association that he's willing to repeal a notorious secrecy provision that he let become law. It was rammed through the Ledge by Pine Bluff's own Knox Nelson, a state senator and oil-and-gas dealer, though not necessarily in that order.

This Knox Nelson Memorial Act keeps the public from knowing how much in tax credits goes to individual oil-and-gas dealers. Now that the powerful senator is stepping down by popular demand, our fearless governor is ready to take him on.

The governor still insists, however, on keeping the Arkansas Industrial Development Commission safe from public scrutiny. After all, the public only pays for it. Through the nose. But the governor couldn't have been nicer about it. At one point, he achieved what must be the apotheosis of Slick Willie. That's when he told the press association: "If you can show me what information you do not have access to now that the public should know about . . . I'll be glad to cooperate."

Got that? All the press has to do is specify what information it doesn't know exists, and the governor will try to have it released. To share the AIDC's secrets, just tell the governor what they are. This is Catch-22 squared. Ah, but it sounds so reasonable if you say it in a hurry and don't think about it. Who do you think is writing the governor's speeches these days — Lewis Carroll or Franz Kafka?

Do you think Mr. Clinton would ask Dave Harrington over at the Arkansas Industrial Development Commission to please release all the files on that plastics plant at Morrilton which seems to have a blank check on the state treasury? It already has benefited from the use of some $750,000 in state funds. That's an impressive vote of confidence in an "extremely financially unstable" company, to use Dave Harrington's own description of this well-connected outfit.

At one point, the state rushed in with a $300,000 loan guarantee when the company was fighting a strike. On what collateral? The personal word of the company's president. That decision now is being challenged in court.

Later, Governor Clinton promised to provide even more support to keep the company going, and its employees working, preparatory to being endorsed by the Arkansas AFL-CIO in this election. Another $500,000 infusion is being readied. That would bring the state's investment in this troubled operation to $1.25 million.

The Clinton administration is nothing if not neutral: It seems willing to dole out public funds to both sides in this labor dispute. Who says Bill Clinton doesn't know how to win friends and influence voters? All it takes is other people's money. Only a few picky taxpayers may object.

Request for information: Have any similar commitments been made to other companies or unions, and, if so, what ties do they have with the governor? Surely that's the sort of thing "the public should know about." Or is that information secret, too?

The Unveiling of an Associate Justice (And of a President)
June 18, 1993

It's only circumstantial evidence — like a little kid standing near the cookie jar with a happy smile and a few crumbs on his face — but one suspects that the nomination of Ruth Bader Ginsburg to the Supreme Court of the United States owes less to her own qualities, however admirable, than to Bill Clinton's headlong rush to the safest port in a continuing storm. The controversies over various other of his nominees, notably Hurricane Lani [Guinier], has yet to fully abate, and the president needs a nice, universally acceptable appointee for a change.

He may have found her. Judge Ginsburg is the perfect choice — for a president who wants only a little peace right now. She represents an extreme of moderation. Liberal, maybe, but not too liberal. She's for abortion, but critical of *Roe v. Wade*'s single-minded sweep. (Her sensitive comments on that decision show a thoughtful mind at work.) It is too early to hazard any but the vaguest guess, but she could turn out to be a David Souter of the mild left — no star, but no embarrassment, either.

Ruth Bader Ginsburg surely can be counted on to uphold the quality of the current court. That's unfortunate, its quality being mediocre. Then again, justices of the Supreme Court have a way of fooling anyone who dares predict their philosophical trajectories. Inside the nice little lady in the Rose Garden yesterday there could be a tiger or, better yet, a Robert Jackson or Hugo Black.

From the purely political point of view — that is, Bill Clinton's — the judge is a twofer, being both (a) a woman and (b) Jewish. Not only would the number of women on the high court double with her appointment, but the old Jewish seat/quota would be reestablished for the first time since Abe Fortas's hasty departure from the bench.

(There are some of us who can remember times when the outstanding legal talent on all sides of great issues invariably turned out to be Jewish. If this society really were a meritocracy, in some periods the country would have needed only a token Gentile seat on the court.)

Alas, Judge Ginsburg would not seem another Brandeis or Cardozo or even Frankfurter — but who is these days besides Arkansas's Richard Arnold? But to have appointed anyone so independent of mind, learned in the law, and gifted with the language would have been to risk excellence. And excellence has a way of doing precisely what the president clearly wanted to avoid: make waves. . . .

Not for the first time, as when the president unveiled Janet Reno as his (third) choice for attorney general, the nominee outshone the nominator. The ceremony was almost over, and everything seemed to have gone without a hitch, when Bill Clinton had to make a scene. The first query from the press turned out to be the last when ABC's Brit Hume dared ask the question on everybody's mind: Was this perfectly safe nomination a response to the hubbub Mr. Clinton had stirred by his nomination and un-nomination of Lani Guinier?

The president acted as if Brit Hume had spoken the unspeakable, as if the nomination of a justice of the Supreme Court at the White House was a purely social occasion and that for any reporter to be so gauche as to mention politics — *politics!* mind you — in connection with a political appointment was, well, beyond him. How any reporter could dare ask such a question after the judge's speech . . . well, the presidential blue-green eyes teared up. (Whatever he lacks in depth or other profound emotion, our president makes up for in sentimentality. He was never so full of admiration and love as when he was tossing Lani Guinier overboard.)

The president then cut off the press conference — an act of collective punishment for the press and other Inquiring Minds that neither Brit Hume nor anyone else might have anticipated. And this just after Mr. Clinton had moved to soothe relations with an increasingly wary White House press corps by playing host at a barbecue. He will doubtless get a good talking-to from his davidgergens about keeping his cool — instead of acting like a camp counselor whom the kids have finally got to.

How explain this tearful overreaction to a natural and, yes, proper and respectful question? Stress, probably. Brit Hume is a gentleman, and, though he asks tough questions, he's polite about it. This time the answer he got could have come from any self-righteous clod with a full set of tear ducts. These days, even when Bill Clinton manages to weather the constant presidential storm, he betrays signs of a political crackup of Scott Fitzgerald dimensions.

The New Class does like its questions from the press tame, particularly at sweet ceremonies. The press, however, insists on asking what's on its and maybe the country's mind. Respectability is for diplomats, not inky wretches. In its own way, Mr. Clinton's non-answer to the question was more informative than any civil response would have been. Bill Clinton's almost practiced huffiness — he didn't pause or stumble over his words or grammar — says nothing untoward about Judge Ginsburg. It does raise some concerns about his own qualifications for a demanding job.

Chapter 8

FORNIGATE

The presidential campaign grew hot with lurid tales once Bill Clinton moved onto the national scene. Nor did the rumors and allegations cease when he became president. But even the most devoted Clinton-watcher and disillusioned Clinton-critic can have trouble working up an interest in the president's after-hours life — if the critic is burdened by a remnant of good taste and the old-fashioned belief that even a president should still be allowed a private and family life that is none of the commentator's business.

TABLOID TREMOR: READ ALL ABOUT IT!
JANUARY 27, 1992

Hot dawg! The tabloids in New York are having a lot of fun with the latest sensational accusations against Bill Clinton in *Star,* one of those indistinguishable supermarket non-newspapers. Front-page headlines depict the presidential hopeful as battling to save his campaign against such stories. Headlines scream. Readers read. The prose is purple: Lies or Lust? Twelve-Year Fling! (How's that for restoring vigor to the White House?)

No sign so far of a classic headline like "FORD TO CITY: DROP DEAD" or "More Mush from the Wimp," but we aficionados of gonzo journalism live in hope. *Star* promises more "sensational sex secrets of JFK-style ladykiller Bill Clinton" and so predictably on. Well, guess it beats Space Aliens Ate My Baby.

The talk shows are not far behind, and last night the Clintons were featured on *Sixty Minutes*. It's getting harder and harder to tell network television from Sally Jessy Raphaël, and a presidential campaign from the fare on Geraldo. Before this is over, the American press may make the British tabs look rather restrained.

The hilarity ceased when the Governor and Mrs. Clinton had to appear on *Sixty Minutes* to address these rumors. Suddenly, they're two real people instead of names in a tabloid. One comes away feeling a bit like a Peeping Tom. Theirs was doubtless a necessary appearance in these nosy times, but one wishes it hadn't been.

The source of all this Pillow Journalism is said to be one Gennifer Flowers — state employee, chanteuse, erstwhile television reporter, and she once claimed, one of the Hee-Haw Girls. . . .

Only spoilsports may wonder why all this interest in a story no reputable paper would have touched if it hadn't demanded refutation. Is it because we have become a nation of voyeurs? Or because it may take a little thought to decide what to do about the recession or the post-Soviet world, while it takes no information or judgment at all to gossip about others? No serious critic of the governor's ever claimed that Mr. Clinton's personal life interfered with his official duties, but now it seems to outweigh minor political views. Hey, what a country!

Ah, but what about the Character Issue? Don't politicians routinely use their families as advertisements? Shouldn't their family life therefore be fair game for public-minded periodicals like *Star*? To answer that line of questioning with another: Why is "character" now limited to sexual mores? Have we forgotten that character once was considered relevant to public affairs, too? Or is this boundless interest in "character" just an excuse for titillation? We don't expect politicians to go into the intimate details of their happy marriages; why demand they specify their failings?

And, finally, speaking of character, what does this intense interest in such matters say about the character of the American press and the American electorate?

THE CLINTON FOLLIES, ACT 11
DECEMBER 17, 1993

Is this an administration or a *Saturday Night Live* skit?

At this rate, tales about Arkansas politics are going to surpass even Louisiana legends like Uncle Earl Long and Blaze Starr. What a movie this Arkansas hayride is going to make some day. I can see Paul Newman in the title role of *Bill!* with Sharon Stone as Gennifer Flowers, Bette Midler as Miss Hillary . . . and a cast of thousands. A Laff Riot, the ads will say, in a game attempt to disguise the fact that most of the material was old last year.

Not everything is quite the same after a year. Arkansas's boy governor is now America's boy president, Slick Willie has been promoted to Slick William, and what Betsey Wright, The Great Explainer, used to call bimbo eruptions have progressed to state trooper eruptions.

The kind of Bill Clinton stories that Arkies used to tell in barber shops now have been retailed by David Brock in the *American Spectator.* His sources: Two state troopers who make their guard duty at the Governor's Mansion sound more like a procurers' patrol.

The more things change, the more explanations, denials, and dismissals come forth from the White House. Where there's smoke, as usual, there's Betsey Wright. Also Bruce Lindsey. Happy days and the old cast are back again. It could be The War Room circa the fall of '92, or maybe last February in the snows of the New Hampshire primary.

The sources of this latest explosion of ribald stories may be new, but there is a kind of tasteless nostalgia about the whole replay. Boccaccio did these things better.

Some may profess themselves shocked — shocked! — at such gossip despite its age. Even if all the tales in this mod *Decamaron* were as factual as the multiplication tables, they would be more pathetic than shocking. As pathetic as the people who only now are coming forth with this stuff, offering juicy tidbits straight from the trash. The year-old trash.

If these goings-on went on, they represent more a violation of a private rather than a public trust. Which is what distinguishes these latest stories from the twenty-year avocation Bill Clinton made of misrepresenting his military record, or rather lack of one. That masquerade did indeed presage his performance as president and commander-in-chief.

The Clintons are still a family as well as news, and it would be nice if even a little distance could be preserved between whatever private lives they have left and the public glare. But so civilized a prospect may be too much to hope for at a time when celebrityhood long ago replaced civility in American life.

One of the great advantages of judging not is that one can leave the gumshoe routine to the David Brocks of this world, and stick to discussing the public actions of public figures. Here and there in this sordid saga, there are indeed some questions involving the public trust — like the accusation that government jobs were used to reward people for their silence about the First Couple's private lives. Those are the only legitimate grounds for investigation or interest in this latest replay of old rumors.

Gentle Reader may just have to hold on as the whole industry of idle speculation gears up again; the result should be an outpouring worthy of any supermarket counter. The usual pack of pundits will soon be discussing what Bill Clinton did to whom, and when and where.

Meanwhile, do you suppose anybody is still interested in what the guy is doing to the country?

Fornigate: Anatomy of a Scandal
December 29, 1993

The latest brouhaha over what Bill Clinton did or didn't do while he was still governor of Arkansas was never supposed to make it into the respectable press. (If "respectable press" is not a contradiction in terms.) This story was going to be contained. It was going to be limited to the *American Spectator* and Rush Limbaugh. The new, gergenized Bill Clinton was supposed to stay presidential, above the fray. This stuff would stay in the tabloids where it belonged. At least that was the plan.

It didn't work out that way.

The dam cracked one Sunday night when CNN carried interviews with the state troopers who had started talking out of school, or rather out of the Governor's Mansion. . . .

The White House claimed the story was "old news," which sounds right. Who in Arkansas hadn't heard such tales for years? But that line of defense only sounds right. What was new, to quote Wes Pruden of the *Washington Times,* was the troopers' willingness "to go on the record." Two lawmen with names and faces were speaking out. Yes, the stories may have been old gossip. But with the addition of identifiable sources, they became new news.

What is news? That's as elusive a question as what is art. News, a British publisher once explained, is anything somebody wants to suppress; everything else is advertising. Not a bad definition, though it is less than comprehensive. There's good news, too, the kind nobody wants to suppress: "NAFTA Passes," "GATT advances," "Interest rates stay low."

That's the kind of news the Clinton administration had been enjoying for weeks. Then along comes this blockbuster, just when the president's approval ratings were approaching those of his first heady weeks in the White House.

Most editors were caught between the temptation to maintain a false respectability (journalism is no more respectable than much of the news is) and the increasing recognition that they were confronted with a news story.

Result: Not even the *New York Times* could blink away the obvious for long. Its bureau chief in Washington may have forgotten that the Iran-Contra story was broken by a scandal sheet in Lebanon, that Gennifer Flowers's allegations first saw the light of night in a supermarket tabloid, and that news doesn't always come in politically correct packages.

Respectability, as Walter Lippmann once observed, has ruined more good newspapermen than alcohol ever did. In practice, liberty cannot be assured without tolerating license. Because it's not always easy to tell the difference between the two until a story has jelled. This one hasn't. It's still in the wet, slimy, stage. . . .

The White House clearly thought the story was worth a response. ABC taped presidential aide Bruce Lindsey doing a bit of damage control when he called Buddy Young, an ex-state trooper and Clinton appointee, right in the midst of a television interview.

And you know things are serious when Hillary Clinton is filmed serving cookies at the White House. There's nothing like a crisis to bring out The Little Woman in Miss Hillary. Under pressure she can revert to the smiling Stepford Wife with astonishing speed.

Betsey Wright, the old expert at bimbo eruptions, was bound to be called on in these circumstances. You couldn't have a proper Clinton scandal without her, any more than you could have a spectacular oil field blaze without Red Adair showing up.

What next? Well, it was Joaquin Andujar, poet and pitcher for the St. Louis Cardinals, who said you could sum up baseball in one word: "You never know." His word count may have been off, but he caught the essence of games like baseball and politics: You never know.

Any violation of a political trust remains peripheral to this scandalette, which essentially involves a violation of more personal matters, like taste. No smoking gun or impeachable offense has yet surfaced. For the moment, Fornigate seems only a combination of sex farce and swearing match. But it is news.

It's more than news. It's a corrosive influence. No matter what subject the president addresses any time soon — the deficit or international trade or foreign affairs — many Americans will be thinking of something else at the sight of him. Just as it's hard to hear Ted Kennedy speak about equality or justice, and not think of Mary Jo Kopechne. Nobody may say her name out loud, but she's there. Like the suddenly renewed presence of Slick Willie in the White House.

This latest scandal will fascinate and repel, at least for a while. Surely it's not the pornographic angle that attracts; there's quite enough of that in the news. It has to be the political prominence of its subject that makes all this news. Americans follow the First Family the way Brits do the royals. And even after this latest scandal fades, its effects will remain.

Ever notice the invisible bubble that seems to descend over the commander-in-chief whenever he visits a military base? It's as if he were covered in some kind of plastic wrap to protect him from the general derision and contempt in such a setting. No one need say a word, but the irony is thick.

The same bubble will now have to be extended to those occasions when Bill Clinton delivers one of his Dan Quayle homilies about morality and family. This tempest in a tabloid won't affect his performance as a political leader in the narrow sense, but the old aura that used to be associated with the pre-Nixon presidency now becomes something else, something close to a smudge.

BORN YESTERDAY: THE CLINTON FOLLIES

JANUARY 3, 1994

The complete absence of a historical consciousness on the part of Bill Clinton and the Clintonoids — no, that isn't the name of a rock group — no longer surprises, but it continues to entertain. Take Fornigate. (Please, as Henny Youngman would say.) Anybody who remembers Watergate knows that the big problem with a top-level scandal usually arises not out of the original offense but in the course of trying to control the damage. Watergate wasn't about a third-rate burglary so much as a fourth-rate attempt to cover it up. That's where Richard Nixon made his politically fatal error.

But to this president, the lessons of Watergate could be as distant as the details of the War of the Spanish Succession. So instead of leaving embarrassing enough alone, Bill Clinton has to start calling state troopers when word leaks that he's about to become the subject of some juicy stories. (And some of us innocents thought the president was spending all of his time on the phone trying to round up votes on Capitol Hill.)

It wasn't the juicy stories that landed our ever-young president in trouble, but his discussing possible federal jobs with a state trooper. That's all it took to raise the question: When is a job offer only a job offer, and when is it a bribe to ensure silence?

The particular jobs the president mentioned were that of federal marshal and regional administrator of FEMA, the Federal Emergency Management Agency. One ex-state trooper, Buddy Young, already has a berth at FEMA, which is where presidential aide Bruce Lindsey called him as Fornigate was breaking open.

Mr. Lindsey's call was taped by a television crew that happened to be interviewing Mr. Young at the time, and if this affair ever makes it into history, that scene will surely be replayed in the documentaries.

Bill Clinton's interest in the details of government is well known by now, but surely it is unusual even for an obsessive president to be recruiting federal marshals and regional-level administrators out of the innocent blue. The call clearly had some connection with the breaking scandalette.

Quick, Betsey Wright to the rescue! The old firefighter took off from her day job to visit Little Rock. Shortly thereafter, an affidavit appeared swearing that the state trooper whom the president had called — Danny

Ferguson — had said the president "never offered or indicated a willingness to offer any trooper a job in exchange for silence or help in shaping their stories."

Or as Trooper Ferguson himself would explain, "He didn't say those words."

Well, of course he didn't. Whether or not you believe all the tattletales told by a couple of other troopers, it defies everything one knows about Bill Clinton to think he would offer anybody a job while reciting the words, "in exchange for silence or help in shaping a story."

After all, Mr. Clinton is not only president of the United States but a lawyer.

Why, one could as soon envision Bill Clinton saying, in the course of breaking some campaign promise, "I am now breaking Campaign Promise No. 187." He would never be guilty of such candor. Some things about Bill Clinton you can count on.

The amount of slick here grows thick. Not the least clintonesque touch is the solemn-looking affidavit itself, which on closer inspection is not from the state trooper but from his lawyer. Trooper Ferguson himself hasn't sworn to anything. Smart move.

I happen to believe the trooper on both counts — that the president mentioned a job to him, and that the president did not say those precise and incriminating words. The president knows better. Unfortunately, he didn't know better than to talk to Officer Ferguson in the first place.

Bill Clinton would have done better to place a call to Richard Nixon and proceed to review the history of Watergate. Then there might have been no need for Betsey Wright to take up her old specialty — putting out bimbo eruptions. What a shame to visit Arkansas on business when there are so many pleasures to enjoy here.

As for the two troopers who have been dishing out the dirt like dump trucks, both readily admit they're not saints. Unfortunately, their records even as state troopers are not unblemished. . . .

If you believe the troopers, both played a supporting role in a succession of sexcapades at the Mansion — one trooper in order to save his job till he could safely retire, the other out of some blind-deaf-and-dumb loyalty to the then-governor rather than to his own dignity.

Conclusion: While besmirching the president's honor, neither of these troopers can pretend to have upheld his own while at the Governor's Mansion.

But remember that you first read about Fornigate in the respectable press (if that is not an oxymoron) and not while eyeballing a tabloid at a supermarket counter. Which indicates that the talkative troopers are motivated by something other than greed, since their stories would be worth a pretty penny, or rather a pretty hundred thousand, in the tabloid trade.

Even if these two troopers were motivated by material gain, it is possible for witnesses to be both greedy and accurate. Gennifer Flowers, who sold her story, now has had it backed up by two uniformed witnesses. Which ought to give anybody who doubted her some second and maybe even third thoughts. (For that matter, did Bill Clinton ever actually deny the substance of Gennifer Flowers's story, or just leave that impression? Between the clinton clauses and clintonspeak, it was hard to tell.)

So what does the Arkansas State Police propose to do in these delicate circumstances? Its director, Colonel Tommy Goodwin, says he and an assistant attorney general are researching the question of — no, not whether a couple of state troopers were offered an inducement to ensure their silence. Rather, the director of the State Police is investigating whether the troopers have violated some law by talking to the press.

It seems to happen every time a government official is accused of an impropriety: The whistle-blowers are investigated, not the high official. Ain't power grand?

But hey, what a country. Against the history of the twentieth century, with its gulags and death camps and transports, where abuse of power has meant not some bedroom farce but war and revolution, terror and torture, and sheer Evil has walked to and fro in the earth from Sarajevo in 1914 to Sarajevo again in 1993, this purported presidential scandal reads like innocence itself.

The only other thing this saucy scenario needs is a French maid, and it could come straight from the stage of Minsky's old burlesque theater. And this is what passes for shocking in America. What a happy land.

God bless America — and this president, too. Over the past year, the whole country has been impressed by the Comeback Kid's remarkable political stamina, and now the troopers' stories depict him gallivantin' till all hours before arising at the crack of dawn to deliver some statesmanlike speech on the education of the young or some such elevated subject. More power to the young man — but may he put it to a better purpose.

From the Fornigate File
January 4, 1994

Fornigate has everything a sit-com needs: sex, political prominence, sex, a plot more involved than it is important, sex, colorful characters, sex, irony, sex. . . .

Irony? Oh, yes, Fornigate has plenty of it. And not just how the intrusion of all the president's men (plus Betsey Wright) ensured that the scandal would grow.

My favorite instance of irony: Those who appear most shocked and at the same time most titillated by these stories, which were retailed at encyclopedic length by David Brock in the *American Spectator*, tend to cite Scripture, chapter and verse, to justify their censure of the young president.

Yet the scriptural tradition — how to put this? — makes a hero of another head of state, King David, that sweet singer of Zion and all-around scamp, whose sins of the flesh are vividly chronicled. Yet young David is described as someone after the Lord's own heart, while The Book depicts tall King Saul as the bad guy of the story. Not only is conventional morality reversed, but Saul has to put up with David's never-ceasing manipulations, too. No wonder Saul had mental problems.

Clintonphobes would do well to give the biblical kind of morality a wide berth. It's full of surprises. And ironies — "for the Lord seeth not as man seeth."

David Gergen, mediameister extraordinaire, has yet to be heard from on this oh-so-monumental affair. Something tells me that he won't be either. He'll just keep pouring on soothing Gergen's Lotion behind the scenes.

If the White House's new ringmaster was quietly appalled at what he found when he first came on the chaotic White House scene, like a parent arriving home in the midst of a pajama party, imagine David Gergen's secret thoughts when this little ol' scandalette broke anew. As Ross Perot would put it in Pure-D Texarkansan, he must have felt as skittish as a long-tailed cat in a room full of rocking chairs. . . .

This whole, overblown production might have closed after a week out of town if the Comeback Kid himself hadn't been contacting state troopers in Arkansas and talking jobs. Bill Clinton doubtless meant to suppress what became Fornigate, but he succeeded in supplying the only legal rationale for investigating it.

Some things a president should leave to others. Richard Nixon could have told him that.

DECLINE OF THE AMERICAN SCANDAL
MAY 11, 1994

bim-bo e-rup-tion, *n.* An accusation of sexual impropriety against a prominent public figure, usually one of a series. Attributed to B. Wright re Wm. J. Clinton, late–nineteenth-century U.S. pres.
> — *Political Lexicon of the Future*

Just when does another scandalous rumor about the president's love life — well, sex life — pass from tabloid gossip into good gray newspaper copy?

Hard to say. Professors and critics of journalism, and even some of us inky wretches who actually practice the trade, have been debating the point at least since Gennifer Flowers.

Some say bimbo eruptions are worth covering from the first hint of a tremor, while the more genteel wouldn't touch the subject till the whole political landscape tilted and began to slide into the Pacific. Nothing short of a Krakatoa scattering evidence worldwide — verified by official seismograph and filmed by Cecil B. De Mille in technicolor — would move these ladies and gentlemen to take note of a b.e.

So just where on this Richter scale of political scandal does one put the allegations of sexual harassment filed last week by a Paula Corbin Jones against one William Jefferson Clinton in the U.S. District Court for the Eastern District of Arkansas, Western Division?

Did this latest scandalette deserve coverage from the moment it was recorded in the *American Spectator*? That publication has become more an actor in these scandals than a spectator, a mix of Distant Early Warnings and false alarms.

There was a time when one could use the *Wall Street Journal* as a barometer of respectability. Back then, the raciest subject in its editorial columns might be the Federal Reserve rediscount rate. Vermont Royster was in his heaven and all was swept up and tidy in Wall Street's world.

Now just mention Arkansas or the Clintons to Bob Bartley, an otherwise sensible and cultivated gentleman with a certain wry charm, and his eyes narrow, his suspicions grow, his paranoia blooms, and all systems are wildly Go! When the subject is Clintonism in any of its pervasive forms in this abortive culture, it's hard to distinguish the editorial columns of the once staid *Wall Street Journal* from the old *Police Gazette.* The Clintons seem to have this effect on editors of delicate sensibilities.

So how long should the [rest of the press] wait till commenting on alleged bimbos and eruptions thereof? Should we contain ourselves till a news conference is held, a reference is made on David Letterman, a formal denial issued, a lawsuit filed, a major motion picture released?

Surely this latest eruption deserved notice from the time it was announced that, in his private capacity, Mr. Clinton had engaged as his attorney the formidable Bob Bennett, whose skills have made him a bipartisan favorite in Washington's tangled web of law, politics, and general barbarism.

Even so, no bimbo eruption worthy of the name can be officially recognized without the attendance of Cliff Jackson and Betsey Wright. They go together like twin locomotives — approaching each other head on. Both tend to lurk in the wings, but unless they appear stage center, like boxers meeting in the ring, and begin exchanging accusations and counteraccusations, the bout cannot be proclaimed a Stellar Attraction by your ringside announcer.

It would take an A. J. Liebling to do justice to these two combatants' different techniques, but the late great A. J. is now occupied elsewhere. In his lamentable absence, a brief and unsatisfactory intro for these title contenders:

In the black trunks, Cliff Jackson demonstrates a polemical style that is drier than dust and about as interesting. Vast quantities of Sensational Revelations have been known to crumble and float away at his very approach. Let this Little Rock lawyer and unintentional firefighter appear at the site of a bimbo eruption, and its scale shrinks from Vesuvius to anthill. He could make tales from the *Decameron* sound like a legal brief, and vice versa.

There is something about the appearance of Cliff Jackson at the side of one more accuser of Bill Clinton, or just in the background, that seems to destroy all interest in even the juiciest accusation, and renders it but another empty rind for *A Current Affair* to exploit. Cliff Jackson's talking about a sex scandal can make doing the laundry sound exciting, even imperative.

Playing yin to Cliff Jackson's yang is Betsey Wright. You can't have one without the other. As any aficionado of these spectacles knows, where Cliff Jackson goes, Betsey Wright is sure to follow, or maybe beat him there. She now has a day job in Washington, but seems to be everywhere an eruption needs denying. A demure denial from Dee Dee Myers at the White House just ain't the same. Maybe it's experience that makes the difference; Betsey Wright has been at this a long, long time.

(This judgment intends no slight to the redoubtable Dee Dee Myers. Her intimation during the late presidential campaign that Bill Clinton spends his nights reading Marcus Aurelius's *Meditations* still stands as an unforgettable classic in the field.)

A true bimbo eruption may not require either a true bimbo or much of an eruption, but it must have the seal of Betsey Wright. The matter of Paula Corbin Jones didn't qualify till Miss Betsey surfaced on *Good Morning America* and denied it. "It simply did not happen," Miss Betsey announced, with the sure air of someone who had been there and seen it not happen. That's when Jones v. Clinton passed from fare for tabloids to fodder for the *New York Times.* Anything important enough to warrant Miss Betsey's attention will soon get the country's, if not for long.

The more of these circuses, the less public interest they seem to draw. The only sure crowd that a sex scandal may now attract is the omnivorous press. In this, the second of the fast-paced Clinton Years, scandals only about sex no longer seem to attract Americans. Perhaps because supply outran demand some time ago.

Only the politically correct — like Anita Hill — can draw a crowd for a discussion of sexual harassment in high places, and it's the high places, not the sexual acrobatics, that titillate. The essential fascination of any contemporary American scandal has become not sex but money or power, both of which objectives now come cloaked in ideological camouflage. The sexiest thing going in scandaldom these days is Hillary Clinton's commodities trades.

To some, this may seem a businesslike step up in public taste, but it strikes at least one observer as another instance of a once rip-snorting republic's sad decline into middle age. . . .

Scandals Then and Now
May 18, 1994

There was a time in American history before bimbo eruptions, namely the Federalist period, when the discussion of such matters might be confined to drawing rooms. And if it couldn't be, the politicians concerned would confront such charges with grace and dignity.

For inspiring example: In 1797, Alexander Hamilton's relationship with a certain Mrs. Reynolds was fully explained — by Alexander Hamilton himself.

It seems that a few years earlier, a congressional committee had been told that the nation's first secretary of the Treasury had been speculating in government debts and had paid one James Reynolds $1,100 as part of a scheme to manipulate their value in his favor.

Confronted with the accusation, Colonel Hamilton invited three of the congressmen, including one James Monroe of Virginia, to discuss the subject in the privacy of his home. They accepted, and arrived armed with what they had been told was incriminating evidence. (It had been supplied by two men accused of embezzling from the Treasury and looking for a way out of their fix.)

Taking the visitors into his confidence, Hamilton fell back on a man's last, desperate defense: truth. Asked to explain his payments to this Reynolds, the secretary of the Treasury said he was being blackmailed by the scoundrel. It seems Hamilton had had an affair two years before with the alluring Mrs. Reynolds. The unfortunate and imprudent but always gallant Hamilton had been seduced by the wife and then blackmailed by the husband, doubtless working as a team.

Oliver Wolcott, the comptroller of the Treasury, also had been invited that evening — to verify that the secretary had not compromised his official duties in any way. Alexander Hamilton was surely the least affluent man ever to hold the office of secretary of the Treasury of the United States. At one point he was reduced to borrowing small sums from friends while administering multimillion-dollar transactions for the still new government, always with great skill and scrupulous honesty.

(On his visit to the United States, Talleyrand, the French statesman, passed by Hamilton's law office and spied him working by candlelight. Talleyrand recorded the scene in his memoirs: "I have just come from viewing a man who had made the fortune of his country, but now is working all night to support his family.")

Once his visitors realized that no government funds had been involved in the secretary's purely personal folly, they agreed to keep the matter in strictest confidence. There were still gentlemen in those days.

Nothing further was said about the unfortunate affair with Mrs. Reynolds — until an unscrupulous editor (but I repeat myself) publicized it years later for partisan purposes. Hamilton responded by publishing a forthright and public account of the entire affair. Accused by the husband of mishandling public funds, he confessed: "My real crime is an amorous connection with his wife. . . ."

The truth was told, justice done, and even the Hamiltons' marriage preserved by the grace of a tender and forgiving wife. To quote one historian, "It was an amazing performance. Never in American history has a public man showed greater candor." Choosing to sacrifice his private life in order to vindicate his public one, Alexander Hamilton had saved both.

It is hard to imagine today the air of confidentiality in which this matter was resolved when it first arose. And it is almost impossible to conceive of a public figure's explaining his private conduct either in such detail or with such grace when the scandal became public knowledge. . . .

Things began to get out of hand in Colonel Hamilton's time, and they had spun out of control by the 1920s, when the ghost of Warren Harding was hounded by Nan Britton's memoirs. By now, these spectacles have gone beyond the ridiculous into the terminally boring, and what once might have caused a scandal induces only a yawn.

After the latest revelations and counter-revelations, accusations and counter-accusations, and trash talk in general, what may entice and interest the most at the moment would be a really good cup of tea. Compared to these politico-sexual eruptions in the news, *The Federalist Papers* would come as a refreshment. (Alexander Hamilton had a lot to do with those, too.)

It may have been Verdi who advised: "Let us return to the past; that would be progress."

Chapter 9

MISS HILLARY AND WHITEWATER

The rise of Bill Clinton will scarcely qualify as tragedy in the Greek sense. It has the inevitability of classical tragedy, and the element of moral choice, too, but it lacks another essential quality: nobility. At best his saga might do as an American tragedy along the lines of Scott Fitzgerald's *The Great Gatsby*, a story not of greatness lost but of success lost.

It's not as if Bill Clinton made some kind of Faustian bargain in which he sacrificed principle for success, since he never seemed much attached to any principle other than political viability, which is more of a technique. The closest he came to a political ideal was a vague notion of "social progress" dating from the McGovernite 1960s. He is one of those politicians who wishes to have a great career rather than achieve great ends. Once arrived, he of course was going to do great if unspecified things; that much was assumed. But only assumed — never very deeply considered, and certainly never articulated. Having risen to the top of the greasy pole early, he has succeeded. There is no tragedy there.

But having arrived, the journey has so shaped Our Hero that it is hard to imagine Bill Clinton accomplishing much except holding high office. Let it be said of this president that at least he has been consistent: Consistently ambitious and consistently successful, but in no clear cause. This is not tragedy but a different and even older story, another vanity of vanities.

The story of Hillary Rodham Clinton is different. It is that of a young idealist with strongly held beliefs, who over the years not only com-

promised those beliefs but lost her once clear identity as well. Both her
political success and personal tragedy can be traced in these comments
over the years, which begin on a note of admiration and hope, and end
in commiseration and sorrow:

PASSING THE TEST
AUGUST 22, 1983

Bill Clinton may still not be ready to commit himself to a tax plan or
a special session of the legislature to aid education, but Hillary Clinton's committee on standards for education is making good, and specific, progress. It just agreed that eighth graders should have to pass a
competency test in basic subjects before being promoted. That would
spell a statewide end to "social" promotion, the bane of public education and one of the more unsocial practices permitted in modern society. It's one reason so many high school graduates turn out to be unable
to read, write, or cipher.

The committee's plan sounds fair, and generous. Eighth graders who
failed the test would be allowed two more chances to pass it during the
summer. And not just students would be held accountable under this
system. If 15 percent of the students in a school failed to pass the test,
that school would be obliged to reconsider its teaching methods. If the
school's students didn't improve their performance after two years, it
could lose its accreditation. That's a big change from passing problems
onto the next grade without ever taking responsibility for them. Competency tests would also be given in the third and sixth grades, but students who fail those would not be held back; that could prove a big
mistake, and lead to lower standards and enormous pressure by the
eighth grade.

But in general Mrs. Clinton and her colleagues on this committee
are to be commended as they begin to establish some clear programs,
rigorous standards, and high expectations. They're showing leadership,
and not taking refuge in vague evasions. Now if the governor would just
do the same, he would pass the test.

BILL CLINTON COMES OF AGE
NOVEMBER 2, 1983

If anyone deserves more credit than Mr. Clinton for awakening
Arkansas to the needs of its young people, it may be Mrs. Clinton. As

chairman of the statewide committee on standards in education, she helped educate a whole state, not excluding her husband. If Bill Clinton has shown a new political maturity these past few weeks, it wouldn't be the first time that the key to a man's growing up would prove to be a woman.

When the anticlimactic announcement was made that Bill Clinton would run for reelection as governor in 1986, the praise for Hillary Clinton was more than tongue-in-cheek. In the fight to give Arkansas some clear educational standards, she had shown herself not only idealistic but a whiz at forging consensus and fighting off special interest groups — like the Arkansas Education Association, which had objected to the state's new (and simple) competency tests for teachers:

Bill Clinton's Announcement
July 26, 1985

Dawgone. We guess this means Hillary Clinton won't be much interested in running for governor next year. Shoot. She might have been the best candidate in the race.

In 1990, by the time Bill Clinton announced he would run for reelection as governor and promised — absolutely — that he wouldn't be running for president in 1992, Hillary Rodham Clinton had become an automatic adjunct to his political career and nigh-permanent First Lady of Arkansas. But after she broke into and virtually took over a press conference being held by another candidate in the Democratic primary, it became hard to think of her as First or any other kind of lady. From then on, she was First Woman:

Sandbagged: Miss Hillary Rampant
May 21, 1990

The look on Tom McRae's face was a study last Wednesday afternoon. It summed up the quandary of a whole generation of nonplussed males in the Age of Lib. There he was, a gubernatorial candidate proceeding to hold a fair-to-middlin' press conference, one that probably would have ranked somewhere between Less Than Sensational and All Right on the DWM (Dull White Men) scale when . . .

Bam! Kapow! Scraatch! Total Demolition! — Hillary Clinton, spouse and knight errant of the incumbent governor, had materialized in the state Capitol to stand by her man. Or rather in his place. It was as if the age of the waltz had met the nanosecond of the lambada. Cameras swung, fingers were pointed, and Tom McRae's press conference wasn't Tom McRae's any more. It was Hillary's show all the way.

Poor Tom. His was the dilemma faced by a whole generation of Americans of the masculine persuasion raised with one set of expectations (stand up when a lady enters the room, flirt courteously, be nice) only to be bowled over by a whole new set, those of Modernity her very self. A modern American male who finds himself standing by a door no longer knows quite what to do at the approach of a modern American woman: open it or arm-rassle her to the ground.

What's a guy to do? (Equally disturbing, the maladapted word *guy* has entered the Southern vocabulary, and is even becoming of indeterminate gender, as in "What do you guys want to do — make some fudge or get our hair done?" It was a better thing when Southerners corrupted French words — picayune, Smackover, lagniappe, bayou — instead of adopted Yankee ones straight.) But we digress. The central question was: What's a guy to do? He usually strokes his tie and settles for a series of stutters-and-stumbles knit vaguely together by a brave smile, which might be a description of Mr. McRae's normal speaking style.

It would have taken a Rhett Butler to win this one ("Frankly, my dear . . ."), but they don't make Southern men like that any more, according to the ultimate authority — many a Southern woman. And of course they won't so long as Southern women do not prop them up, also known as love-honor-and-obey. That ritualistic formula is becoming as rare as the hoop skirt. It's no secret that women won James Thurber's War Between the Sexes long ago, but victory does not seem to please. Perhaps that's because to any true warrior, it is the combat and not the outcome that matters.

The New South is afloat in steel magnolias, but ladies and gentlemen seem fewer and fewer. We should have known the times they were a-changin' when those once distinctive titles were conferred promiscuously on rest room doors as synonyms for Men and Women. Certain

distinctions have faded, and the results are all around. Like eighteen-
wheelers bearing down on us.

The only title of nobility Americans seem to recognize officially,
despite the formal prohibition in the Constitution, is First Lady — a
term for the wives of chief executives. It denotes only marital status,
not manners, as in: "The First Lady of Arkansas interrupted a news conference yesterday at the state capitol, neatly sandbagging her husband's
political rival . . ." After that spectacle, perhaps First Woman might be
a more exact title in this state, given the muliebrile times.

(With admirable British reserve, our trans-Atlantic cousins have
declined to title Maggie Thatcher's husband First Gentleman or even
First Spouse, which is a relief. Of course they have serried ranks of other
titles to amuse royal-watchers; we ourselves have wondered about the
difference between squire and esquire, palsgrave and margrave, but,
being American, not for very long. There are some things it is difficult
to sustain an interest in, like cricket — another great English mystery
with a fascinating vocabulary.)

This rendezvous between Ms. Clinton and Mr. McRae at the Capitol
— they really can't go on meeting like this — said less about politics
than about times and mores. According to Ms. Clinton, who is a kind
of steel edelweiss, it was something of a chance encounter — debate at
first sight. She just happened to be at the seat of state government to
"pick some things up" and decided to fire a few rhetorical rounds while
the cameras were on. She just happened to have with her a four-page
prepared statement. She also just happened to mop the marble floor
with her husband's opponent. The poor guy apparently could never
decide whether to fire back or offer her a chair.

Mr. Clinton, who may not have been fully briefed, didn't described
these goings-on as exactly happenstance: "She told me this morning she
might go up there. . . . She said, 'I just think I ought to do it.' I told her
to have at it. . . ." She did. The mister seemed to approve. "I hear she
gave him a good lickin'," he said proudly. He could have been a fight
manager recounting a protégé's debut at Madison Square Garden.

Once upon a time kids used to have Big Brothers who could beat up
anybody who picked on them. Now grown-ups have attorneys ("My
Lawyer Can Beat Your Lawyer," to quote one bumper sticker) or a
spouse. In the case of Ms. Hillary, she's both. Formidable. Not since Say
McIntosh [a Little Rock activist who often made the headlines] has a

public appearance been disrupted with such determination, although Ms. Hilary reminds us more of Willie Pepp. We would not advise anybody to encounter this First Lady in a dark alley.

In his race with Governor Clinton, Tom McRae finally got the one-on-one debate he's been saying he wanted, but it turned out to be with the tougher Clinton. That'll teach him to want things; he just might get them. As for what was actually said, that was of secondary importance in an era when fame lasts fifteen seconds and television is validation. Lincoln-Douglas it wasn't; it was more Mammy Yokum – Mister Peepers. The essence of Hillary Clinton's case was that Tom McRae had approved of many of her spouse's objectives and policies; the essence of Tom McRae's defense was that he could do a better job carrying them out. Ho hum.

So what's a guy to do? In a different time and place, with enough preparation, Tom McRae might have managed to be both chivalrous and effective. A thousand ripostes doubtless have occurred to Mr. McRae by now. The French call it staircase wit — the things we should have said, but that only occur to us after we have left the party. But even if Tom McRae had summoned the most courtly of responses, would the rest of us recognize courtliness by now? "All the pleasing illusions, which made power gentle, which harmonized the different shades of life, and which, by a bland assimilation, incorporated into politicks the sentiments which beautify and soften private society, are to be dissolved. . . . All the decent drapery of life is to be torn off." Edmund Burke saw it coming in 1789, with the French Revolution.

This wasn't so much a debate at the Capitol as a *Kulturkampf*, a battle between two cultures, old and new, and Mr. McRae was burdened with too much of his to fight back. It was only further evidence that we Southerners are last becoming totally modern, fully Americanized, and unabashedly advanced. For some reason, the news does not please.

THE GOVERNORS TWO: VOTES
BEFORE EDUCATION
MAY 1, 1990

Having defeated Tom McRae in the Democratic primary, Hillary Clinton is still running hard for governor. The state's First Woman took advantage of a speaking engagement at Girls' State to adamantly deny that the governor(s) of Arkansas are for consolidating school districts solely because of the districts' small size. "It's just not true," said Miss Hillary, "and I resent the heck out of it." Resentment tends to be Ms. Clinton's stock in political trade; she rolls it out the way other pols do patriotism. "Over the last seven years," she went on, and on, "both of us have said we don't believe in consolidation based solely on size. It's a lie and I'm tired of it."

Some of us are tired of supporting a grand total of 329 school districts and therefore 329 separate school superintendents, plus staffs and perks, to turn out an inferior brand of education. But reform groups like A Plus of Arkansas can scarcely expect any succour from Arkansas's first couple, this being an election year. After all, the school district is the biggest local industry around in some small towns and fields.

This is scarcely a problem confined to Arkansas, though this state is one of the more blatant examples of how to organize an educational system as wastefully as possible. Americans in general spend a far greater percentage of the Gross National Product on education than most if not all industrialized nations, yet the quality of the finished product continues to be gross — if worldwide rankings are any guide. Maybe it's not the *amount* we spend that's the problem so much as the wasteful ways we spend it.

For example: Last year this small state with its 329 districts spent $14,209,314 just on school superintendents' pay. Fourteen million, two hundred nine thousand, three hundred and fourteen dollars. That's an increase of half a million dollars over the year before. And that figure covers only the superintendents' straight salaries — not their insurance, retirement benefits, secretaries, staffs, cars, or assorted fringes.

What is Arkansas getting for this duplicative, top-heavy school organization? Fifty-six percent of the state's high school graduates who go on to attend college in Arkansas require remedial courses in English, math, or reading. They apparently aren't getting the basics. And the gubernatorial candidates just aren't getting the message, or at least they're afraid to repeat it. That would take courage. That would take candor. It would mean offending all the interests that support small, inefficient school districts. Some places might even lose their own football teams. It's more politic to cite the rare exception ("Small School District Offers Physics and Sanskrit in First Grade/Patrons Pass New Tax Every Election") and pretend that it's the rule.

Meanwhile, the state still can't decide whether to require a C average of students who want to play ball. This is said to be too "complicated" a question to resolve now. It's not the question that's too complicated, of course, but the politics of it. Requiring higher grades for extracurricular activities would offend both popular feeling, also known as football fever, and the kind of educators who never were that enamored of the basics.

Miss Hillary's remarks at Girls' State will be of great comfort to the forces of illiteracy and bureaucracy in Arkansas. Other candidates for governor may not have said anything better this year, political realities being what they are. What rankles about the governors' stand, or rather their lack of one, is its pretension and hypocrisy. The governors Clinton put themselves forward as champions of education when they're really only for ameliorating ignorance if that can be accomplished without too much political risk. That's what we resent the heck out of. It's clear where the Clintons' priorities lie: Votes first, education someplace else.

Sure the governors know better. If they don't, the future of Arkansas may be even more foreboding than these latest educational statistics.

THE LADIES MACBETH
FEBRUARY 27, 1992

Why is it that when Hillary Clinton stands by her man, she's well on her way to becoming America's Sweetheart, another Eleanor Roosevelt, and a gallant defender of hearth and home — but when Marilyn Quayle, the vice president's wife, promotes and defends her spouse with similar determination, she's pictured as a combination of Dragon Lady and Lucrezia Borgia?

What accounts for the separate but opposite coverage of Arkansas's First Woman and the country's Second Lady in places like the *Washington Post* and *Time* magazine?

Maybe it's the gliberal biases of the Beltway press at work again in America's ongoing *Kulturkampf*, which is German for a heckuva fight over taste. When a forceful, aggressive liberal — or even a moderate — gets her dander up, she's a Portia come to judgment. When a forceful, aggressive conservative starts firing back, she's a scheming Lady Macbeth. At least in the more fashionable media.

There's another possible explanation — one that might occur to women more readily than men. In terms of mental agility (let's leave character out of this) Bill Clinton would seem to offer a wife more promising material to work with in developing a presidential husband.

The disparity between the Clintons in terms of intelligence, ambition, and sheer mental rigor would seem slight; surely most folks in Arkansas would agree that Mr. Clinton doesn't lag far behind his wife in any of those categories, and may even equal her ambition.

But the gap between the bright, tough, and determined, not to say zealous, Mrs. Quayle and her vague vice presidential husband amounts to a chasm. It's much easier to imagine Marilyn Quayle in the role of feminine Svengali manipulating a male, blond, innocent, golfing version of Trilby. Besides, Mrs. Clinton's public style is much too open for a Svengali.

There's nothing remarkable in our conventional culture about a bright, eager, upward-bound man marrying a slightly vacant but nice-looking woman. But when it's the woman who's the thinker and the man who's essentially ornamental, society begins to invent sinister scenarios. Who says the double standard doesn't still exist? The trophy husband is still a novel American concept.

Hillary Clinton doesn't make nearly as satisfying a sinister mastermind as Marilyn Quayle. First, because Mrs. Quayle tends to stay behind the scenes. And second, Lady Macbeth has to be all of a piece — consistent, unchanging. It's a character role. And Marilyn Quayle has been the bright lawyer, overly supportive wife, and not-so-hidden tigress since she first came onto the public scene. She doesn't change from act to act.

Mrs. Clinton, on the other hand, has undergone a considerable transformation since she came into public view, and not just in looks. She doesn't even have the same name as when she moved into the Governor's Mansion at Little Rock. Then she was Hillary Rodham — in keeping with the days when everybody knew who Gloria Steinem was. In the '70s, a wife's keeping her own name was the equivalent of a feminist declaration of independence — an ideological test that the certifiably With-It had to pass.

But after her husband lost an election for governor of Arkansas in 1980, Ms. Rodham became Mrs. Clinton. Not just the name changed. The Yale Law grad became a Stepford Wife, at least on public occasions. She mastered the customary adoring gaze expected when the male of the family is in full rhetorical flight. Greater love, or at least political ambition, hath no modern woman.

I remember the first time I ever heard a speech by Hillary Clinton. It was love at first word. She was Hillary Rodham then, and she was speaking in the ballroom of the old Sam Peck Hotel in Little Rock. It was a grand hotel, and a grand speech — one I wouldn't trade for any of her star turns now. She wasn't a headliner then, only a feisty law professor fighting an already lost battle against a new vogue called the National Endowment for the Humanities.

Her talk that day was an acute, uncompromising defense of intellectual freedom; it rose above party, ideology, or self-interest. She put it plain: Any scholar who thought he could apply for a government grant and not find himself adjusting his views to fit official specifications was only kidding himself. And his soul was in danger. Miss Hillary was not pretty then in the cosmetological way she is now, only ravishing.

I can't imagine Hillary Clinton delivering such an impolitic speech now, with its potential for alienating academics, bureaucrats, and respectable types in general, yet it seemed to come naturally to Hillary Rodham. The Hillary Rodham of the '70s has since been replaced by the newer, more successful model that shows Bill Clinton's smooth influence. Of course Hillary Clinton is no Lady Macbeth; who ever heard of a Lady Macbeth whom her Macbeth could direct?

Hillary Rodham had to go; she was a political liability. But there are some of us who miss her still.

———————

The first trickle of Whitewater can be detected in Bill Clinton's heated defense of Mrs. Clinton, Esq., when a question arises early in the presidential campaign about her correspondence on behalf of "a savings-and-loan connected with a friend and business partner" of the Clintons':

TWO FOR ONE: THE DOUBLE STANDARD LIVES

MARCH 23, 1992

When Bill Clinton rushed to the defense of his wife and informal running mate in one of the most recent presidential debates, the effect was less then impressive. For a number of reasons:

First, Miss Hillary can defend herself quite well, thank you, and is even better on the offense. Remember how Arkansas's First Woman took over a press conference of Tom McRae's during the last gubernatorial contest? Poor Mr. McRae offered no resistance, since he comes from the old school which holds that a gentleman never retaliates against a member of what used to be called the fair sex. Tom McRae could do little but smile wanly as Hillary Clinton fought like a man — another increasingly antiquated figure of speech. Hillary Clinton is no Little Woman dependent on her plumed knight; she's an articulate, high-powered lawyer.

Second, indignation is not an adequate substitute for information. "I don't care what you say about me . . ." Bill Clinton told Jerry Brown in one of his less credible sallies of the evening, "but you ought to be ashamed of yourself for jumping on my wife. You're not worthy of being on the same platform with my wife." At the time, Mr. Brown was sharing the platform with Governor Clinton, who took refuge in sheer outrage rather than answer accusations that the Clintons had a conflict of interest. "You're always trying to attack," Jerry Brown complained. "You never answer the question."

Third, Mrs. Clinton's name was dropped with a clang more than once in correspondence between the state securities department and her law firm about a savings-and-loan connected with a friend and business partner of the Clintons'. This happened even though Ms. Clinton used to contend that she did not represent clients of her law firm before state agencies. Now she says she had "no substantive involvement in the work that was done before the securities commissioner." Does this mean she had an only insubstantial conflict of interest?

Ms. Clinton also used to claim that she took no share of her firm's fees from cases involving state government. Does that apply to this case, or to the firm's profits from representing the state in bond sales? Should it? No clear answers are in yet from the otherwise highly articulate Mrs. Clinton.

It's time for less indignation from Governor Clinton and more information from Counselor Clinton. If she is going to campaign, advise on policy, and be advertised as part of a "two-for-one" package — to borrow a phrase of the governor's — then her record should be just as open to public scrutiny as his. Not just Ms. Clinton's financial ties should be available for examination but her political and legal philosophy. This may be a co-president we're electing, or perhaps an acting attorney general. The public has a right to have its questions addressed, not dismissed in a husbandly huff. (Besides, Bill Clinton looks ridiculous in even rhetorical armor.)

Conclusion: The Clintons can't have it both ways. Either Hillary Clinton is only the candidate's spouse — and therefore exempt from the rough-and-tumble of the campaign, à la Barbara Bush or Margaret Thatcher's quite properly seen-but-not-heard husband — or Hillary Clinton is the tough partner and contender she appears to be and therefore as open to being attacked by the opposition as any other political scrapper.

The double standard is gone, or should be. Women's Lib should have freed not only women from some constraints, but men.

CRACK IN THE FACADE: ARISE YE BISCUIT COOKERS
MARCH 26, 1992

So far in this presidential campaign, Hillary Clinton has conducted herself with admirable composure. Only rarely does an impolitic remark break through the gritted teeth and almost mechanical composure of Mrs. Clinton in her Stepford Wife mode. It happened on *Sixty Minutes* when, in a kind of joint State of the Marriage address, she let slip her contempt for Tammy Wynette's stand-by-your-man ethic. She barely escaped the full wrath of the country-music culture by offering some quick explanation we've forgotten; maybe it was so unconvincing it deserved to be.

Now she's in trouble again. Goaded by Jerry Brown's talk about her having a conflict of interest as a lawyer, Ms. Clinton responded by noting that he'd have nothing to say if she hadn't pursued a professional career. "I could have stayed home," she added, "and baked cookies and had teas."

Uh oh. She soon heard from women who had chosen to stay home, but who were quick to explain that being a homemaker means a lot more than baking cookies and serving tea. Swift as she is, Miss Hillary moved to soften her remark almost as soon as she had made it, explaining that she had meant only to defend any woman's right to choose her way of life. But the damage was done. Once again she had come across as contemptuous of women who had not made her choices.

Surely she did not intend to. But having been provoked by an expert at it, she reached for the first rhetorical stereotype handy. The one she chose — and the instant reaction to it by women across the country — is revealing. What it reveals, in addition to differences of class and culture, may be a time gap. Under pressure, Miss Hillary showed not grace, but a tendency to revert to a pejorative, sixties stereotype of a mother who works in the home. But this is the nineties, when that kind of parent is staging a healthy comeback — not just in the psychology texts but maybe even in fashion. And this new New Woman is not about to be cowed by talk of doing nothing but baking cookies and having teas. Miss Hillary had managed to stir up the folks Witt Stephens used to call not cookie-bakers but the "biscuit cookers."

Unfortunate as this resurgence of tradition may have been for Hillary Clinton, it's a good sign for the country and its future. For too long fashionable American couples have wanted to have children the way they wanted to have a nice house or car — not to cherish and rear, with all the labor and care that it implies, but as a profession or status symbol, something to be tended to in their spare time.

There are some of us who hold that the root cause of many problems in American institutions is the collapse of that basic human institution, the family — and that no work is more important than rearing children and making a home. We were not amused by Miss Hillary's dismissive comment, or much persuaded by her explanation in place of an apology.

Should it matter to the electorate what Hillary Clinton thinks about the future of the American family? Yes, if she's going to play as prominent a role in a Clinton administration as she's now playing in the Clinton campaign. To quote her: "If you vote for him, you get me." In that case, the American electorate needs to know what it's getting.

One Life to Live: Politics as Soap Opera

April 14, 1992

The great thing about Hillary Clinton is that on occasion the plastic wrap slips and you get a glimpse of a real person. She gives the listener some traction, even abrasion. One needn't approve of what she says or does (though often it is highly approvable) to recognize her as *real.* What a relief from her spouse. Even his boyish tantrums have a practiced sound, not to mention his run-on speeches. But the co-candidate on the Clinton ticket remains ever so slightly unpredictable, thank goodness.

Miss Hillary's mix of intrigues and idealism, intelligence and irksomeness, provides a relief even from herself, at least in her Stepford Wife incarnation. Committing an indiscretion in an interview, she's human again. It's as if Hillary Rodham — the fighting feminist — has been resurrected.

This time her mask slipped in the course of an interview with Gail Sheehy of *Vanity Fair,* the only part of which worth preserving was the less than discreet suggestion that the press investigate George Bush's love life. (Meow.) Ms. Clinton referred specifically to an old Washington rumor that has never been more than an old Washington rumor. Hell hath no fury like a wife whose own family has been put through the tabloid mill. Correction: make that Meow a low growl. As in Tigress.

For just a moment, the curtain in the quadrennial opera that is an American presidential contest had failed to come down on time, and the audience could see the diva whispering to the stage manager, and hear her plotting against the basso.

Why, having been subjected to the tabloid treatment herself, would Hillary Clinton want to wish it upon another family, even a Republican's? There are any number of plausible explanations for her behavior — stress, fatigue, the kind of campaign pressures that make everybody a little crazy — but no good reason.

Hillary Clinton has the one indispensable prerequisite for such a misstep: Ambition. With a capital A. The kind of ambition that can overwhelm not just manners but even an extraordinary intelligence. The newsweeklies have a phrase for it: Blonde Ambition.

As soon as her quote was reported, Miss Hillary realized her mistake. It was, as the French say, worse than a crime; it was a blunder. Did she ever actually apologize? In any event, she was clearly sorry for what she had said, or at least that it had been reported.

Alas, Ms. Clinton swiftly produced one of those stream-of-excuses statements that will come from people who don't know how to apologize simply and properly. She explained that her comment had been "a mistake. People were asking questions at the time and I responded. Nobody knows better than I the pain that can be caused by even discussing rumors in private conversations and I did not mean to be hurtful. . . ." and so lugubriously on.

As usual, the apologetics were worse than the deed. Can anyone above the age of reason in this country believe that an interview with Gail Sheehy is a "private conversation"? And if Hillary Clinton wasn't speaking for quotation, what was she up to? Sicking the press on the Bushes in hopes we would do her dirty work for her? (Any newsman knows that approach. It's quite common — in more than one sense of the word.) Accomplished and talented as she is, Hillary Clinton was again outclassed by Barbara Bush, everybody's ideal aunt. Mrs. Bush's reaction to the rumor: "Baloney!"

Much of American politics is inevitably and intensely personal, and probably should be if it is to remain in keeping with the American character. The way the British conduct their elections with brevity, economy, and a stiff upper lip may excite our envy, but it is too formal for this wide-open society.

Americans are electing not just the leader of an administration but a commander-in-chief, head of state, and first family. Our presidential race needs to be wilder, longer, and more personal than a proper parliamentary election. Far from standing apart from the "real" issues of a campaign, a candidate's character may be the most real of issues in a system that places so much authority in a single individual. It's quite a show, but it can't be helped.

What can be helped is the quality of the drama. A presidential election doesn't have to be low entertainment. Instead of resembling an episode of *Designing Women*, it could aim for *Sunrise at Campobello* or *Death of a Salesman*. Happily, the country faces no great crisis. Unhappily, normalcy does not usually produce great dialogue.

The memory of the fine job Hillary Clinton did in raising Arkansas's educational standards a decade earlier was still fresh when her husband appointed her as head of the commission that was going to give the country a better system of health care. I can almost hear myself applauding the president's choice even while seeing the pitfalls ahead:

TWO WINNERS: HILLARY CLINTON AND THOMAS PICKERING

FEBRUARY 5, 1993

Bill Clinton could not have done better in filling two important, not to say, crucial positions this week — one at the center of this country's challenge at home, the other at the center of the dissolving world facing American foreign policy.

The first was Hillary Clinton — counselor, politician, and a synonym for competence here in Arkansas and some ways beyond. Oh, yes, she's also First Helpmeet, and Mr. Clinton is to be commended for not letting that additional distinction stand in the way of appointing the best person in the country for the job.

The job is to head a commission charged with straightening out the country's unsystematic system of health care. It's an assignment that would make setting the Augean Stables in order look like a piece of cake.

Miss Hillary has done this kind of thing before, if on a smaller scale, and done it with remarkable patience and fairness. In 1983, she chaired a committee that came up with some tough new school standards for Arkansas. Night after night, meeting after meeting all over the state, she brought everybody into the process and, more impressive, made sense of it. Not everybody liked the results — a sure sign she was willing to offend some special interests — but everybody had a chance to speak up and be heard.

Let's hope Hillary Clinton and her fellow commissioners can do as much for health care when they gather in the War Room of the Old Executive Office Building. To win this war will require the same kind of fairness, openness, and judgment that Ms. Clinton brought to education in Arkansas. Without those qualities, not even her expertise will untie this bureaucratic knot.

Here's hoping her commission reaches its conclusions after, not before, it studies the problem. If the deck is stacked, and Ms. Clinton sets out only to put into law the president's empty campaign plank on health care, the country will reap not reform but confusion. And health care will remain an American quagmire. The system does not need patching; it needs replacing.

Not at all encouraging is the talk about "managed care," which could prove a euphemism for too much management and not enough care. More radical reform is needed — one that empowers the individual American, makes health insurance in this country universal and portable, respects the patient's right to choose, and uses competition to control prices. That's a tall order, but Hillary Clinton has experience at formidable jobs. Tangling with the Arkansas Education Association at its feistiest might have been the best possible preparation for her new job. . . .

TO YOUR HEALTH: A LETTER TO MISS HILLARY
MAY 12, 1993

Dear Hillary,

Hope I'm not annoying you with these opinions from outside the Beltway about health care. But you did ask.

A plea: Beware of what is called "managed care." It may not be either. That phrase has become a euphemism for price controls, and they haven't worked at least since Diocletian tried them in the last stages of the Roman Empire. Instead, control prices by encouraging competition among providers, and expanding free choice for consumers. That's how the cost of prescription glasses has been controlled — by letting suppliers compete.

Only when folks are given a choice of health plans, and can choose the DeLuxe or Economy-Sized model, and maybe from several in between, can costs be kept under control and quality maintained. That's how health insurance for federal employees works. And it works well.

Note that the cost of the program covering 9 million government employees has not risen as much as plans sponsored by private employers — even though the federal program keeps adding more benefits and includes 1.5 million retirees and their dependents, including those without Medicare.

It pays to give people clear, simple choices. Allow folks to save on insurance premiums if they will settle for only a basic program of health benefits. In short, if you pass the savings on to the consumer, there may be more savings. Ever notice how modest our needs may become if we're the ones paying for them? Bill them to an insurance company or your employer, and the sky's no limit.

One more thing: Avoid the kind of bureaucracy that price controls, alias Managed Care, may bring. Bureaucracy is expensive and distracting. One of those revealing numbers in the list *Harper's* magazine publishes regularly is sixty-eight. That's how many new employees American physicians hire [every day] to handle paper work. No wonder so little of the money supposedly spent on health care is spent on actual health care.

No, not all doctors are greedy, but it's a wonder that all of them who have to deal with the mountain of indecipherable paperwork dictated by Medicare and Medicaid haven't gone nuts by now.

Imagine a system that claims to rank the relative value of seven thousand different procedures performed by five hundred thousand physicians and adjusts largely fanciful figures every year to take into account inflation, technological change, the number of beneficiaries and, for all we know, the phases of the moon. At one point — June 5, 1991 — the Feds "determined" that the value of having a finger abscess drained was equal to fifty minutes of psychotherapy. You don't have to be crazy to understand such equations, but it might help.

Here's how the *Federal Register* summed up the formula for figuring physicians' fee schedules under Medicare: "Payment equals ((RVUws times GPC(wa) plus (RVpes times GPCIpea) plus (RVUms times GPCIma)) times CF." Competition in a free market is so much simpler, and so much cheaper. Why not base medical costs on it?

Miss Hillary, please write, wire, or walk over to the Heritage Foundation, 214 Massachusetts Avenue N.E., in Washington and take a look at its model health plan, which is not too different from the one now used by millions of federal employees.

To quote the conclusion of the foundation's latest study on the subject: "(A) health system that works with market forces, and not against them, is the best way to achieve the goal of controlling health-care costs and expanding access to millions of Americans. . . ." Consider that a word to the wise, an once of prevention, and a stitch in time. Please don't give us just the present system slightly changed and hyped in new phrases like Managed Care.

Stay well, don't work too hard, wrap up when you go out, and don't let the actuaries, bureaucrats and special interests sell you a system of health care that's even more out-of-control than this one. Remember: They're the ones who designed this one. Woo pig sooey.

— Arkie

Within a frighteningly short time, Hillary Clinton fell under the sway of a platitudinous guru who had her talking about the Politics of Meaning — and revealing a mastery of philosophical issues that would have done justice to the most blank-eyed sophomore. The whole episode demonstrated once again that upwardly mobile political types shouldn't be allowed anywhere near important questions. It also showed that Hillary Clinton is a quick study, since she stopped talking philosophy shortly thereafter, and the guru was soon demoted to unperson at the White House:

It Hurts Too Much to Look
June 4, 1993

. . . Something else to pass over lightly is the unfortunate interview that Hillary Rodham Clinton granted the *New York Times*'s Michael Kelly the other day. Mr. Kelly, who has a merciless streak, let Ms. Clinton talk and talk and talk about her personal philosophy, and then had the poor taste evidently to report every overwrought word:

> What do our governmental institutions mean? What do our lives in today's world mean? . . . Let us be willing to remold society by redefining what it means to be a human being in the twentieth century, moving into a new millennium. . . . We have to first create a language that would better communicate what we have to say, and the policies would flow from that language. . . . I think this has to be thought through on a variety of planes . . . attempting to come to grasp with some of the inarticulate, maybe even inarticulable, things that we're feeling . . . (the) prevailing acquisitive and competitive corporate life is not for us. We're searching for a more immediate, ecstatic and penetrating mode of living. . . .

It was a bit like being seated next to a voluble teenager for the duration of a trans-Atlantic flight. And one who was going through a Crisis of the Soul at that. A little intense. And a lot *bo-ring.*

Not that there would be anything wrong with such an outpouring of gush in an adolescent approaching confirmation — on the contrary, it would be appropriate and the young person's search for meaning commendable. But you would think that by the time one has become the parent of an adolescent, it would have dawned that the greatest and most difficult service one can do the world is to tend to one's own soul, rather than save everybody else's by executive order. Which seems to be the object of the faddish new Politics of Meaning our co-president has picked up, much as one might contract a mild childhood malady at an improbably late age. One hopes she gets over it soon. In the meantime, surely the kindest thing one can do is to edge gingerly away and hope it's only a light case.

This is not an infrequent malady. Often somebody quite capable in a specialized field — a physician or attorney or businessman — will decide one day to wander off into faith and morals, and begin paddling wildly and loudly in the deepest waters, splashing sentiments every which way, apparently under the impression that all of this is as new to the rest of us as it obviously is to the speaker.

The late Henry Wallace, who was quite adept when he stuck to marketing hybrid seed, went through something like this back in the era of FDR, and never quite came out of it. We have every hope that Miss Hillary's seizure will pass quickly. For one thing, she's a lot tougher than poor Henry ever was. And before this episode, a lot more tough-minded.

I would recommend a week or two back home in Arkansas, where everybody would be happy to see her, and serious pretensions don't stand a chance. Not after exposure to the healing waters and down-home laughter.

This endless interview in the *New York Times Magazine* is enough to make one devoutly wish Miss Hillary would stick to the administrative minutiae of health care, where folks could disagree with her ideas respectfully, and not have to repress an irrepressible giggle, or hold back a slow, sad shake of the head. After the first few pages, which seem to last an eternity, the eyes roll back.

It's hard to follow all this cut-rate Kierkegaard, or maybe Social Gospel warmed over, or equal parts of each sautéed in a mild existential angst, or whatever this socio-eco-theo-ideological Aquarian stew is, without suddenly remembering a prior engagement that requires one's immediate attention elsewhere.

I confess I didn't read the whoo-o-o-le thing. (My admiration for Michael Kelly's stoical powers of absorption has never been greater.) I just felt I owed Ms. Clinton that much. One does not stare at a lady while she's overcome by an irresistible urge to do a yuppified imitation of Norman Vincent Peale.

If the almost uniform reaction to this interview (embarrassment for her) doesn't teach Miss Hillary to steer clear of anything that smacks of the Meaning-of-Life, nothing will.

THE DANGERS OF A CO-PRESIDENCY

FEBRUARY 27, 1994

Remember how, during the presidential campaign, voters were promised a twofer if they went for the Clintons? Vote for one president, get a co-president free?

Sounded like a good deal at the time — and still does for many. In a recent poll, Hillary Rodham Clinton came in second only to Eleanor Roosevelt as The People's Choice for greatest First Lady. (That office is nowhere to be found in the Constitution, but it seems to satisfy a frustrated American hunger for the titles of nobility that the Constitution explicitly forbids.)

Miss Hillary's energy and her leadership do appeal, and her highly visible and influential role in this administration has been widely praised. Sometimes it's not clear just who is helping whom in the White House — who is top banana and who is understudy.

At least before the Whitewater whirlpool started swirling, there was some half-humorous, half-wistful talk about the wrong Clinton having been elected to the office, just as there used to be in Arkansas when the Clintons were in the Governor's Mansion. (At least with Miss Hillary in office officially, the public might get some straight answers; she's seldom been shy about taking a stand and sticking to it, right or wrong.)

It may not be fashionable, but there is a case to be made for a less obvious style in presidential partners. My own role models in this regard are Bess Truman and Grace Coolidge — the kind of spouses who could keep their mates out of trouble with a single sharp glance, or at least never made any trouble of their own.

Much like Caesar's wife, a presidential spouse should be above suspicion — or, even better, so obscure as to be below it.

In terms of foreign models, it spoke well of both Margaret Thatcher's and Golda Meier's husbands that it was hard to remember their first names. They had faded into the background with practiced ease.

Granted, neither Mrs. Truman nor Mrs. Coolidge was very modern (another advantage), but there was little risk that the political interests of either might conflict with her husband's. It is hard to picture either Harry Truman or Cal Coolidge having to choose between (a) exposing a spouse to a special counsel's widespread net or (b) stonewalling as if he had something to hide. That was pretty much the choice that Bill Clinton faced when he was confronted by demands for a special counsel to investigate Whitewater's complexities.

As time passes, it may become clearer why the Founding Fathers did not choose a plural executive, even one consisting of Mr. and Mrs. President. The framers may have known some things we moderns have forgotten. Maybe it was watching the intrigues among royalty that convinced the framers of the American Constitution that a government has enough problems without providing for a First Family to head it.

Doesn't a president of the United States have to balance enough conflicting interests without having to take into consideration whether, by protecting a political flank, he might endanger his spouse's? What an impossible choice: Political astuteness vs. family values.

Even good ol' Barbara Bush — America's sweetheart, or maybe America's favorite aunt back in long-ago 1992 — was a bit too politically active for my hopelessly outmoded tastes, especially when she took the stump at the Republican National Convention to do her bit for husband and party.

Government would be a better and clearer enterprise if even the most popular First Ladies, and in time First Gentlemen, were contented to smile from the sidelines.

In an ideal world, First Spouses, like vice presidents and children, should be seen and not heard. That way, there would be no doubt about whom the voters elected chief executive of the Republic. And a president could act like a president without any compunctions about endangering a spouse's political base; there would be none to endanger. The presidential couple would be husband and wife, not running mates. Many might find that arrangement quaint by now, but it would also be clear and simple.

Maybe too clear and simple for a politically correct age that hasn't quite figured out the lines of authority when the White House comes equipped with His and Her political interests. People used to marry for better or worse, for richer or poorer, and vow to stay together in sickness and in health. All of which would seem a daunting enough challenge without having to take on the obligations of a coalition government as well. Important institutions, like marriage and the American presidency, would seem to have enough burdens as it is.

MISS HILLARY'S BIG DEAL
MARCH 25, 1994

Is anybody who knows Hillary Clinton supposed to be shocked — shocked! — that she made a cool hundred thou or so speculating in commodities back in the late '70s? And that she did it with a little guidance from a friend? Sounds very American to me. Good for her.

This news only adds to the store of flattering things known about Hillary Rodham Clinton as a strong mother, advocate, politician, and, now, commodities speculator. Nobody in the know has ever denied that Hillary Clinton is a tough negotiator, or that she likes money any less than the rest of us, or that she has good friends willing to help her. None of those attributes is a crime, last I checked. They may be forbidden only by the canons of the Politics of Meaning, a frail craft Miss Hillary launched a year ago and then wisely let sink without a trace. Nobody ever said she was a philosopher, or at least a strong one.

Only those innocents who have gone for the Saint Hillary routine will be surprised at her success in knowing when to hold 'em and, even more important, when to fold 'em in the futures market.

Of course Hillary Clinton would be found anticipating the '80s and the Reagan Boom, otherwise known as the Decade of Greed in more partisan circles. She is not only a tough cookie but a style setter in matters ideological, moving through names and lifestyles the way lesser models do clothes closets.

As an ardent Nixon-hunter in the '60s, she might have passed as a hippie among the unknowing. By the '70s, she was riding the crest of feminism as Hillary Rodham, well-known lawyer and not as well-known commodities trader. (There are some things, it turns out, she can indeed be shy and retiring about — like her business contacts and mercantile prowess.)

During the '80s, political necessity being what it was in Arkansas, she became Hillary Clinton for a decade. Now she has emerged full blown as Hillary Rodham Clinton in the '90s. Contrary to Shakespeare's Juliet, there's a lot in a name, and the repeated choices of same.

Belated congratulations to Miss Hillary on making a killing back in the '70s. Say, you don't think she might be interested in managing a small account or two, do you? . . .

THEY'LL CHEAT YOU FOR LESS
APRIL 6, 1994

WHITEWATER LAGOON — It's the calm before, and after, the storm. Anybody who has been a Clinton-watcher all these years will recognize this period as one of those quiet lulls during which All of This Is Being Put Behind Us, preparatory to All of This or maybe All of Something Else breaking loose again.

This is not the end of Whitewater Madness or even the beginning of the end; it's a welcome intermission before the next really dramatic act erupts. Most of us might not be able to take the roller-coaster spins and turns, but people who live from crisis to crisis seem to thrive on it. . . .

Why, if all the facts and income tax returns and trading reports are so innocuous, did the Clintons wait so long to dribble them out? There is no hard evidence here, just scads of teasers, clues, and false leads everywhere, all of which may never be sorted out. Mainly because only a CPA could be interested in some of this stuff. (Has the shade of Agatha Christie come back to write the Whitewater Saga in accounting-ese?)

My wholly unsubstantiated theory is that the Clintons' reticence was a cultural thing, like so much else in American life. Hillary Clinton — she would have been Hillary Rodham back then — turns out to be not a hippie lawyer but a secret commodities trader. You might as well picture Mother Teresa playing a little blackjack for fun and profit. The political problem isn't so much how Ms. Clinton, nee Ms. Rodham, made her money, but the money itself in a culture where Rich is automatically Bad. The populist mind — well, mentality — resembles a muddy swirl of concepts like filthy lucre, root of all evil, usury. . . . It resembles a mix of the Hebrew Prophets and The Collected Works of

Coin Harvey. (Historical footnote: William "Coin" Harvey was the popular pamphleteer, conspiracy theorist, and economic crank of the last century who built his great redoubt against the money changers in the mountain fastness of the Ozarks.) Populism, like art, isn't easy to define but you know it when you hear it, and you also know that land speculators and commodity traders are not populist role models.

Better and more concise than all the writings of Richard Hofstadter about the populist spirit in America history was a sign I once spotted above a used car lot somewhere in the vicinity of Malvern, Arkansas — WE CHEAT YOU FOR LESS.

The phrase is part of a whole, now largely underground redneck argot, though occasionally a Lewis Grizzard will validate it in print. Behind this particular piece of eloquence lies the Jeffersonian assumption that all commerce, or at least all successful commerce, is a cheat — unlike the noble returns of a now largely gone agrarian life. Such is the myth, and myths are shaping even and especially when they go unarticulated.

The thought of young Hillary Rodham speculating in cattle futures through a trader with a checkered history taints her carefully crafted iconography. The nineties are proving a highly suspicious, media-mad, Rush-Limbaugh-listening, ill-tempered time.

Until recently, the Clintons played on its themes like twin virtuosi (The Greedy '80s and all that), and now it turns out that The Enemy Was Them. It's a bit of a letdown, like finding out that Ross Perot is really a Japanese-owned subsidiary.

The irony is a bit embarrassing, and all the more difficult to fight because the problem is more hinted at than spelled out. The presidents Clinton are up against the same class prejudices they've done so much to cultivate and exploit. It's the Clintons of '94 against the Clintons of '92, and that's tough competition — as bumblers like George Bush and James Baker discovered.

The Whitewater Rapids are still just around the bend despite this stretch of calm water. The best guide to them isn't some Commodity Trader's Guide, or a bunch of yellowed income tax returns, but an ostensible work of fiction, *The Great Gatsby*.

Yes, there are some obvious differences. F. Scott Fitzgerald was a simpler, more credible writer than the history of the 1990s has been to date. And the principal characters in Whitewater, with the notable exception of the late Vince Foster, would seem to lack an essential quality for tragedy — nobility.

Gatsby and Whitewater do share a tragic sense of inevitability. And the principal characters in both melodramas seem to share an awful carelessness about things — mainly finances, people, the company they keep, commitments, ideas, law and ethics . . . . This may explain why *Gatsby* and Whitewater have the poignant sense of a failed dream — specifically, the American Dream.

STYLE VS. CONTENT: HILLARY CLINTON BOFFO HIT

MAY 2, 1994

According to my unofficial ringside score, here's how Miss Hillary did in her final, complete, definitive press conference that's-going-to-put-Whitewater-behind-us-once-and-for-all No. 1:

Style. A-plus.

No one can be nicer than Hillary R. Clinton when she wants to be, or more effective in a Young-and-Rubicam way. Oh, the discreet charm of the New Class once it's gone to purring: The soft pink sweater and soft pink voice and soft pink deflections of tough questions. Ah, the demure yet businesslike effect. The conversational setting. The simple armchair. (No podium to distance her from the audience.) The candid manner, if only manner. The winning apologies, although for exactly what may not be clear, certainly not for any less than appealing fault. Hillary Clinton has learned that, if one must apologize, to do it for some admirable trait everyone can understand, like protecting the family's privacy. Perfect. "Contrition as Weapon," said the headline over one analysis of her news conference.

Maureen Dowd of the *New York Times*, who has an eye for these things, noted "it was clear that a lot of thought had gone into how today's performance would be staged. Hard right angles were avoided. Even her chair was set at an oblique angle, cater-corner to the angle of the chair in which Lincoln sat contemplatively in the darkly gleaming oil portrait above."

Cool as gun metal, Miss Hillary didn't need a single sip from that glass of water at her side. To quote one summation of her style, it was "somewhere between Grace Kelly and Edward Bennett Williams."

The Grace Kelly was evident; the Edward Bennett Williams lurked in the text. Did she get any special treatment from her commodities broker? Not a flat denial but a lawyerly, "There's really no evidence of that."

Why no margin calls on her trades? Was it favoritism? Again, not a definite No but words which leave that impression: "I don't think there's any evidence of that." Or this variant of same: "I had absolutely no reason to believe that I got any favorable treatment." She was just another ordinary Arkie working hard and living by the rules. All of us here in Arkansas made $100,000 or so in cattle futures circa 1979–80.

It would be wrong to call such a performance slick. That would be criminal understatement. It was deft. It was elegant. It was dang near perfect. The First Woman's formidable memory was outshone only by her brilliant forgettery. For example: Why didn't she ever get any margin calls when other investors might have? "I do not remember any of those details."

This was not the Hillary Rodham who a couple of years ago came barging into a press conference called by some poor rival of her husband's in the state capitol and left him rhetorically sprawling. Then she was Carry Nation reborn, wielding a verbal ax and taking no prisoners. Miss Hillary can change personas as easily as she does hairdos, wardrobes, and last names.

A phenom in politics, Hillary Clinton would have made a splendid actress. Maybe she *is* making a splendid actress. Politics is not altogether different from showbiz, though its best practitioners do not let on.

Content. F. What do the American people know or suspect about Whitewater now that we did not know or suspect before? Pushed aside only temporarily by Ms. Clinton's words and manner, the same unanswered questions about Whitewater and related puzzles still lie there like land mines.

Among them:

Why did the McDougals lose so much more in this deal than the Clintons, although Whitewater was supposed to be a fifty-fifty deal?

Why the long series of false and contradictory explanations of Hillary Clinton's commodity trades that have issued forth from the White House without a single demurrer from her before now?

How did she manage to parlay a $1,000 investment into $100,000 despite the astronomical odds against profits on such a scale? For that matter, how did she manage to make $5,300 on a $1,000 investment the very first day — a feat some old pros still can't explain? Just what trades did friend and mentor Jim Blair place for her, and how could he do that if, as she contends, "I made the trades"?

What was her chief of staff doing in Vince Foster's office after his suicide was reported? What papers were removed? Why was Vince Foster working on the Clintons' personal affairs at all as a member of the White House staff? And how justify the administration's taking charge of these records, and this evidence, rather than leaving all this to the police supposedly handling the case?

And why was her chief of staff involved in that series of highly improper meetings between Justice Department higher-ups and presidential aides to talk about a criminal referral in which the Clintons were mentioned? And if such meetings weren't improper, why is Bernard Nussbaum no longer counsel to the president? And why was he the only top aide obliged to resign over this scandal, which involved so many others?

How can Ms. Clinton still deny her conflict of interest in representing the federal government against a friend, supporter, and contributor to the Clinton campaign? By explaining, as she did Friday, that he was not a close friend and that she put in only a couple of hours' work on his case. How long does it take a lawyer to influence a settlement? Or is a small conflict of interest no conflict of interest?

Counselor Clinton also tried to justify signing a letter on behalf of Madison Guaranty to a banking commissioner whom her husband had appointed, and who in turn addressed her on a first-name basis. At her press conference, Miss Hillary explained that all she had done was to let her law firm put her name on the bottom of a letter. What else would her law firm need to exert her influence?

Those looking for further defenses/explanations of Whitewater have a growing number to choose from, including earlier assertions by Ms. Clinton's spouse that she "has never lobbied me or any state agency that I'm aware of . . ." (Bill Clinton, March 16, 1992) and that when she did, it was minimal. ("That was basically the extent of her representation. Now, all I can do is tell you that she believed there was nothing unethical about it." — Bill Clinton, March 24, 1994.) Or are these explanations now "inoperative"?

No, there was no shortage of explanations at this press conference, but once they wear off, there won't be any shortage of questions, either.

Rhetoric. A.

Note this rousing defense of the American free enterprise system, which came when Ms. Clinton was asked whether her killing in cattle futures contradicted her and her spouse's earlier attacks on the 1980s as a Decade of Greed:

> I was raised by a father who had me reading the stock tables when I was a little girl, and I started doing that with my daughter when she was a little girl. I mean, I don't think you'll ever find anything that my husband or I said that in any way condemns the importance of making good investments and saving, or that in any way undermines what is the heart and soul of the American economy, which is risk-taking and investing in the future.

Hurray, attaway, and woo pig sooey! In light of Ms. Clinton's all-American pride in her investments, one wonders only why she did not publicize them earlier, but waited until she had to. Modesty about her financial acumen, no doubt.

Other authorities might take a more critical view of Hillary Clinton's making a 10,000 percent profit on her investment in cattle futures. For instance:

> "The 1980s were not just a decade of greed and self-seeking, they were a decade of denial and blame."
>
> — Bill Clinton, September 22, 1991

> "The 1980s were about acquiring — acquiring wealth, power, privilege."
>
> — Hillary Clinton, speaking last May

> And: "The 1980s ushered in a Gilded Age of greed and selfishness, of irresponsibility and excess and of neglect."
>
> — Bill Clinton, speaking in October of 1991

The new, born-again, commodities-trading, capitalist-tool Clintons, whom even Daddy Warbucks would find amenable, certainly are preferable to the fiscal puritans who campaigned for president. Not only can they make cattle futures sound like a nice conservative investment for a struggling family, but with a little help from a friend or two, Miss Hillary can make 'em pay off like slot machines that show only jackpots. And never a margin call. Anybody who can do that has to be talented. In one way or another.

THE RISE OF HILLARY CLINTON
MAY 4, 1994

Each time seems to produce its own characteristic scandal, and Whitewater says much about ours. It is complex, confusing, suspect, and most of all upwardly mobile. It's also an equal-opportunity scandal: Hillary Clinton must be the first wife of a president to speak about her financial affairs at such length, or need to.

The most intriguing little puzzle in the big puzzle that is Whitewater has to be Hillary Rodham Clinton's run of luck or something in cattle futures. Mrs. Clinton now has told the press that there was "no evidence" of hanky-panky in her running $1,000 into $100,000 in the commodities market.

No, and there may not be any evidence that somebody who hits the winning number every time she plays roulette is the beneficiary of a fixed wheel, but the pattern will arouse suspicion, not to say disbelief. The mathematical probabilities are so unlikely.

Or as the Baltimore *Sun* summarized Ms. Clinton's remarkable success in the commodities market, "It certainly doesn't smell right."

It doesn't smell right. That summation might apply to the whole swirly mix of fact and falsehood, impropriety and conflict-of-interest, suspicion and hypocrisy, excuse and indignation known as Whitewater.

Nobody should be condemned on the basis of nothing more than a fishy odor, but strange smells should not go uninvestigated. They only tend to get stronger.

Whatever Whitewater turns out to be or not to be in national politics, it has cast an illuminating light on state politics.

For just a moment, the people of Arkansas have got a peek at our state's invisible government — a subterranean network of friends and mentors, kingmakers and pols, fund raisers and campaign spenders. In short, the whole messy nexus of personal connections that lies behind the carefully arranged scenes and slick lines. The curtains of a glittering production now have parted prematurely, and some of the stagehands and a producer or two are caught wandering about the stage, handing the actors their checks. It's been fascinating for those of us who wonder from time to time how these special effects are produced.

The Rise of Hillary Clinton would make a great title for a novel if only it had more sympathetic or interesting characters. Unfortunately, various aspects of the story already have been extensively explored in

American literature — in *The Rise of Silas Lapham, The Octopus, The Financier, The Great God Success,* and *The Great Gatsby.*

A great novel should also have a great hero, and one might have to wait for the sequel, *The Fall of Hillary Clinton,* for one to emerge. Robert Fiske? Jim Leach? Surely not Alfonse D'Amato or Henry Gonzales.

Besides, it's not at all clear whether that most repetitive of authors, History, has any plans to publish such a sequel. Any work of fiction featuring a mysterious character named Red Bone would surely be dismissed by the critics as too improbable even for fiction.

This would all be standard fare for British politics, in which Whitewater wouldn't cause a ripple. In that more stratified society, it is an accepted practice for older and wiser heads to take promising young politicos under their wings. ("I say, old sport, what a pity someone as clever as yourself, with such a bright future, and as keen to serve the realm, should be without an independent income. . . . I know of a smashing little limited company whose shares should double in a fortnight. Why not have a go at it? Little or no risk, all quite cricket, and I would be happy to guide you through the sticky spots. . . .")

Naturally the process would be speeded up in the bigger and better American version of upward mobility, with cattle futures producing a 10,000 percent profit in no time.

Just as naturally, nothing would be said about the politician's incurring any obligation. But who wouldn't be much obliged for a lesson in how to make a fast hundred thou? It was Fiorello La Guardia who said that the first qualification for public service should be "a monumental ingratitude." Not many of us could be so impolite, not to say inhuman, as to be wholly ungrateful for such guidance.

Masterpiece Theatre could bring off a British drama along these lines, but such politic arrangements don't fit the requirements of the American Dream Theater. This country prefers stories about the self-made man, the barefoot Rhodes Scholar, the Little Girl from Little Rock, the forgotten middle-class Americans who work hard and play by the rules. . . .

After all, how could Hollywood make an inspiring campaign film about a young but aspiring commodities trader who is shown the ropes by a Tyson lawyer? You see the problem.

For now this unsatisfying drama — it won't die but it won't rev up, either — seems to have reached an interminable intermission. There's no telling just when the curtains will part unexpectedly, catching the actors off guard again. Keep your ticket stubs handy; this could still be quite a show.

AND THE WINNER IS . . .
JUNE 27, 1994

No doubt about it — the envelope, please — the winner is, has got to be, couldn't be anybody else but . . .

Hillary Rodham Clinton! (Tumultuous, Barbra Streisand–scale applause.)

First Woman took the cake and a brief respite from Whitewater on the strength of a virtuoso performance back in April. So says *TV Guide*, which gave Ms. Clinton its award for "best performance in a drama . . . or press conference."

In this surreal world, those two categories became interchangeable some time ago — at least since the Age of Reagan. Ronald Reagan didn't so much end his acting career when he became president as extend it. Certainly the drama was heavy at Richard Nixon's press conferences about Watergate, too, though he never seemed comfortable in the role of president or hardly any other. (Mr. Nixon was always something of a bad actor.)

This latest award for drama confirms what a lot of us have always suspected: that Miss Hillary has been a closet thespian all along. She has performed under various names during a long and distinguished career:

First there was Hillary Rodham, the earnest young McGovernite. This is still my favorite performance. Not since Loretta Young of the whirling petticoats has innocence been captured so perfectly. So perfectly that some of us still don't believe it was an act. It was more a character role. Of course this is the Hillary who would try to enroll in the Marines and go on to make a bundle in the commodities market. The U.S. Marine Corps missed a good bet.

Then she played Hillary Clinton No. 1, who not only stood by her man but mowed anybody down who got in his way. Just ask Little Rock's Tom McRae, who had the temerity to run for governor of Arkansas against Mr. Clinton four years ago and was promptly sandbagged by Ms. Clinton. At the state Capitol. At what felt like High Noon. Miss Hillary walked in on his press conference and proceeded to take it over. She came on like Gangbusters, the U.S. Marines, and a one-woman Demolition Derby. Bam! Kapow! Scraaatch! Total Dee-Mo-Li-Shun! It would take a Tom Wolfe to describe the rhetorical carnage. . . .

No sooner had one become accustomed to the New Hillary than the script changed again. Hillary Clinton No. 2 emerged in the 1992 presidential campaign as the perfect Stepford Wife — complete with fixed, adoring gaze for her lord and master and candidate. This role seems to have ended with the campaign, and a good thing it did. None of us, surely including Miss Hillary, might have been able to bear it a second longer. One more Nancy Reagan pose and we all thought we'd scream, or Hillary would. Now there is the many-faceted Hillary Rodham Clinton, the absolute whiz on health care but just Poor Li'l Ol' Me when it comes to intricacies like commodities trades and savings-and-loans.

TV Guide was right: Her press conference displayed a range that would have made Yma Sumac envious. She was superb — from the brash Shoulda-Coulda-Woulda dismissal of a leading question to the complete Southern Belle innocence about high finance. Compared to Hillary Clinton, Bette Davis was one-dimensional. The effect of the press conference and star turn was great while it lasted, which was about half an hour. Then, as the magic began to wear off, it occurred that this woman's superb memory was matched only by a superber forgettery.

TV Guide couldn't have made a better choice, but there's always a quibble with us critics. It wasn't the performance that impressed so much as the costuming, the stage setting, the choreography, the perfect sight lines, the just right angle of alignment with the Lincoln portrait, the pinkish suit, the hairdo, the perfect tonal modulation . . . the whole ensemble.

When it was over, one wanted to shout not Author! Author! but Designer! Designer! As in the box scores, some unknown ought to get credit for a great assist.

There are various nominees for the dubious honor of Greatest Collapse of the Clinton administration — American foreign policy, for one. But surely the great Health-Care Plan That Wasn't would be among the Top Ten candidates. What happened to that dream? How did a savvy operator and well-regarded organizer like Hillary Clinton preside over such a debacle? Part of the explanation may be found in some

documents that are now part of the public record — over the adminis-
tration's understandable protests. These papers from her Health Task
Force indicate that, if Hillary Rodham Clinton was willing to change
her persona for political advantage, she could hold onto some unreal-
istic ideas all too long:

THE SECRETS OF MISS HILLARY'S TASK FORCE
SEPTEMBER 21, 1994

No wonder Hillary Rodham Clinton didn't want to reveal the working papers of her Task Force on National Health Care Reform. She suc-
cessfully stonewalled for some eighteen months before releasing 234
boxes of documents, each containing about 2,500 pages of material. Her
task force was able to maintain its secrecy much longer than the one
amassed around Haiti, but of course Miss Hillary's outfit had a more
determined commander-in-chief.

And what do the first, cursory dips into this library of healthspeak
show? That almost from the first, officials within the administration
were making the kind of devastating criticisms that, in the end, sank
this Task Torce. The criticisms were ignored, but nobody can say that
Ira Magaziner, who was supposed to coordinate the uncoordinated
effort, wasn't warned. Hillary Clinton should have been able to detect
the torpedoes, too. They started coming early:

- On February 17, 1993, a senior economist at Treasury — James
  R. Ukockis, described the administration's health-care planners
  as having gone "from frenetic to frantic" in trying to answer
  unanswerable criticisms in his work. It was clear to Mr. Ukockis even then that the White House "was not interested in a balanced evaluation" of its plan, but just looking for "someone to
  make the best possible case for a specific price control program."

  Somehow this does not surprise. Rather than conducting an
  objective study to find the best solution to the problems of
  American health care, the organizers of the Task Force seemed
  out to confirm their own preconceptions. True Believers are
  like that; they hold onto their cognitive dissonance as if it were
  an article of faith, confident that sheer willpower can make two

plus two equal five. Or at least four and a half as a negotiated compromise. Can this be what Bill Clinton, in his 1992 presidential campaign, used to deride as "brain-dead politics" in his opponents?

■ A month later (March 23, 1993) Mr. Ukockis surveyed the jury-rigged plan being assembled, and warned: "Every option has fatal flaws, which, although passed off as problems 'still under examination,' are actually major roadblocks to successful implementation." It would take more than a year for the administration to tacitly admit as much when it agreed to scuttle the Task Force's plan. The challenge now is to make a strategic rout sound like a great victory.

The big problem with the Clinton Plan was that, instead of making only incremental changes, or beginning anew, it attempted to make coherent changes — well, changes that seemed coherent to its theorists — in a health-care system that isn't a coherent whole to begin with. How did health insurance in America ever get tied to employment in the first place? Because war industries . . . set up their own medical systems to care for their workers, and everything else just grew from that quirk. If the American (non)system of health care had a name, it would be Topsy.

Eventually the country would develop an arrangement under which insurance companies make medical decisions, lawyers' fees determine insurance rates, competition has less effect on price than do government dictates, coverage tends to end when the job does, employees have an HMO instead of a doctor, taxes are called "mandates" . . . and the whole, ramshackle system continues to grow in all directions, or maybe shrink.

One cannot make changes, however rational in theory, to selected parts of this clanking, uneven machine without throwing off all the other parts. The economist at Treasury had identified the big problem with the Clinton Plan early in the game: "Every option had fatal flaws" that could be disguised as "problems still under examination" only for so long. Eventually the American people, to judge by the polls, caught on, Congress followed suit, and ClintonCare was undone.

Here's a memo from Treasury that affords a glimpse into how things worked on Planet Clinton: On April 1, 1993, when the administration was asked to provide some reliable figures on how much its health plan would cost, the health planners "sat around the table making guesstimates of the savings to be realized" by their ever-changing plan. Conclusion: "It was an appropriate exercise for April Fool's Day."

What we have here is the familiar triumph of theory over mere reality: First concoct a program or a policy, and then find the numbers to justify it. The administration's health-care plan, like Dr. Johnson's description of second marriages, was a triumph of hope over experience.

The administration was able to pursue this complex mirage for more than a year, but inevitably it fell apart. What reason cannot teach, time must. And now Congress is considering only incremental reforms that could have been passed in President Clinton's first year in the White House, or maybe even President Bush's last.

The True Believers are in retreat for the moment. What is remarkable is not that they had to retreat, but that they held out against the facts for so long. Ira Magaziner's leadership style, which might best be described as extraterrestrial, lost touch with reality early, while Hillary Clinton did not give up the struggle until late, apparently under the impression that arithmetic was another sneaky Republican plot that must be foiled at all costs.

Whatever all this says about the health plan, it demonstrates once again that the Clintons make a perfectly balanced political couple: If the president seems to have no conviction he won't sacrifice for political advantage, Ms. Clinton has entirely too many.

Chapter 10

REELECTION '96

Will this president win reelection in 1996? Those of us who have watched Bill Clinton make comeback after comeback know better than to bet against him. He's been finished as an American political figure as many times as Richard Nixon, only to surface again. Defeated for reelection as governor of Arkansas after only one two-year term, Bill Clinton came back. When his presidency cracked up early in the spring of 1993, Bill Clinton managed to put it back together again. At midterm, his party suffered its worst defeat in forty years, but Bill Clinton was repositioning himself before the year was out. Up or down, this perpetual campaigner keeps on truckin'. Don't count him out yet.

THE BUBBLE BURSTS
JUNE 11, 1993

The telephone calls were the first signs. The same reporters and pundits who only a few months ago were deep into Arkansas Chic and eager to learn the secret of the Clinton charm, the Clinton magic, the Clinton touch . . . now call and ask about the Clinton disaster.

"What happened?" they want to know, as if they had never been warned, as if somehow I or maybe Arkansas was responsible, and owed them an explanation.

American politics knows no golden mean. Either we're celebrating the coming of the Millennium outside the Old State House here in Little Rock, the political capital of the known universe, or all the imitation Edward R. Murrows of the televised world are putting together one of their oh-so-profound analyses of Another Failed Presidency.

Crowds that cheered on cue now boo at the mention of the suddenly former Conquering Hero. Audiences that once couldn't get enough
of America's Hope change the channel. . . .

Mercurial thing, public opinion in this televised, computerized,
atomized mass democracy that has all but replaced the Republic. One
hesitates even to call it public opinion; it is more like mass moodiness.
The gladiatorial games at the Coliseum must have attracted the same
kind of instant, unthinking reactions now painstakingly recorded by
the Harris and Gallup polls . . . and revealed with a mystical solemnity
formerly reserved for messages from the oracle at Delphi.

The story is told that Alexander Hamilton, on hearing the majesty
and wisdom of The People invoked just once too often, turned on the
invoker and sneered: "Your people, sir, are a great beast." He had probably got too many calls from out-of-town pundits the night before.

If the people in its collective majesty and wisdom bear a certain
resemblance to a great beast, surely it is to a dinosaur — a massive car-
nality with a pea-sized brain, a behemoth that with one flick of its great
tail vaults a particular politician into not-exactly-everlasting fame, and
then fifteen minutes later tosses the same pol back into obscurity, or
even obloquy. Invariably, said pol is left with the unshakable impression that his rise was entirely self-propelled, his decline the fault of
incompetent aides who need to be replaced at once. . . .

Vanity of vanities.

Those of us who for our own perverse reasons make a business of
watching ambitious politicians rise and fall have seen it before, and no
doubt will see it again. It is a cycle as old as Ecclesiastes. We're much
like the field hand in the great opening paragraph of Robert Penn Warren's masterpiece, *All the King's Men*. Now and then we look up from
our humble hoeing at the sound of another automobile in the distance
going off the shimmering road, leaving behind only "the little column
of black smoke standing up against the vitriolic, arsenical green of the
cotton rows, and up against the violent, metallic throbbing blue of the
sky."

And all the field hand can say is, "Lawd God, hit's anudder one done
hit." The bubble Popularity makes a treacherous and unforgiving god.

One thing for sure: Whenever a president enters that downward spi-
ral, and begins to feel the road give way beneath him, no matter what
his politics, he remains convinced that it is not he who is at fault, and

that if only people better understood that, all would go well. That's why the press secretary is often the first to go.

Quick, bring in a davidgergen to handle PR. It's never the star attraction's fault but his handler's, and all the president needs is a better handler. (Remember when James Baker was going to save George Bush's faltering presidential campaign?) Does anyone around the White House dare whisper the suspicion that the fault, Dear Brutus, lies not in our stars, or even in our press secretaries, but in ourselves?

If nothing succeeds like success, as it did last November, nothing fails like failure. Those of us who were pointing out The Candidate's little problem with character (namely, the lack thereof) now find our doubts amplified and simplified by the great chorus called the conventional wisdom. It may be singing our song, but what we wrote in sorrow (and, all right, maybe with a little pity and contempt) now seems to come out all anger. It's like having Rush Limbaugh agree with you.

I find myself wishing Bill Clinton would go off to the desert for forty days and forty nights, and substitute a diet of locusts and honey for his usual Big Macs, and find himself. Or any self. It would beat more staff changes, slick speeches, and cute foto-ops. Think I'm kidding? Forty days from now, will the president be any better off for having stuck to his usual rationalization and escape clauses?

Last fall, the style-setters were explaining that Candidate Clinton's, uh, flexibility was not so much a lack of character as a new, up-to-date version of it. Now even Maureen Dowd of the *New York Times* has caught on. She was so shocked by the president's abandonment of poor Lani Guinier that she has begun to raise some questions that sound eerily familiar: "Who is Bill Clinton? What does he stand for? Is there any principle or idea for which Mr. Clinton will unflinchingly fight — any person?"

Now she asks.

Everybody seems to be catching on at once. The effect is like the roaring of [Hamilton's] great beast. Pat Caddell, Jimmy Carter's old pollster, says Mr. Clinton is "the first president who has the ability to stand up and just deny he has been involved in something that he has been involved in."

How soon they forget Richard Nixon.

Bill Clinton is scarcely the first American president who seems hollow at the core, and the Nixonian aspects of his administration grow evident with alarming speed and comprehensiveness. Says one analyst, as if it were news: "He is a pinball moving back and forth to the pressures of external events, without any internal gyroscope to guide him." Tell me about it.

The president's hurried response to this crisis of confidence that has been brought on by his own confidence games is to . . . rearrange his staff. He continues to switch around policies, principles, and appointees, innocent of the possibility that it is not his policies, principles, or appointees that have got him in trouble. It is his inability to stick by any of them. Or by anything. Elastic Man is running out of convincing contortions.

The country senses the lack of direction, the vain attempt to substitute manipulation for leadership, the void at the center. ("It is not the compromises that he has made that trouble so much as the unavoidable suspicion that he has no great principles to compromise." — *Arkansas Democrat-Gazette*, October 28, 1992.) The-Boy-Who-Cried-Wolf effect already begins to set in, and the question arises whether this president would be believed even if he somehow came up with some strong beliefs.

Even at this distance, one can sense the rising panic in the White House as another administration veers off the road, fighting the steering wheel all the way, losing control, cracking up, blaming the passengers or fate or somebody, anybody else.

THE SPIRIT OF '94: THE MEANING OF MIDTERM

NOVEMBER 21, 1994

When it's all over including the shouting, and the last analysis of these midterm elections is in, and the last politician has explained that he engineered this great victory, or bears only a share of responsibility for this great defeat, and the last pollster has told us what we really think and feel about it all, how best sum up the significance of this electoral earthquake? Try this:

The American people have set their mind on Freedom.

It was one of the last of the Whigs and first of the Republicans, Abraham Lincoln, who asserted that public opinion was supreme in politics, and in his homely wisdom Mr. Lincoln went further. He said that public opinion, shift as it might from issue to issue and position to position, always had some central impetus, some motivating idea at its center around which all the other issues and tendencies and thoughts of the time revolved.

Mr. Lincoln understood, and demonstrated, that for the politician to become a statesman, he must trace and find that central theme — not just gather up every popular notion that comes along and throw the whole, artfully arranged bunch at the voters. Mr. Lincoln understood that the American people would eventually demand that statesmen grapple with some central issue, rather than forever dance around it.

In the elections just past, the triumphant Republicans offered the American people a ten-point Contract that touched on a wide array of issues and promoted any number of ideas and interests. But throughout that Contract With America, whether the promise was lower taxes or a balanced budget or support for families or tort reform, a central theme emerged: More power to the people — or rather to persons, to individuals.

To sum up the promise: More power over one's own earnings, more assurance of personal safety, more opportunity for work, more emphasis on the family and, conversely, less power to government and fewer perks for the politicians. Now let's see if Republicans remain as fond of those objectives when they control Congress.

These midterm elections may not signify a partisan victory, but they do represent a partisan defeat: Not a single Republican incumbent in Congress or in gubernatorial office was ousted, while Democratic incumbents went down one after the other. Could it have been because the Democratic Party was not able to unite behind a single motivating idea?

The Democrats certainly had a single recognizable leader in the White House, but that may have been a crippling disadvantage — since his leadership consisted of whatever issues and ideas may have sounded good at the time. Bill Clinton mastered the means of politics some time ago; his talent at synthesizing ideas and combining interests remains unmatched. But to what end all this unceasing political activity? That much has never been clear, and it is still not clear.

To sum up Clintonism: All sail, no anchor. To say the president stands for change is to say nothing. What matters is the direction in which change will take the country, and in the Age of Clinton direction has never been a priority — only movement. Or at least the appearance thereof.

The one sustained error of which Bill Clinton has been capable, not just in his presidency but throughout his years of political prominence, has been an inability to recognize that principle matters. This is not to say that he has betrayed some central moral theme, only that he has never engaged one for very long. Even when it comes to abortion, the one policy he has supported most consistently in deed, the president shies away from endorsing it in word.

For a historic moment this president succeeded in fashioning his party in his own vacuous image. But in the wake of these midterm elections, it gasps for breath, unable for the moment to touch bottom, to find any sure ground on which to rebuild. Its world has shifted. Suddenly the Democratic Party's cognitive dissonance, so comfortable only a little while ago, is no longer deniable. And the questions that no smug party likes to face cannot be put off much longer: What now? Where to?

Republicans had much the same experience two Novembers ago. They seem to have learned much from defeat, the world's most unforgiving and effective teacher. Victory, as Republicans are about to discover, will not prove nearly so educational. In politics as in war, the most disorganizing experience a force can encounter is sudden and sweeping victory; it teaches overconfidence and inflexibility. It reinforces tactics most effective in the past. It is the enemy of mental and spiritual growth.

The Democrats now have the great advantage of being able to see their leader more clearly: This president has had slogans aplenty, and he is never out of touch with the latest fadthink, but underneath all this ferment, has anyone ever sensed solid rock? Would anyone ever confuse his politics with Mr. Lincoln's engagement with the central, motivating theme of public opinion in his time? Abe Lincoln, too, was nothing if not flexible, shrewd, and ambitious; his political record is replete with many a maneuver and compromise. Yet throughout his many swerves, he kept his eye on those twin stars, liberty and union. He may never have been sure how to get there, but he knew where he was going.

This is not to deny that many a politician has enjoyed a successful career temporizing the central issue of his time. Mr. Lincoln's debating partner, Stephen A. Douglas, confused moral irrelevance with statesmanship and vision. He thought of slavery as an unfortunate diversion from the manifest destiny of American expansionism. Not until too late did Senator Douglas come to realize the disaster a nation invites by forever putting off the central moral issue that confronts it.

Even now, one can hear the gears grinding again in the White House as the newest, rearranged constellation of presidential advisers and experts — all those hot numbers — work out still another policy to deal with the economy and maybe everything else. Dee Dee Myers will explain all this yet. Problem is, no one may buy the explanation, not even the explainers.

Somewhere in the White House or in James Carville's ever-fecund mind, there may even be some effort to work on what George Bush used to call the Vision Thing — as if it were not the essence of leadership but one more separate issue, like tariffs or grazing fees.

In this administration, there doesn't seem to be a central, organizing theme in sight or sound. No wonder it gets harder to distinguish the Clinton crew from Bush II. Its policies may differ, but the sense of inertia, the feeling of hopeless drift rather than patient mastery, is all too familiar. So are the doubts: What do these people believe? Where would they take us? *Whatever happened to the Happy Warrior?* Style is all in such matters, but it cannot be maintained independent of spirit and substance. And vision. Not that Americans seem in the market just now for some alternative vision out of the White House; the election results would seem to indicate we've set our minds on Freedom.

THE FORGOTTEN MAN
JANUARY 11, 1995

With all eyes on Congress, the great challenge of the suddenly forgotten executive branch this past week was not how to take the initiative — some things are no longer within the range of hope — but to remain relevant.

The vibrant voices from the House and Senate reflected the hopes and dreams, the fears and forebodings, of the American people. The president's voice on the evening news had acquired the tinny, dated sound of a historical film. Just what he said tended to slip the mind. George Bush would understand what was happening. The country was turning toward the future.

How did it happen? When did it happen? Those were a couple of the questions posed by a visiting editor who dropped by to talk shop the other day. A Clinton enthusiast in 1992, he couldn't understand how it all could have happened by 1994. This out-of-state editor hadn't paid much attention to any storm warnings from Arkansas, figuring they were just a case of familiarity breeding contempt. It seems to happen in every presidential candidate's home state. He had no idea things would go this far this fast.

How did it happen?

When did it happen?

Every failing, flailing president must ask himself the same questions when he finds himself in the midst of a dark wood, unsure just how he got there, or why, or when. Or if he will emerge to see the stars. By the time one asks the questions, it may be too late for the answer.

It would be too cruel, because all too accurate, to suggest that this sense of failure was inherent in the way success was achieved, that the end was only the natural outcome of the means. Sheer expediency may win the day, but not the years. People get tired of being told only what they want to hear.

The simplest explanation of Bill Clinton's latest slump is an old one: "It is true that you may fool all the people some of the time; you can even fool some of the people all the time; but you can't fool all of the people all the time."

Surely most Americans would recognize that well-known sentence attributed to Abraham Lincoln; most might not be familiar with the sentence that immediately preceded it: "If you once forfeit the confidence of your fellow citizens, you can never regain their respect and esteem."

There is a kind of raw justice that is hard to distinguish from cruelty. Here is the most talkative president of the century, perhaps of the presidency, the wonk-in-chief of policy wonkhood, a politician who seeks out every counselor to explain the wisdom and appropriateness of his policies at every stage, and what he really meant all along, and why he is the most misunderstood, the most unfairly abused of all presidents, and how he can still pull it off and . . . and nobody seems to be listening any more.

The very sound of that deadeningly familiar hoarse voice, still making points in a game that may have ended months ago, still eager to explain everything just one more time, is enough to produce a gigantic, continental click as television sets switch channels from coast to coast — or just go blank, as Americans turn to the rich, honest, meaningful sound of silence.

Bill Clinton is not without spiritual resources, or precedents. Other presidents have rehabilitated themselves, if not while in office. It was reported last week that Mr. Clinton had met with Anthony Robbins, "a motivation expert who specializes in peak performances," and Steven R. Covey, author of *The Seven Habits of Highly Effective People.*

Naturally, Bill Clinton and these management mavens convened at Camp David, the presidential retreat. Richard Nixon used to go there to think things through, too. Reading this little item in the news, one thought of Bill Veeck hiring a psychologist to bring the old St. Louis Browns out of their slump. It didn't work.

The president might have done better to consult William Shakespeare, an expert in tragedies. To paraphrase one of the playwright's motivational studies: The fault, dear Brutus, lies not in our efficiency experts, but in ourselves. . . .

THE CALM BEFORE THE CAMPAIGN

APRIL 17, 1995

The president and the presidency are at ebb tide now. The center of attention and gravity in American politics has shifted like some continental plate. The Speaker of the House delivers a wrap-up of the First Hundred Days of the new Congress, but what he is really talking about is the State of the Union. Congressional government is coming back into its own after something like a century of eclipse under strong presidents. As for this president, he appears not so much unpopular as ignored. "I don't consider myself a titular head of state," Bill Clinton said the other day — the surest sign that he knows many others do. It is definitely time for All the President's Men to counsel together.

At least two camps have formed among the president's counselors. According to Michael Kelly, now the *New Yorker's* resident clintonologist, the "What, Us Worry?" school of thought in the White House is represented by Hillary Clinton, James Carville, George Stephanopoulos, and Harold Ickes. Mr. Kelly quotes Harold Ickes as explaining that the November landslide was no seismic shift to the right after all, but only a failure of the Democrats to communicate:

> I do not think the country is any more conservative as much as I think it is more nervous, and more scared and more unsure of itself. I would analogize the country in terms of the Great Depression. I think we are going through enormous social changes — changes that have been building, to some degree, for a decade or

more. People are wondering what the new direction is, what the new social compact is. People are very nervous about their jobs, their futures."

Right. The election of the first Republican Congress in four decades, and of Republican governors in thirty states with almost three-quarters of the country's population, and the shift of national focus to the GOP's Contract With America, and the sense of movement anybody outside the White House could feel . . . all that is a passing case of nerves. Right. The 104th Congress is really no more revolutionary than the Republican 80th in Harry Truman's time, Newt Gingrich is just another stolid, 1946ish Joe Martin, and the moon is made of green Camembert.

Once again the clintonoids are underestimating the dynamism, the sense of adventure, the sheer confidence, the eagerness for a new start out here in the rest of the country. In always revolutionary America, the folks who are "very nervous about their jobs, their futures" may be most highly concentrated in the Clinton administration.

The surest sign of the president's own frustration at events is the frequency of his passing tantrums. Todd Purdum of the *New York Times* reported Monday that Mr. Clinton "exploded in anger" during a White House meeting when a Democratic congressman from Texas, Lloyd Doggett, dared say the obvious — that the American public believes Bill Clinton lacks conviction.

The president must know — and occasionally he indicates — that simply to go on as before won't do. The Clinton White House in 1995 has begun to take on the dispirited air of the Bush White House in 1991. The long slide into irrelevance, barely perceptible at first, may prove unstoppable unless some sharp change of course is made.

Harold Ickes's is the kind of advice Republicans can hope this president not only gets but takes. That's unlikely. Mr. Ickes's title may be senior adviser, but Bill Clinton is his own senior adviser, campaign manager, and chief strategist. Sure, he's going to listen to Mr. Ickes and Mrs. Clinton, to the Ragin' Cajun and all the stephanopoulii, and just about everybody else. It is hard to have a conversation with Bill Clinton without being mined for information, counsel, support, tips . . . or at least being used as a sounding board.

Bill Clinton was networking before network was a verb. So he will also be listening to those who still believe he can be the New Democrat who was elected president aeons ago in 1992. Notable among them:

Al From of the Democratic Leadership Council and Al Gore, Roboveep. But he'll listen to himself most, and for good reason: There's not a better campaigner in the country.

This president may be no great shakes as an executive (he's about as hands-on as the Venus de Milo), but he's about to come into his own as election year approaches. This is just his fallow season, like the brief hiatus in his political career after he lost a gubernatorial election in Arkansas in 1980. That was a shock, too, like the midterm elections of 1994, and it took Bill Clinton a while to recover, but recover he did. Every Clinton-watcher is familiar with these seasonal changes. If there is such a thing as a deciduous politician, it's Bill Clinton.

The conventional wisdom may already have counted this president out, but wait till the alternative is not some abstract Perfect Opponent, but an actual Phil Gramm or Bob Dole or Lamar Alexander or, Democrats can hope, worse. Wait till Bill Clinton hits the campaign with the zest of a natural politician who can't wait to stop being The President and start being The Candidate again.

The *New Yorker's* Mr. Kelly wonders if Bill Clinton will follow the lead of the "What, Us Worry?" school of advice, or act more like a Me-Too Republican. Will the 1996 model Clinton appeal to fear and envy, or moderation and compromise?

The answer, Michael Kelly sees almost immediately, is "all of the above." The president, he writes, will be presented as "(1) a constructive leader," "(2) a conservative at heart," and "(3) a solidly liberal Democrat." And those personae are just a start. Wait till the others start popping up on the campaign trail like multiple personalities in a psychologist's case file — realist and idealist, moderate and revolutionary, pragmatist and theorist . . . all depending on what different issues and different polls demand.

Mr. Clinton's, shall we say, versatile approach to politics is actually faithful in its way — not to any principle, of course — but to his political history. Who says Bill Clinton can't be consistent?

To Irrelevance and Back
April 24, 1995

Tuesday night, the president of the United States held a press conference, and here is a brief but complete summary of what he sought to convey: "I am not irrelevant!"

Of course Bill Clinton said it at much greater length. (Doesn't he always?) And the message was about as convincing as Richard Nixon's stirring declaration, "I am not a crook!"

The president also said that he'd said all he was going to say about his draft record, a most prudent decision in his case.

A couple of the television networks — NBC and ABC — passed up the opportunity to broadcast this news event for the good reason that it was more event than news.

The most affecting and welcome part of the president's presentation was his ending it. He seemed to half wander, half wobble down a long, empty hall, as if unsure on which side to exit. (Somebody should have put up a sign: "This Way to Irrelevance.")

Once upon another time, no network would have ignored Ronald Reagan in prime time, perhaps because The Gipper understood that presidential appearances are more than a way to defend policy or build a following. They are of the essence, not just a means to a political end. They can unite, inspire, and invigorate not just a presidency but the country.

Unfortunately, Bill Clinton makes a presidential press conference sound more like an oral interview for a Rhodes scholarship. Rather than inspiring, he rattles off facts and figures and what sound like test-marketed responses. His might be just another voice hawking just another product — himself — on teevee. There is the dignified intro, the premeditated presentation, the practiced ad libs, and the clincher at the end. (Step right up! Something for everybody! Your questions answered, your doubts put to rest! And, yes, your responses to polls instantly translated into presidentese.)

As always, Bill Clinton made sure to include as an Extra Added Bonus a few applause lines, though they no longer seem to generate applause. At the end, Mr. Clinton walked not into the sunset, but retreated down that hall, seeming to shrink in the distance, his invisible veto wrapped around him like Linus's security blanket.

Ronald Reagan — president, commander-in-chief, and trouper — would approach the microphone as if he were coming out of the wings, and when it was over he would stride, not slink, away. Indeed, as has been noted before, Ronald Reagan was to television what Franklin Roosevelt was to radio.

In post-Reagan America, as in post-Thatcher Britain, the press conference has become an exercise in ennui, a purely ceremonial occasion that must be performed with or without an audience. It's as if Ameri-

cans had turned their attention elsewhere and left their presidents to
go through the motions.

Bill Clinton isn't the first chief executive to become an afterthought
in the American mind. Much the same thing happened to George Bush
as his term dwindled. Nobody seemed to be listening. The country was
looking for new leadership and new ideas, or just for leadership and
ideas.

Even the inaugural poet, Maya Angelou, seems to have caught on to
the secret of this president's failure — "trying to be all things to all people." If by Tuesday night even she had figured it out, who wouldn't?

Wednesday afternoon, this president was back before the television
cameras, and this time no television network major or minor was missing. Oklahoma City looked like Beirut, the country was fighting shock
and rage, the full extent of what had happened had yet to sink in, and an
America in sorrow and anger once again turned instinctively toward
the White House.

Bill Clinton seemed to have cast off political calculation like yesterday's shirt. His voice was as familiar as those instantly recognizable
accents out of Oklahoma City. Pretense and politics had become yesterday's news, and they may be tomorrow's, but this was no time for
The Game. This was real.

In a few brief moments, the president had expressed a nation's rage
and sorrow, and utter determination. He asked Americans to pray for
that grace that has been so showered upon this nation, and even before
he spoke the words, it had been granted him and us. Beyond the shock
and anger, an iron resolve was forming.

"A great people," Learned Hand once reminded us, "does not go to
its leaders for incantations and liturgies. . . . it goes to them to peer into
the recesses of its own soul, to lay bare its deepest desires; it goes to
them as it goes to its poets and its seers." . . .

In the president's voice Americans could hear not a candidate but a
friend and neighbor. We could hear ourselves. His message reflected the
country's own elemental decency and dignity and determination, as if
the words hadn't been written but crystallized out of American feelings.

The president was saying some simple things that needed to be said: "The bombing in Oklahoma City was an attack on innocent children and defenseless civilians.

". . . We will find the people who did this. When we do, justice will be swift, certain and severe. These people are killers and they must be treated like killers. . . .

"I ask all Americans tonight to pray; to pray for the people who have lost their lives, to pray for the families and the friends of the dead and the wounded, to pray for the people of Oklahoma City. May God's grace be with them.

"Meanwhile, we will be about our work."

And then he had said enough. There were now words by which to realize the work at hand and go forward. The country was knitting together. The message, not the messenger, had become what mattered again. Like most Americans at some point or another during that long, long day, he had gone beyond self; he had risen to the occasion, if not beyond.

Chapter 11

BILL CLINTON'S
FUTURE—AND
AMERICA'S

The associated pundits of America — we really ought to form a trade group — keep trying to define the essence of Clintonism. The big problem is that it has none, but this will not stop us. As another presidential election approaches, watch for any number of oh-so-deep, scholarly variations on the wispiest of themes. ("Bill Clinton: The Man, the Presidency, the Prospects.") Much will be said about the defining policy or basic philosophy of this president without overemphasizing their absence. In short, we inky wretches will find ourselves in the position of your average account exec at your average advertising agency who may have only a vague idea, but would very much like to sell it. And we will call it a . . . concept. As in, "What a concept!" When it is really more of a mood, an extended shrug — an elaborate, hyperverbalizing way to follow the course of least resistance.

Trying to define Clintonism is as easy as nailing Jell-O to a wall, yet the effort is worthwhile. Not only because of what it says about what the country can expect from Bill Clinton and his administration in the future — some days I can almost smell those steak dinners I have riding on his reelection — but because of what such an examination says about America in the '90s. And about what has happened to American standards. For when this president is at his most reelectable, and he's one heck of a campaigner, he is only reflecting our own desires, our own

266

increasingly tenuous values. We really know Clintonism very well; it is the spirit of our age.

THE CLINTONIZED CULTURE
AUGUST 2, 1992

clin-ton-ize: to make over in the image of Wm. J. and H. R. Clinton, fin-de-siècle political leaders and cultural avatars of late 20th Cent. U.S.A., parents of C. Clinton, noted scientist and humanitarian who led reaction against Clintonism in 21st Cent. 2: to reform in decadent manner. 3: to make fashionable. See Clintonism, Nouveau, and Upward Mobility.

— Universal Biographical Microchip, Moon City, 2159.

The Democratic National Convention and the Clinton-Gore buscapade are but the beginnings of a new style about to sweep the country — as distinctive as the New Look of the Eisenhower Era or the tie-dyed inelegance of the Age of Aquarius and McGovern.

Politics and culture feed off one another, and it's hard to tell where one stops and the other starts. Just as it would have been unthinkable for the intellectually fashionable in the '50s to vote for anyone but Adlai Stevenson, so Bill and Hillary Clinton are rapidly becoming the cultural icons of the '90s — like it or not, ready or not. Style, that most continuous of tyrannies, doesn't give either its exemplars or subjects much choice. We're all going to be clintonized together. The turnaround in the polls has been mirrored by portents in the high pop culture. It hasn't been too long since the cartoon in the *New Yorker* magazine . . . depicted a matron shopping for a tailored jacket but "nothing too Hillary." That had to be the low point. Some of that feeling persists, but it begins to fade in the reflected glow, or maybe glare, of the Democrats' masterfully orchestrated national convention and all-inclusive be-in. Convention week in New York, Hillary culture-stock had risen to the point that she was being quoted in a blurb for a new musical. (" 'Simply magical!' — Hillary Clinton.")

Camelot, like the mini-skirt, is making a comeback. The Candidate's visit to the convention hall in mid-roll call was consciously imitative of John F. Kennedy at his 1960 zenith. The Clintons walked over from Macy's basement, an unconscious statement about the merchandising of the presidency in the 1990s.

The rhetorical attacks at the convention on the insidious influence of special interests alternated with elaborate receptions sponsored by special interests. (Big Business tends to shake the hand that slaps it.) This, too, will be a hallmark of the coming, clintonized culture: a gap between preachment and practice that will be hailed as the new, tough-minded idealism. The officially designated Best and Brightest of the generation coming to power will master this split-level morality, which will be called sophistication.

The clintonized style will not be limited to the campaign and its hangers-on, or Democrats in general, or the more fashionable quarters of the press. Independents and Republicans and malleable youth without previous political affiliation will also be drawn to Clintonism with all its Vigor (another favorite Kennedyism).

Such is the influence of fashion that the most hard-bitten Republican plutocrats and exemplars of American codgerhood will soon find themselves using clintonized expressions, wearing clintonized clothes, and thinking — or rather not thinking — in acceptable, clintonized clichés. Back in 1961, even the dullest of tycoons eventually switched from the Trumanesque double-breasted suit and Eisenhowerian homburg to the single-breasted, hatless Kennedyesque look.

More lasting will be the intellectual fashion being ushered in. Like many of the best things being said in this mediocre time, the following observation and warning comes from Czechoslovakia's successful dissident and failed president, Vaclav Havel:

> They say a nation gets the politicians it deserves. In some senses this is true: politicians are indeed a mirror of their society, and a kind of embodiment of its potential. At the same time — paradoxically — the opposite is also true: society is a mirror of its politicians. It is largely up to the politicians which social forces they choose to liberate and which they choose to suppress, whether they rely on the good in each citizen or the bad. . . . Those who find themselves in politics therefore bear a heightened responsibility for the moral state of society, and it is their responsibility to seek out the best in that society, and to develop it and strengthen it.

The Czech playwright and politician only spelled out what is meant by Role Model, a term that could come into currency only in a society that badly needed one. The clintonized culture of the '90s will affect

Americans not yet born but already registered for law school or headed for the abortion clinic, two of the more popular destinations in this definitely lower-case culture.

The Age of Clinton will be poll-driven. Pollsters now play the role oracles did in ancient Greece. Stan Greenberg, The Candidate's pollster, is well on his way to becoming the George Gallup of the '90s, or maybe the Pat Caddell, who ran Jimmy Carter's polls.

The clintonized-gored culture taking shape will blend a thoroughgoing careerism with an unexamined sentimentality. Its ideology will be anti-ideological. It will be for Us, the country's semi-intellectual elite. (The wholly intellectual need not apply; they're dangerous and, worse, they're losers.) It will be a culture resolutely against Them, those incorrigibly stodgy, unsentimental types with cast-iron Republican souls forever lost to the cultural mainstream.

As for those who play by the rules, they will be praised in speeches but it will be made clear enough that only a fool would emulate them and expect to get ahead in the Age of Clinton. The motto of the coming, clintonized age: It's our turn now! The '90s will be an era of instrumentalism: The principal use of political thought will be to advance careers, of religion to improve society, and of culture to be ornamental rather than influential. For example: The other day, The Candidate's press secretary, the always entertaining Dee Dee Myers, was quoted in the *New York Times*, that sure guide to clintonization, as saying that The Candidate makes it a point to re-read the meditations of Marcus Aurelius every couple of years. Her statement stood out from the dull gray type like the news that Richard Nixon was taking up Zen. I could not have been more struck than if someone had told me that Marcus Aurelius spent his spare time reading the collected speeches of Bill Clinton. Stay tuned. A decade of such ironies awaits.

IS THE PRESS BIASED?
SEPTEMBER 16, 1992

Dear Diary —

Appeared on a panel discussion last week. Good company. Same old topic: The press, currently going under the alias of The Media, as in Medusa. Last seen everywhere.

The inevitable question: Is the press biased?

The answer: Is a bluebird blue?

Next week's topic: Is the world round?

That the press is biased has become part of conventional wisdom, which is the usual fate of the obvious. The one thing that escapes the eagle eye of the press is the obvious. We have a genius for the unconventional, the obscure, the irrelevant, and above all and below all the trivial. (Which may help explain the quality of this presidential campaign.) After all, why tell the public what it can plainly see? We inky wretches of the press have elevated ourselves to the gnostics of American politics.

One need not specify in which way the bias runs. That's so obvious it's understood: In favor of liberals, now known as moderates, however immoderate in their views, and against conservatives, often known as ultra-conservatives, anti-choice voters, the radical right, and Them.

As in most philosophical disagreements, victory goes to whoever seizes the high ground: the language. The title of Moderate is the Little Round Top of this engagement, and the press occupied it for Bill Clinton at the outset of the campaign. (See "The Anointed/Bill Clinton, nominee-elect" — by Sidney Blumenthal, the *New Republic*, February 3, 1992.)

Sure the press has its share of right-wing zanies, too. And yes, the usual critics on the Left argue that the press is biased, but against them. The more honest and observant of them will not say news coverage favors the Right, but rather the center or center-left, or wherever Bill Clinton is at the moment. No one dares call him left-wing or liberal except Republicans.

Stipulations: this charge of bias applies to the media in general, as an institution, as a culture, as — forgive me — a Lifestyle. Not to every single member, including William F. Buckley and Rush Limbaugh. There are numerous exceptions to the domination of the left (on talk radio, for example, and out in the country) but the bicoastal culture sets the style.

The news angle and politically correct language filter down from Washington and New York. The party line doesn't need to be enforced, just pronounced in the right places, and the Young Upwardly Mobile news types in the business fall into line. Fashion and peer pressure are a lot more powerful in this country than anything so brutish as censorship.

Note the different receptions accorded the media at the national conventions. The Democrats tolerated, even welcomed, the media. The

Republicans stood up and jeered at the teevee boxes high above the Astrodome. (One of the more popular buttons at the Republican confab read: "It's All My Fault — I'm With the Media.") People don't have to be told who their friends are, or who wishes them ill. They can sense the obvious.

This is more than a political dispute; it's a cultural divide. Being Republican or Democrat is only part of it. This *Kulturkampf* separates puritan from cavalier, Hollywood from Main Street, and the adversary culture from the straight-and-narrow. Advocates of the New Covenant confront those who still cleave to the Old. Believers in regulation fight the apostles of deregulation. It's condoms vs. abstinence, National Industrial Policy vs. the free market. The press vs. Capital-D Decency. Hillary vs. Marilyn, Barbara, and maybe Tipper, Al and Bill.

The culture gap hasn't been this clear since the Lost Generation took on the Holy Rollers in the '20s, and H. L. Mencken was covering William Jennings Bryan's last stand at the Scopes trial — about as objectively as National Public Radio covered Nicaragua. Only Mencken had the honor not to pretend to objectivity.

If any documentary evidence of bias is needed, there is the news and editorial coverage in the *New York Times, Washington Post,* and *New Republic.* On the eve of the Republican convention, the *Times* runs a lead story on the front page quoting entirely unidentified sources saying George Bush is planning to bomb Baghdad the night of his acceptance speech. A typical news judgment from American journalism's cultural elite. Conservatives are again taking refuge in Little Magazines, like *National Review.*

The press is on an "anti-Bush kick" and "stories have set an unrelenting positive tone about Clinton that contrasts sharply with the skeptical, adversarial stance toward Bush." No, that bulletin does not come from Accuracy in Media or any of the Right's other media watchdogs, but from Mickey Kaus of the *New Republic,* who describes himself as a "liberal activist."

Consider how differently the media treated Gennifer Flowers and Anita Hill. Both made unsubstantiated charges against different men; one becomes a joke and the other a heroine. (If either had more circumstantial evidence to offer, surely it was Ms. Flowers with her tapes and state job.) It wasn't just the class factor or the checkbook journalism that made the difference in how the establishment press treated each accuser. It was the media's own predilections.

Finally, suppose George Bush had permitted the execution of a self-lobotomized black man convicted of murder? Is there any doubt that the best-known name at this point in the campaign would be Rickey Ray Rector? George Bush would have been denounced from coast to coast (though perhaps not in between) as a killer, racist, and bloody opportunist who used capital punishment to prove he wasn't soft on crime. The resulting uproar would have made the brouhaha over the Willie Horton commercial four years ago look as unjustified as it was.

Instead, Bill Clinton presided over the execution, and Rickey Ray Rector is not only a dead man but a forgotten one.

The prosecution rests.

"Shut Up," She Explained
October 7, 1992

Not that the polls seem to care, but Bill Clinton has been caught in one more (a) lie, (b) memory loss, (c) misinterpretation, or (d) act of disingenuousness. The correct answer depends on Gentle Reader's own capacity for euphemism and tolerance for falsehood. The benefit of the doubt given The Candidate was stretched to the breaking point some time ago, and a story published Saturday — in the *Arkansas Democrat-Gazette* at Little Rock — represented just one more confirmation that Bill Clinton's excellent memory is surpassed only by his astonishing forgettery.

It seems that, back in a 1982 gubernatorial campaign, Slick Willie's opponent, Frank White, got off a rhetorical shot about Bill Clinton's never "having run anything in his life except anti-war demonstrations." Mr. Clinton's straight-faced response at the time? He said he had "no idea" what his opponent "could be talking about."

The Candidate was the picture of innocence at the time; he added only that Mr. White must be "desperate" to make such an accusation. And the public and press bought it. So much for the fabled cynicism of newspaper types.

Not until this year's presidential campaign did the most reliable of witnesses surface to second Frank White's assertion: the young Bill Clinton himself. It seems the twenty-three-year-old had written a letter to the colonel in charge of the ROTC program he had joined, then slipped out of. In his letter, Young Clinton was candid enough to confess:

I have written and spoken and marched against the war. One of the national organizers of the Vietnam Moratorium is a close friend of mine. After I left Arkansas last summer, I went to Washington to work in the national headquarters of the moratorium, then to England to organize the Americans for the demonstrations Oct. 15 and Nov. 16.

Twelve years later, no longer as young or as candid, Bill Clinton didn't know what Frank White was talking about when he said much the same thing. Twenty years later, he couldn't even remember being drafted. The metamorphosis into Slick Willie was complete.

Betsey Wright has an explanation, of course. She's the Clinton campaigner's explainer-in-chief and can smooth out every discrepancy, embarrassment, and bimbo eruption (her classic phrase) in Mr. Clinton's not very long but crowded lifetime. She stays busy. Contrary to Frank White, she says Bill Clinton never "ran" any antiwar demonstration but only "helped organize" a religious service against the war. Miss Betsey has a talent for making distinctions without much of a difference.

What's more, she adds, Frank White's accusation back in '82 was "silly hyperbole." Which is a neat way of conceding the truth at its core while sounding as if she were denying it.

Any more questions? Ms. Wright has an answer for those, too: "This is red-baiting crap that you are playing here. This is just nitpicking, silly little stuff you are into." That's high praise from somebody who's not bad at nitpicking herself. Note the fine distinction between running an antiwar demonstration and organizing an antiwar service.

Ring Lardner, thou shouldst be with us at this hour. Mr. Lardner would have no problem summing up Betsey Wright's hardball style in only a few deadpan words: "Shut up," she explained.

Do you think it would be possible to have Miss Betsey accompany one when the time comes to face the Recording Angel and try to sneak through those Pearly Gates? My own record would look a lot better if I could just get her to explain it.

As for Bill Clinton himself, he has no Final Statement just yet on Inconsistency No. 487 in his campaign. Earlier this year, he did tell *Spectrum*, a Little Rock weekly, that his opposition to the war in Vietnam was well known. And he added: "I've never hidden what I felt about it or what I did."

That's strange. He didn't know a thing about his antiwar organizing when Frank White referred to it in '82. Never fear. Miss Betsey can explain that away, too. Seldom at a loss, she's got a lot more where her last explanation came from. Listening to her, one is reminded of the good ol' boy on the stand who, when required to tell the truth, the whole truth, and nothing but the truth, had no problem. "Sure," he responded. "Which one do you want?"

None of this is likely to make any more difference in the election of '92 than the word "Watergate" made in the election of '72, the Nixon landslide. Only later, when the usual election-year mists part, may it occur that Bill Clinton's falsifying his past for twenty years might have been of some significance in foretelling the general standards of American culture, 1993– .

For now the clintonized culture descends on the U.S. of A. like a glitzy curtain, or a gauzy backdrop for one of Flo Ziegfeld's follies back in the '30s. Happy days are about to be here again. The gloomy past — or any past — is about to vanish, at least so long as Betsey Wright is running the orwellian Ministry of Truth in downtown Little Rock, where history is mutable and truth one of the plastic arts. The Arkansas Repertory Theater isn't the only place in town where fiction can be made art.

In the clintonized culture, all the wrinkles in time are pressed out, all the unfortunate blemishes spot-cleaned, and a selective memory makes [the past] consistent. There's no more need for the usual fundamentalist, reactionary hang-ups — confession, repentance, atonement, and all that oldthink. Only a little wordplay is required to provide cheap grace.

Welcome to the '90s, the decade of genuine, authentic phoniness. The past isn't even prelude in this clintonized culture. It isn't, period. What went before didn't. Here the world begins anew every day — a theory said to be enthusiastically embraced by political theorists, geese, and the American electorate. The Age of Clinton dawns. It's going to be hilarious. Great copy, as we say in this business, which long ago became a branch of showbiz. You ain't seen nothin' yet!

Zoe Baird Turns Everybody Off
February 1, 1993

The one appointment of Bill Clinton's that caught the imagination of the country — the one nominee who got more people excited than any or all of the new president's cabinet — turns out to be a demure corporate counsel from New Haven. Zoe Baird no longer needs an introduction to the American people; she achieved instant unpopularity. Not since Imelda Marcos has a public figure inspired such contempt. Zoe Baird became an overnight failure, which means she's no longer a person but a symbol — apparently of everything Americans begin to loathe and despise about the nineties, a.k.a. the clintonized culture. How did she manage to offend so many so quickly? Let us count the ways:

Elitism. Laws that applied to others — laws that she proposed to enforce with consummate confidence as attorney general — did not apply to her, at least not until they became an impediment to upward mobility. That is the usual point at which yuppiedom's attention is finally engaged.

Moral amnesia. She said she'd done wrong, so what was the big emotional deal? That should have been the end of it. Anything more than reciting a verbal formula now constitutes cruel and unusual punishment. The past should have no unpleasant consequences in the future, certainly nothing that interferes with career plans. This would seem to be one of the few guiding principles of the coming Age of Clinton, yet here Zoe Baird was being denied the nomination. Of course the lady was perplexed.

Condescension. Particularly noticeable were the times Ms. Baird acted as if she deserved a medal for living in New Haven, with its crime and violence and other almost standard accessories of life in America circa 1993. (I've known folks like that wherever I've lived — Pine Bluff, Shreveport, Chicago, New York — even in Little Rock, now the center of the political universe. And you probably have, too. Every town has its share. In their more martyred moments, they humbly confess how unappreciated they are in this burg, the implication being what a favor they're doing the rest of us by living here.) It never seems to occur to the Zoe Bairds that it is they who ought to be grateful to their town for tolerating them. How'd you like to live next door to somebody who harbors illegal immigrants? And then doesn't pay their Social Security? (And what about unemployment? Did she skip that, too?) Talk about ruining the neighborhood. Not all undesirables look scruffy.

Spiritual emptiness. Yep, that's what I said, though you won't see this clear and present danger mentioned in all the oh-so-sophisticated, psycho-social analyses of the Baird Affair & Explosion. All those picky labor laws in the Old Testament — don't take a poor man's cloak in pawn, don't let the sun set on a laborer's wages, provide for the widow and orphan, the worker is worthy of his hire — have a monumental message: The poor are people, too. Not units of production. Not conveniences for their betters. They are not to be reduced to complete dependence on their employers. Or to use the language of the twentieth century's ebb, they are not to be treated like undocumented aliens. (For that matter, The Book has some strong things to say about the rights of aliens. Turns out they're made in the image of God, too.)

Even those who aren't very articulate about their religious beliefs knew there was something about Ms. Baird's actions that they Really Did Not Like. The reaction to her cool-as-a-cucumber confession wasn't confined to neo-conservatives or neo-liberals. It was in great part a reaction to the neo-pagan veneer that covers this mod, upwardly mobile society. Zoe Baird actually did us all a great service by demonstrating that people still reap what they sow. It's a lesson to keep in mind. There but for the grace of. . . .

Euphemism. Even while accepting Ms. Baird's wise decision to withdraw, Bill Clinton was still referring to her "child-care situation." Not her ignoring the law or neglecting ethical obligations. Ms. Baird herself talked about how she had let her feelings as a "mother" take precedence. What had taken precedence was her career. Euphemism is always the first sure sign that something unsavory is being sold. This time it was No Sale. The public was repelled. You bet Bill Clinton & Co. are scurrying to find another nominee for attorney general ASAP. The spotlight cast by this fiasco is all too revealing. The sooner the subject is changed, the better for the populist image of this new leader.

Class. "I've just never felt so strongly about anything before," said a forty-three-year-old nurse at Georgetown University Hospital. She works with single mothers who must struggle to find day care, and who somehow manage to do it without breaking the law. "I don't think it's fair," said an assistant manager quoted in the *New York Times.* "I raised my kids while I was working. I worked days. My husband worked nights at the post office. Our in-laws filled in when they had to. This makes me mad." Such comments were typical of the national reaction. Zoe Baird somehow managed to unite the country — against her. The poor were resentful. The middle class, with its respect for the proprieties, and maybe inspired by a little old-fashioned class envy, was teed off. And the upper class, with its tradition of noblesse oblige, was not amused. Who was this person, and how dare she treat her servants so shabbily? It was embarrassing.

W-a-a-it a minute. How could this be a case of class division if Zoe Baird offended all classes? Because she represents a new class. Decades ago, Milovan Djilas called it just that — The New Class — and wound up in prison for his insight into communist society. He was talking about those who enjoy class privileges while ceaselessly praising the classless society.

In the quondam Soviet Union, the new class was called the *Nomen-klatura* — a word for the old nobility. In this country, the new class is being augmented every year by our most prestigious institutions of higher learning, law schools prominent among them. Congress is only the tip of this privileged caste. For a fairly representative sample of the new class, see the Clinton cabinet, which only looks diverse. It is dominated by lawyers. Its members articulate their ideas endlessly. Any ideals or principles remain mainly subjects for speculation, hidden in a fog of politically correct platitudes. This is the new, technocratic aristocracy.

The most frightening aspect of *l'affaire* Baird is that Bill Clinton was unable to sense, when he made this appointment, that his nominee's little ol' problem with illegal aliens was a great big one. Maybe his sophistication obscured it. A simple country boy would have smelled trouble from the first. Bill Clinton has learned how to manipulate populist symbols deftly, but he didn't anticipate how this nominee would strike the country — smack in the face. At such times, his allegiance to the values behind the symbols can be seen as only campaign-deep. Our new president turns out to be an all too typical representative of the new class himself.

NOTES ON THE NEW CLASS
JUNE 16, 1993

It has been almost forty years since a Yugoslav (there were still Yugoslavs then) by the name of Milovan Djilas gave the world what remains the best sociological study of communism (there was still a communism then) by concentrating on its ruling class, its *Nomen-klatura*, its Beautiful People . . . what he dubbed its New Class. That class has vanished along with communism in Europe, or at least changed its loyalties, but the new classes rise elsewhere, too.

Every society has an elite, but not every society knows its elite. Such studied innocence is particularly true of systems that not very accurately call themselves classless, like the happily former Soviet Union and the happily extant United States of America. If only America had Milovan Djilas, or if the general run of sociologists could write, the New Class in this country would make an ideal subject for an academic journal. Failing that, the task must be left to journalists and such.

So far commentators have only a slippery grasp of America's new class. Just what the clintonized culture has wrought is, like the Clinton administration itself, only in its opening throes. But already certain phrases begin to hint at a new phenomenon or at least style in matters American: the governing class, the political class. . . . Clearly or not so clearly, a new elite has come to the fore. Call it the New Class.

The first and perhaps most obvious characteristic of the New Class is its commitment and compassion. You can tell because its members are always talking about both, and always in the same undeviating order: first the commitment, then the compassion they express when breaking it. When a member of the New Class tells you how sorry he is, how much he loves and admires you, what a wonderful person and real champ you are . . . watch it. You are about to be stomped on. Hard.

This New Class may be stronger on commitment and compassion, in precisely that sequence, than any other elite the country has ever had. The stronger the commitment made, the more flowery the professions of Caring, Feeling, Admiration, and Love when it is broken.

Nobody is better at this than Bill Clinton, president-for-life of the New Class. His treatment of Lani Guinier represents a heretofore unmatched example of the commitment-compassion cycle. Yes, something of the same pattern may be noted in his treatment of others (Zoe Baird, Kimba Wood, Haitian refugees, Bosnian Muslims, Chinese dissidents, the American middle class . . . the list grows steadily), but Professor Guinier's case presents a textbook example of New Class commitment followed punctually by New Class compassion.

First came the commitment: strong, unquestioning, repeated, good-humored, tough, lower-lip-biting boyishly capital-S sincere:

Tuesday, May 11: "I want to say a special word of support for Lani Guinier. I went to law school with her, and I announced at the Justice Department the other day . . . that she had actually sued me once. Not only that, she didn't lose. And I nominated her anyway. So the Senate ought to be able to be able to put up with a little controversy in the cause of civil rights and go on and confirm her. . . ."

Friday, May 14: "I nominated her because there had never been a full-time practicing civil rights lawyer, with a career in civil rights law, heading the civil rights division. . . . I still think she's a very well qualified civil rights lawyer, and I hope she will be confirmed."

Later that same day: "I would never have appointed anybody to public office if they had to agree with everything I believe in. . . . Based on my personal experience, you will believe me when I say I am confident that she will follow the Constitution and the laws of the United States."

Wednesday, June 2: "I want to reaffirm two positive things about her. One is that everyone can see she is a first-rate civil rights lawyer. . . . Secondly, I think any reasonable reading of her writings would lead someone to conclude that a lot of the attacks cannot be supported by a fair reading of her writings. . . ."

But that was before, one whole day before, Bill Clinton gave her writings his own fair reading — and joined Lani Guinier's attackers.

Thursday, June 3: "At the time of the nomination, I had not read her writings. In retrospect, I wish I had. Today, as a matter of fairness to her, I read some of them again in good detail. They clearly lend themselves to interpretations that do not represent views that I hold very dearly . . . I cannot fight a battle that I know is divisive . . . if I do not believe in the ground of battle."

Now it was time for the compassion to ooze and mount and flow and finally break like a great, magnificent, all-inclusive wave. R. W. Apple, Jr., of the *New York Times* was there to record it all when the president rolled out the compassion at a White House dinner. (Public expression of undying love for one another is another hallmark of the New Class's members, particularly when the press is there to record it.)

You could tell from Mr. Apple's account in the times that here was a deeply troubled, sensitive president taking full responsibility for his decisions while having a perfectly plausible excuse for each and every one. Why, he had granted his soon-to-be former nominee an audience that lasted for more than an hour in which to explain her controversial views before kicking her overboard. Gently, of course.

The ordeal had made him two hours late for the dinner. By the time he arrived, many of the guests were halfway through their beef Wellington and on their second glass of cabernet. It was clear the president wanted to talk about his day at the office. It had been "a brutal, heartbreaking day," he sighed. Mr. Apple's story doesn't speculate on what kind of day it must have been for Lani Guinier.

The president did say Mrs. Guinier had resisted his decision to drop her, a decision "which must have hit her on the head like a two-by-four." (Gosh, why? Can she have taken all his words of support, encouragement, and commitment seriously, silly girl?) In the end, Bill Clinton was able to say, she "was a champ." And that wasn't all:

"I love her," he professed to the assembled businessmen, journalists, apparatchiki and glitterati dining that evening in the Green Room. "I think she's wonderful. If she called me and told me she needed $5,000, I'd take it from my account and send it to her, no questions asked. It was the hardest decision I've had to make since I became president. . . ."

There couldn't have been a dry eye in the house by the time the president finished. "If not a historic moment," Mr. Apple wrote, "it was a highly dramatic one." Well, a melodramatic one, anyway. If the New Class lacks any profound emotion, it abounds, it overflows, it floats on sentimentally. Particularly for anyone whose hopes and dreams it has just gutted. Bill Clinton just loves Lani Guinier to death.

If only Mrs. Guinier had wanted the loan of $5,000 instead of an opportunity to defend her honor, there would have been no problem. But honor is not very high on the New Class scale of values. It tends to interfere with essentials like political viability.

Members in good standing of the New Class soon learn to follow the Four Way Rule whenever they've done something extraordinarily cloddish: (1) Talk endlessly about how sorry they feel for the victim. (2) Talk endlessly about how sorry they feel for themselves. (3) Talk endlessly. (4) Forget it. This last point must be scrupulously observed so that, having learned nothing from the commitment-compassion cycle, they can go on repeating it.

George Stephanopoulos, who's still vaguely around, told the press that the president "feels very badly about this. . . . It was a very painful decision for him. He feels very sorry for Lani Guinier." This wasn't as elaborate a performance as the president's, but all the members of the New Class can express postcommitment compassion with passable proficiency on the shortest notice. They get so many opportunities to practice it.

The Search for Meaning
July 4, 1993

American intellectuals are molting again.

It seems to happen with ever greater frequency, like changes in computer technology or audio reproduction. Intellectual costumes, too, seem to need changing with ever greater frequency.

Sometimes the latest fads even double back on one another. Family values were denounced as some kind of fascist plot when they were being touted by Republicans at their last national convention. Now they're back under new management and a new name. Hillary Clinton has noticed the unraveling of not just the American family but the American school, neighborhood, and the society. Her response has been to urge a search for meaning in politics, life, or maybe the universe.

Americans are uneasy, the nation's First Woman has discovered, and Ms. Clinton says we need to decide what it means to be an American at the dawn of a new millennium. But this state of uneasiness is not a monopoly of any one time or place; it may have something to do with being human. In the species as a whole, it is known as anxiety. It tends to drive *Homo sapiens* toward God or various unsatisfactory substitutes therefore, notable among them politics, ideology, art, and perhaps most common, self-worship. It is the oldest temptation. "Ye shall surely not die," the serpent assured Eve, urging her to eat of the fruit, for then "ye shall be as gods, knowing good and evil."

The search for meaning seems to grow particularly intense when we grow impatient with being creatures and decide to create ourselves anew. Surely, we tell ourselves, we could do a better job. All we have to do is decide what this New Man should be like.

This new American should have an "ethos of caring," says Miss Hillary, which is unsatisfying modspeak for: Love One Another. Unsatisfying because it smacks of social engineering rather than divine command, which used to have a certain authority. One may do things out of sheer love or awe that mere reason would never prompt. (Note the things friends and family will do for one another.)

You can tell a lot about the worth of an idea by the words in which it is expressed. Love is personal, even when it is love of an abstraction like justice. The ethos of caring, like a Title IV program or Werner Erhard's latest Ultimate Answer, is a kind of social gospel without the gospel.

This is scarcely the first time Americans have been prodded to find a collective meaning. The current search for meaning in politics, and maybe out of it, is enough to bring back one of the more futile ventures in American bureaucracy, the presidential commission on national goals. Was it back in the Age of Eisenhower, or part of the Kennedy Camelot? It doesn't matter because the commission didn't. It is now happily forgotten and deserves to be.

Oh, yes, the distinguished commissioners decided that the American goal was "to preserve and enlarge our own liberties, to meet a deadly menace, and to extend the area of freedom throughout the world." As if we hadn't known.

Well, three out of three ain't bad. Viewed from 1993, America seems to have been remarkably successful in triumphing over communism and extending freedom. It could also be argued that liberty has been extended at home. But the dignitaries who devised those goals could have saved themselves some long and oh-so-solemn deliberation. They could have settled for the words of the first commission on national goals, a.k.a. the Continental Congress. Its report was issued 217 years ago today:

"We hold these truths to be self-evident, that all men are created equal, that they are endowed by their Creator with certain unalienable Rights, that among these are Life, Liberty and the pursuit of Happiness . . . ."

The words can still make you breathe a little deeper every time you hear them, unlike Search for Meaning. Okay, but where in the Declaration is the road map, The Answer, the 12-step guide, the meaning of American life? It's not there because the essence of America is to leave that decision to the individual.

Mr. Jefferson in his famous declaration spoke of life, liberty, and no, not happiness but only its pursuit. He was asserting a right, not demanding a guarantee. Wise man. The right to succeed has to include the right to fail, or it isn't freedom. The right to define ourselves has to include the wrong definition, or it isn't a choice.

Those systems that guarantee heaven have a way of producing hell. (See the history of this simultaneously most advanced and most brutish of centuries.) Those regimes that supply the meaning of life for their subjects tend to collapse into meaninglessness. There are some decisions that government should leave to the governed, like the meaning of our lives.

Alas, America now has developed its own little gray people who, dissatisfied with their own lives, announce that they have discovered how everybody else should live. After all, why should people be allowed to muck up their lives when government can do it so much better?

For a disheartening example, see the present welfare system. At long last, the new world seems to have produced an institution once found only in the old — a proletariat, a permanent underclass doomed to dependence generation after generation. To belong to it was a fate people used to come here to avoid, not meet.

Yes, terrible things can happen to Americans who have nothing and no one to fall back on. The fruits of freedom can be bitter. But they can be sweet, too. Now more and more is guaranteed, including poverty, ignorance, dependence, and self-loathing. Next year, who knows, maybe even the meaning of life will be provided by official fiat. By that time surely some other shibboleth will be in the air. You can already sense this one fading. Meanings of Life have terribly short shelf lives themselves in this speeded up society.

Happily, every July the Fourth, the words of the Declaration of Independence remind that we have no business imposing our own, duly researched, government-certified Meaning of Life on others. Which is something to celebrate.

NOTES ON THE NEWS
JULY 8, 1993

There are certain advantages in coming from Arkansas — or any other state where the civility index is still high. One is being taught how to apologize. Anybody who doesn't know should be handed a videotape of Mack McLarty's remarks at his press conference Friday. It was his finest hour.

As chief of staff, Mr. McLarty took responsibility for the mistreatment of the innocent employees who were fired wholesale from the White House travel office and then made to look like suspects under investigation by the FBI.

Mack McLarty apologized not just to them but to their friends and families — the way a real person would. He made it clear that the administration would make amends, and that those who had been dismissed unjustly were now eligible for jobs of comparable rank.

There is an art to apologizing, and Mack the Nice now has demonstrated it.

Mr. McLarty also reprimanded by name those on his staff who had thrown their weight around or otherwise abused the reputations of innocent people. That these oh-so-helpful aides will only be reprimanded showed remarkable leniency on his part; one hopes his kindness will be justified by their service in the future. Their signal disservice to the chief of staff in this affair makes that only a hope, not an expectation.

As for the twenty-five-year-old cousin of the president's who went in as boss of the travel office, she's now on her way out. Mr. McLarty also questioned the role of the president's buddy and inaugural impresario, Harry Thomason, in this fiasco. And the chief of staff announced new policies intended to prevent any repetition.

Political pundits who never had the benefits of a Southern upbringing may talk about the White House's political blunder and what a blow having to apologize was. They don't understand. A gentleman never stands taller than when taking responsibility, acknowledging error, and correcting it by deeds as well as words.

In the past few months, Americans seem to have grown disillusioned with slick politicians in high office, not excluding the president of the United States, who act as if they have all the answers, particularly when those answers seem to change every Tuesday and Thursday.

What an inspiration it was to watch somebody in the White House who knew what had to be done and did it without wavering or making excuses. It kind of made me proud — not just of Mack McLarty but of the Arkansas that produced him.

Bill Clinton now has managed to unite both timber workers and the environmentalists in the Pacific Northwest — against his compromise plan to control logging there.

How strange: During the campaign, he promised all would be pleased when he both protected the environment and the timber industry. Those who said somebody would have to sacrifice something in a compromise were denounced as offering a "false choice." That phrase became the chorus of the Clinton campaign whenever The Candidate came perilously close to taking a position. About the only time he endorsed Choice unequivocally was when it meant abortion.

The candidate who promised the best of all possible worlds to both sides of almost every issue now is hearing from both sides of this one: A spokesman for the Wilderness Society said of the Clinton compromise: "It's a plan of a thousand cuts." A spokesman for the timber workers said: "He is cutting off at the knees one of the most productive, efficient, and vital American industries, leaving stranded thousands of workers and our families."

The Clinton plan would save the wilderness and destroy the logging industry, or maybe vice versa, depending on who's complaining at the time. But it does have the sure sign of a genuine compromise: Both sides seem to hate it. Contrary to the Happy Talk of the campaign, not all choices in this world are false. And when they're made, somebody has to give — spotted owls or people or both.

One suspects that it's not the pain of having to give something up that infuriates those complaining. It's the disintegration of the central message of the presidential campaign of '92 and maybe of every other campaign year: Nobody but the other guy will ever have to give anything up, there are really no hard choices in life, and anybody who points them out is only painting a "false choice."

That message is almost the spirit of the age. No wonder Bill Clinton was elected. Here is what Bruce Reed, the president's deputy assistant for domestic policy, was saying back when he was a campaign aide: "If ever there was a false choice, it's the one between owls and jobs." What a hoot. Not even the owls might believe that one now. Even if they could be retrained as squirrels, the employment adjustment would involve some sacrifice. . . .

Bill Clinton managed to make it to a $1,500-a-plate fund-raiser for the Democratic Party last week, though many of the tables at the lavish dinner were empty by the time he spoke at 11:15 p.m. That was okay; the lobbyists seem to have sent money instead. It was the most lucrative bash ever for any American political party, pulling in $4.2 million. When the ever-tardy president did get to the podium, he spoke about health-care reform. He spoke about welfare reform. He did not speak about campaign reform. He may not even have mentioned those terrible fat-cat Republicans. Who says the man has no shame? . . .

Confirming the Condomized Culture

July 21, 1993

The confirmation hearings this week on the nomination of Joycelyn Elders as surgeon general of the United States are worth watching. Not because the outcome is in any doubt. Dr. Elders will surely be approved. She's the president's choice. Her party controls the committee holding the hearings, and it should be able to control the vote on the Senate floor. There won't be much suspense about the outcome, but the hearings will say a lot about American civilization *circa* 1993, or what's left of it.

This is the Age of the Condom, that magical solution to every ill — teenage pregnancies, abortion, the AIDS plague, and maybe double parking. And this nominee has been the great champion of condom clinics in Arkansas. She represents a new morality that bears a striking resemblance to the old immorality. Day is night today, night is day today, anything goes . . . so long as it has the authority of Science. That's why the condom has become the mod version of absolution, and Safe Sex is becoming as morally mandatory as virginity once was.

The notion that individual self-restraint might play some role in averting the general unraveling of American society isn't so much denied as dismissed. "Everybody knows" such an approach is unrealistic, antiquated, unworkable.

And not just in sexual matters. Listen to Jim Guy Tucker, Arkansas's governor and Dr. Elders's nominal boss, talking about her being paid as both head of the state Health Department and consultant to its federal counterpart. What does he say about the good doctor's double-dipping — her being allowed to draw $42,119 from the state every three months while collecting $550 a day plus $135 per diem from the Feds?

"To your average taxpaying citizen and to this average taxpaying governor," says Jim Guy Tucker, "it just doesn't look right, and the folks up there (in Washington) should have known it and shouldn't have permitted it."

Of course. It's the Feds' fault. They're always a reliable scapegoat in these latitudes. The Folks Up There must have bound and gagged poor Dr. Elders, dragged her off into a dark alley, and made her accept $675 a day, those fiends.

Besides, after some judicious bookkeeping with vacation days — she accrued fifteen hours of vacation time a month — surely it will be shown that she was working for the Feds only while on vacation and lunch breaks. Her records better be in order. Rather than a graceful leavetaking from her state job, Dr. Elders's resignation Sunday had a forced, awkward look about it.

No doubt the official figures will also show that her crusade for condoms has held down the rate of teenage pregnancies in Arkansas. After all, it rose "only" 17 percent under her stewardship, compared to 18 percent nationwide.

W-a-a-it a minute. Didn't Arkansas's teenage birthrate go from the fourth highest to the second highest in the nation during Dr. Elders's tenure as director of the state Health Department? Didn't the rate of teenage pregnancies reach a ten-year high? Wasn't there also an alarming increase in the incidence of syphilis and HIV among Arkansas teenagers? Could it be that Safe Sex really isn't safe?

At least one expert on infectious diseases — Robert C. Noble at the University of Kentucky — has pointed out that Safe Sex is a fraud. A dangerous fraud. "We should stop kidding ourselves," says the doctor. "There is no safe sex. Condoms aren't going to make a dent in the sexual epidemics that we are facing. If the condom breaks, you may die."

Forgive me for sounding like a medical textbook, but it should be noted that condoms have a 14 percent failure rate in vaginal intercourse and offer even less protection in other, high-risk sexual behaviors. Technology has not improved that much since the Marquise de Sevigne in the seventeenth century dismissed the condom as only "a spider web against danger."

Dr. Steven J. Sainsbury of San Luis Obispo, California, who treats teenage patients every day, has reached the logical conclusion: "AIDS is a killer disease, and any measures taken to prevent its transmission must be 100 percent effective. For condoms to be the answer to AIDS, they must be used every time and can never break or leak. Neither criterion is ever likely to be met."

So what does Dr. Sainsbury advise? He says his recommendation "lies buried in government reports but has always resided in common sense: that the only safe sex is no sex until one is ready to commit to a monogamous relationship with an uninfected person. The key words are abstinence and monogamy."

Isn't that unrealistic, naive, old-fashioned? Responds the doctor: "Well, perhaps a return to a few old-fashioned concepts is what's needed to stem the tide of AIDS, unwanted pregnancies, and venereal disease. Just as we try to teach our children to be honest, kind and gentle, perhaps we can also teach them to be chaste. Why do we harbor such reluctance to teach abstinence and fidelity?"

Because those quaint values conflict with the fatal spirit of this unbuttoned age. Just last week, the Census Bureau reported that nearly a quarter of the country's unmarried women now become mothers — a trend that crosses racial, ethnic, and class lines. Murphy Brown is no aberration.

The new, condomized culture threatens not just the basic institution of society, the family, but young lives. Yet in the condomized culture of 1993, sexuality may not be thought of as only a blessing or instrumentality; it has become a god in the politically correct pantheon. It must not be restrained, only followed and accommodated — even with makeshift precautions that invite disease and death.

In terms of medical effectiveness, the record of our modern condom clinics would make a sexual ethic like that prescribed in a primitive, nomadic code like the Old Testament look positively scientific. Morality aide, such an approach would mark a great step forward just in terms of public health.

But anyone concerned about what this newest idolatry — call it condom worship — is doing to a generation of young women should prepare to be denounced as anti-woman.

Yes, the confirmation hearings this week should be enlightening — not because of what they may say about Joycelyn Elders, who is but the personification of the conventional unwisdom, but as an illustration of how widely and deeply entrenched, and how smoothly rationalized, a mindless promiscuity can become in an alleged civilization.

THEY JUST DON'T UNDERSTAND
AUGUST 31, 1994

The *New Yorker* magazine, like much of New York itself, seems mystified by Howell Raines, who is still fairly new as editorial page editor of the *New York Times*. The mystery: Why is a perfectly good liberal saying those awful things about Bill Clinton — and in the editorial columns of the formerly good gray *Times*?

How the enlightened must miss what Peter Boyer, writing in the *New Yorker*, calls the "faceless gray space" that is the natural milieu of editorial writers. Ever since Mr. Raines came to town, the editorials have taken on color and, worse, bite. This strikes New Yorkers as unnatural.

I know what they mean. There was a time when, teaching a journalism class nights, I could use that day's editorials in the *Times*, or any day's, as the perfect example of how not to write an editorial. Can't do that now that Raines reigns. Most shocking, the editorials in the *Times* routinely compare Bill Clinton, liberalism's last best hope, to . . . Richard Nixon.

Talk about *lèse majesté*. In the rarefied precincts of the *New Yorker*'s press criticism, apparently nothing is more mysterious than the self-evident. It may have escaped Mr. Boyer's notice that the Nixon funeral was one occasion on which Bill Clinton seemed to speak with genuine conviction, rather than his usual transient sentimentality. Here was a predecessor whose style this precocious president didn't just study for pointers, but with whom he could identify. . . .

It's hard to believe that even the present-day *New Yorker* has failed to notice that Bill Clinton is doing to liberalism what Richard Nixon did to conservatism: Reduce it to an empty adjunct of his own political viability, thus depriving a vibrant political philosophy of constancy, legitimacy, conviction, integrity, moral force . . . and a fair chance of working.

Not till after the memory of Tricky Dick faded did American conservatism revive. Who knows when or whether an authentic American liberalism will rebound after Slick Willie has hollowed it out?

Yet the *New Yorker*'s Mr. Boyer seems to share the White House's mystification at why an editor who generally takes the Clinton line on issue after issue should find this administration "easily the most reckless in interfering with the integrity of federal investigative agencies since that of Richard Nixon."

Why would a liberal write such things, and why would the publisher of the *Times*, the semi-official organ of American liberalism, publish them as editorial opinion? Surely the obvious could be overlooked, or at least softened, in the interests of the party line. Isn't that how politics is supposed to be played? Even if this president is something of a Hollow Man, shouldn't a maker and shaper of editorial opinion remember that he's *our* Hollow Man?

Mr. Boyer struggles with this mystery that really isn't, and actually comes close to an answer a couple of times in his piece, then backs off apparently none the wiser. The first time is when he notes that Howell

Raines is a writer before he is an editorial writer. (His Pulitzer was for a memoir of his Alabama boyhood.)

Words seem to mean something to Howell Raines. You can tell he wants to put them together for their own sake, not in order to Shape Public Opinion. He's the sort who is not about to destroy a sentence in order to save a politician. Which explains a lot about those refreshingly honest Clinton editorials in the *Times*.

Mr. Boyer touches on a second and even better explanation for the *Times*'s curious integrity on the subject of Bill Clinton, at least when the subject is ethics and character and the nigh-eternal Whitewater mess. It's "a Southern thing," he quotes White House aides as explaining. Indeed it is, but Peter Boyer associates the Southern thing with some kind of personal animosity, or just a lust to bring down whoever is momentarily atop the greasy pole.

The Southern Thing is embarrassing to have to explain, because if one has to use words to argue for honor, for character, for duty, for a code that words can only hint at . . . well, it's just embarrassing. Like having to point. Not a habit one would want to encourage.

You wouldn't have to use words to explain all this to a Barbara Jordan or Ralph McGill. The *New Yorker*'s Mr. Boyer does recognize that this president "sometimes seems like a compromise in a suit," but that's as close as he gets to the essential problem. (What do you suppose he means by *sometimes*?)

Strange: The Southern Thing is not a matter of words — often it is expressed by a heavy-laden silence — yet it may explain why the South has become the great incubator of American writing in this century. In the South of our fevered imaginations, which day by day we create or betray, meaning still attaches. Words can be twisted only so far, and then there is simply no saying them.

Or, conversely, an Alabama boy may recognize something about a politician or an administration or a whole fin-de-siècle age with so merciless a clarity that there is no *not* saying some things, even in an editorial for the *New York Times*.

How could a Southerner help but react to the slippery maneuvers, verbal and political, of the New Age? The new, flexible, up-to-date standards of truth and honor on display in the Whitewater follies would be instantly recognizable to any Southerner with a sense of history; today's yuppies are just yesterday's carpetbaggers.

For that matter, Southerners of all regions understand. All it takes is a code of one's own that takes precedence over any personal advantage. Nobody would have to explain all this to a Jim Leach or George Shultz, either, or for that matter to any old-fashioned New Englander.

As for why the *New York Times* would place its imprimatur on Howell Raines's outdated instincts, on his broadsword virtues, his politically awkward and certainly politically incorrect views . . . well, it might help to remember the Southern roots of the *New York Times* itself. They go back to the last century and Adolph Simon Ochs of Chattanooga, Tennessee, a carpetbagger-in-reverse who arrived in the big city to introduce that strangest of journalistic wares, a sense of propriety. He, too, must have mystified sophisticated New Yorkers. Then as now, there was no explaining such an attitude to those who just can't see the point of it.

BILL CLINTON TWO YEARS LATER
OCTOBER 14, 1994

There was no getting around it. It was time to pay the Danegeld.

It's been two years since Danish Broadcasting had set up its cameras at the *Arkansas Democrat-Gazette* during the presidential campaign. It seemed everybody in the world had wanted to know who this Bill Clinton was, which was understandable, and had expected journalists in Arkansas to know, which wasn't.

The answer isn't any clearer now, but here are the Danes again. Frank Esmann and his cameraman, Thomas Haas, are back brandishing cameras and mikes and questions. Last time the world's curiosity about Arkansas's native son was such that these not very melancholy Danes had to share an interview with the BBC. Now we're alone in the big conference room and the madding crowd has disappeared. At last the supply of information/speculation about Bill Clinton may finally have exceeded demand.

The first thing I want to know is what I had said two years ago. Columnists, like politicians, want to stay consistent, and how can we if our unforgettable comments have been forgotten?

"You were right!" my Danish interviewer says. He specifically remembers my having used the term Hollow Man in reference to Bill Clinton. "You were actually right," he muses. He sounds surprised.

Then he has to add, "At least the perception of Bill Clinton now fits squarely with what you said." Which is not the same as being right, not at all.

On the contrary, when a minority report becomes the conventional wisdom, it tends to unnerve those of us who have never been altogether comfortable with conformity — on the principle that two hundred million Americans can't be right. There may be hope for Bill Clinton after all if he has managed to offend, not just dishearten, the great majority.

And has Europe soured on our president, too? Oh, yes, says my interviewer. Europeans are "quite skeptical" — have been ever since Warren Christopher came visiting and made it clear he would follow Europe's policy toward the war in Bosnia, which was to let it go on. That's when it dawned that the new president "never really intended to follow through" on his campaign rhetoric, but only to raise "false hopes."

Well, it only turned out that way, I say to myself. No doubt Bill Clinton was sincere at the time. He always is. All sentimentalists are when, eyes brimming over, they make promises they would certainly keep if it wasn't so much trouble. The Balkans are trouble, always have been, and so the war and suffering have been allowed to go on for two more years.

[Another year of war would pass before the administration gave up on European mediation, the United Nations bureaucracy, and general apathy. Faced by another rapacious Serbian offensive, and news accounts and photos of the massacre and expulsion at Srebrenica, the United States, at the head of NATO, unleashed the first serious aerial campaign of the war against Serbian positions, opened the way for a Croatian counter-offensive, negotiated/imposed a settlement, and dispatched an expeditionary force, including a projected 20,000 American troops, to enforce it.]

European diplomats traditionally have been "cynical pragmatists," my visitor explains, unnecessarily, and the world has looked to America for moral leadership. No more. In only a few blood-soaked years in the Balkans — George Bush's last in the White House and Bill Clinton's first two — Washington has adopted Europe's cynicism. Everybody is just waiting for the Serbs to win, my visitor explains, so peace can be declared.

It's an old European solution, dating back at least to Tacitus and his description of the Romans' foreign policy: They make a desolation and call it peace. Now the United States, too, is just waiting for the blood to settle.

Forget the theory of American exceptionalism; we have decided to be a nation like all other nations. Isn't that what maturity is all about? And if so, how does it differ from decadence? Nobody seems to feel very good about it. Which may be another reason for the general irritation abroad in the land. Maybe even those Americans who aren't idealists want their presidents to be.

"Say, are you interviewing me?" Frank Esmann asks. He's caught on. If a cab driver isn't available, a journalist will gladly interview the nearest journalist. If I can't turn a camera on our visitors, I can at least turn the tables. . . . My interviewer has spent the last five years in Washington. Before that, he covered London, Poland, the Middle East, Africa . . . "London must have been nice," I suggest. Oh yes, he agrees, but "Britain got a little boring after the fifth miners' strike."

Then it's his turn: "What's been the worst thing about the Clinton administration?" Worst? This isn't a worst or best administration, just a sloppy one — confused and ineffectual. Often incoherent. Perhaps because its CEO has this stormy, not to say incompatible, relationship with truth.

Not that it's easy or even possible to divine the truth of things, but Bill Clinton seems to believe it is always negotiable. At a time when the world is dissolving into a combustible, pre-1914 soup of nationalisms, statesmen should be making some sense and order out of it all — an ordered freedom. It can be done. This administration finally acted in Haiti after a useless embargo, and it acted in the Persian Gulf. This president may prove educable after all. Pity it's too late for a couple of million people killed, wounded, or displaced in what was once Yugoslavia. There, Warren Christopher still dithers and calls it foreign policy.

Happily, there are wholesome exceptions to the gathering chaos: Israelis and Arabs are moving toward peace, Boris Yeltsin is still holding Russia and himself together . . . the administration is to be complimented for not getting in the way of some trends. Where things are going in the right direction, inertia is preferable to policy any time.

But what a waste of precious years. Later it will be even harder to develop a vision and to exercise the leadership necessary to fulfill it. It's as if this generation had been given a second chance after the terrors of the twentieth century, and we're muffing it again.

At home, the same sense of drift dominates. There have been exceptions: The move toward free trade, and a welcome but unfocused, almost incoherent, crime bill. But the challenges of the time seem to have been tabled, or papered over, or approached only peripherally: Education that doesn't educate, gaps in health care, the welfare trap, and, most dangerous of all, the growing distance between the governed and those who govern . . . all those problems seem to have been postponed, or approached in ways that make them bigger or worse.

The American people tend to demand a president who can give us some traction, even if it's only the kind that makes us oppose him. Remember Harry Truman? Not a very popular president toward the end of his tenure, but there was little doubt about where he stood — on almost anything.

This president doesn't have enough definition for a dynamic society to rally 'round or against him. Sometimes he seems only a reflection of his polls and focus groups, in thrall to a public opinion he constantly courts but may not understand. An administration that has only one goal — reelection — is not likely to achieve it.

One can sense "a condition of excitement and irritation in the public mind," to quote Teddy Roosevelt just before the Progressive Era burst on the American scene. Term limits may prove only the precursor of a housecleaning, restoration, and general shake-up whose tremors can be felt even now in the public's increasing impatience with the politicians.

Come back in two years, I tell our intermittent visitors, and see.

Caution: Politician Talking Philosophy

July 14, 1995

When he talks politics, which seems all the time, Bill Clinton is merely boring. But when he starts talking philosophy, he can be positively dangerous — like a two-year-old playing with a loaded pistol. Because ideas have consequences, some of them highly dangerous. This friendly reminder is inspired by the president's speech at Georgetown University last week. He described it as "more of a conversation" than "a formal speech," but it turned out to be an extended monologue. And maybe a preview of his '96 campaign.

The performance lasted about an hour, and somebody counted seventy-five issues covered in forty-four minutes, twenty-six favorable mentions of the middle class (the one Americans automatically identify with), nine references to "middle-class dreams," and forty-nine endorsements of the work ethic, a.k.a. the Puritan Ethic or the Protestant Ethic.

These times, they have definitely changed since Dan Quayle was hooted down for plugging family values; now those values are the height of political fashion. You can tell because Bill Clinton is now repeatedly, exhaustingly, monotonously for them. He sounded like a buttonholer you might be seated next to on an airplane, and who doesn't let up for a minute from Little Rock to Cincinnati.

The heart and soullessness of this one-way conversation was summed up by the president's assertion that culture really isn't all that important in this society: "There is a group who believe that our problems are primarily personal and cultural. Cultural is basically a word that means, in this context, there are a whole lot of persons doing the same bad thing. And . . . if everybody would just sort of straighten up and fly right, why things would be hunky-dory. . . ."

Free translation: It's still the economy, stupid. One would never guess from this dismissive view of the culture that Dick Morris — who's attuned to the public's attachment to the middle-class values — had supplanted James Carville as the president's spin Ph.D. This twist must be Mr. Clinton's own. Deep inside all those layers of political viability, he has held onto the spirit of his youth. Unfortunately, his youth was spent in the sixties.

The point of this rambling presentation, if it had one, seemed to be: If we can just compete better in the global economy and keep median income from going down the way it has the past couple of years (the president seems to be running for reelection against his own record) than all will be well.

Even now Bill Clinton seems oblivious to the possibility that cultural values are far more likely to determine the success of an economy than the other way 'round. (Surely it's not just coincidence that Calvinism and bourgeois capitalism came onto the Western scene together. There's that Puritan Ethic again.)

Instead, the president put in a good word for the sixties, which he said weren't all bad. No decade is, but in terms of planting the seeds of the social, cultural, and yes, economic unraveling of America, the sixties were gosh-awful. Trace the origins of the destructive trends that plague American society in the '90s — violent crime, illegitimacy, family breakdown, welfare dependency, functional illiteracy, sexually transmitted plagues, the drug culture . . . and the trail leads unerringly back to the '60s. When the culture of *Happy Days* ended with the fifties, so did the happy days.

The connection between the breakdown of the family and the growth of poverty has become undeniable:

In 1959, 28 percent of poor families were headed by women. By 1992, 52 percent were, or more than half. Is there a more vivid illustration that poverty is largely a family problem?

The poverty rate in this country was falling steadily before the 1960s, but ever since the Great Society launched its war on poverty in the '60s, the poverty rate has remained virtually the same.

Something is terribly wrong, and it isn't that government is spending too little on anti-poverty programs.

It's the competitiveness-of-the-global-economy that's to blame, our president explains. The fault lies not in ourselves but in impersonal economic forces. Uh huh. The late Warren Brookes, whose economic analysis is still sorely missed, saw through that kind of globaloney even before the 1990s were upon us like a wolf upon the fold. Here is what he was saying in the summer of 1988:

> There is abroad in our land today a perception, right or wrong, that the decline in our relative economic position in the world may have more to do with a decline in our values than our political leaders are willing to admit. People sense we are much more threatened by the rot within than from an increasingly competitive world without. We know that neither growth nor protectionism can dampen the demand for drugs, or stiffen the spines of parents and teachers, or strengthen the curricula and performance of school systems. In city after city, record-breaking help-wanted advertising is falling on the deaf ears of ghetto youths who kill each other in drug turf-wars. Bright economic dreams do not easily develop in broken homes, nor does development flourish in a drug culture, and education cannot be [left to] metal detectors.

People can overcome material poverty; Americans have done it time and again. Franklin Roosevelt had the right order of priorities when, deep in the deepest of economic depressions, he thankfully noted in his

First Inaugural that the country's problems were only material. The American spirit was still strong.

But a poverty of the culture, a crisis of the spirit, a breakdown of the family . . . all those interrelated problems can be far more dangerous, and lasting, than any economic crisis. Indeed, a cultural collapse can bring on economic crisis — and make it chronic. Hard as it may be for our Advanced Thinkers to admit, the public interest cannot be divorced from private virtue. We're all in this society together, and our actions affect more than our own future. The culture matters — and in ways far beyond the cultural.

Back in the 1980s, the National Bureau of Economic Research conducted a comprehensive study of young people in America's inner cities, and came up with a curious finding: There was only one statistically significant factor in the lives of those young people who managed to escape the crime, violence, drugs and desperate poverty of their environment. And that factor was . . . regular church attendance.

Maybe that finding isn't so curious. Not that there's anything magical about occupying a pew, but church attendance may bespeak other cultural patterns, like self-discipline and family solidarity. All of which may explain why, among young people in the inner cities, attending church was associated with 20 percent less involvement in criminal activity, 23 percent less drug use, and, please note, a 47 percent increase in potential income.

Last week Bill Clinton was back preaching his New Covenant, but maybe it's the old covenant that could use more emphasis just now — the one that starts with Genesis and ends with Malachi, the original puritan ethic with all its atavistic emphasis on, yes, family values. The demand for social justice in the scriptures is sufficiently unrelenting to please the most ardent reformer, but that old covenant never makes the mistake of pretending that the great crises in a nation's life come about because of economic rather than moral conditions.

Oh, dear. I seem to have done it again: stopped meddlin' and gone to preachin'.

The More Bill Clinton Changes . . . The More He Remains the Same

November 12, 1995

This president still can't be trusted to stick with a political position, or even admit taking it, for more than one news cycle. By now Bill Clinton has got the old flip-flop down to a neat three-step: assert, deny, and split the difference. It's the grand Hegelian pendulum of all history — thesis, antithesis, synthesis — reduced to roughly twenty-four hours. (Everything is faster in the internetted nineties.)

Remember this Arthur Murray step and you won't have to wonder where Our Leader is going in these protracted negotiations with Congress over the budget: forward, back, and on to reelection. It's the new tango — without the old mystique. Because by now there's little doubt where this master of the fast shuffle will come out: wherever the poll numbers and his latest guru lead him. This president leads by following, or, to be more precise, he follows by following.

The air of unreality about this presidency grows thick when Bill Clinton steps out of his presidential persona and kibitzes his own performance, like a pitcher stepping off the mound to broadcast the game. Did you note his exposé not long ago of his own tax program? "Probably there are people in this room still mad at me," he told a fund-raiser in Houston, "because you think I raised your taxes too much. It might surprise you to know that I think I raised them too much, too."

The president flatters himself; surely nothing he thinks or says (there doesn't seem to be much of a difference in his case) should surprise the country by now. Particularly because one can see the retraction attached even as the president speaks. (It's even got a name by now: the clinton clause.)

This latest confession set off the usual flap among those Democrats who had stuck their necks out for him. After all, they had helped him pass his budget in 1993 — a budget he was backing away from with the approach of election year 1996. In what must be a practiced maneuver by now, the White House moved quickly to soothe any bad feelings about the president's statement by explaining that he hadn't made it: "The president has absolutely no regrets about the deficit reduction plan he and the Democrats passed in 1993. None. And he didn't mean to leave any other impression." — George R. Stephanopoulos, former press aide and current head of the administration's ministry of truth.

After decades of exposure to the Clinton style, this country editor didn't think that still another quick zoom around the Clinton cloverleaf rated editorial comment. But the president's backward flip in Houston did make the news columns of the *Arkansas Democrat-Gazette;* the item ran deep inside page 9A ("Clinton reverses himself, says he raised taxes too much in '93"). But elsewhere, especially in the oh-so-sophisticated East, it was BIG NEWS. The president's latest reversal made page 1 in the *New York Times.* ("Clinton Angers Friend and Foe in Tax Remark").

Some observers seemed shocked — *genuinely* shocked — by the latest flip and immediate flop. Even the usual apologists for our Plastic Man of a president seemed momentarily discomfited. Across the country, one could almost feel analysts catching on, and beginning to wonder whether there was any point in analyzing policies that would be outdated before the paper hit the streets.

Poor, dazed Carl Cannon, White House correspondent for the Baltimore *Sun,* sounds as if he has just about had it. "This president," he complained, "salts his remarks with so many inventions, half-truths, and self-serving exaggerations that reporters who cover him often have to choose between truth-squadding every speech or ignoring his fibs."

The exasperated Mr. Cannon sounded familiar. To be more precise, he sounded like an Arkansas editor adrift in Bill Clinton's third or fourth term as governor when at last all the Benefits of Doubt had run out, and one was face to face with the possibility — no, the probability — that there was no Bill Clinton at all, but only his political position du jour. Welcome to the vast club, Mr. Cannon.

The big question about presidential policy these days is not what it is — because whatever it is, it'll change — but whether it matters. Can anything so fluid be worth examining even if it could be caught and held up to the light?

Instead, the pundits begin to see that, in this administration, policy is another name for the latest, ever-changing campaign tactic. One can hear the enthusiastic cheers now when the Democrats assemble at Chicago to renominate the president: "Stay the courses!"

Daniel Patrick Moynihan, the astute senator and pixie from New York, figured it out some time back: "I don't know where the White

House is going now. They're not governing. They're just doing the War Room."

The president's comment in Houston was but a capsulized version of his long, convoluted, and still continuing courses on the budget. When he sent a budget to Congress earlier this year, it was such a transparent farce it didn't rate a single vote in the Senate, Democratic or Republican; it was turned down by something like 99–0. Since then, he's been all over the road, swinging and swaying under the guidance of his new-old guru, Dick Morris.

While exposing the president's tricky approach to the budget, Robert J. Samuelson in the *Washington Post* still couldn't help but be awed by the sheer nerve of the guy:

> The ultimate aim is to reach an agreement with Congress, but to do so in such a way that Clinton can claim credit both for balancing the budget and for protecting programs that people don't want cut (but which will have to be cut). In fact he isn't doing either. Only someone with Clinton's indifference toward the truth could even attempt this maneuver. . . . Clinton's whole strategy has been, as much as possible, to avoid the necessity of choice and to excite public anxieties about any choices that might actually be made. The audacity of his political posturing (and its essential dishonesty) is now to project himself as an eager proponent of a balanced budget. . . . Clinton's behavior is defined only by the constant pursuit of personal political advantage.

To paraphrase Rex Harrison as Professor Doolittle, "I think he's got it!" Mr. Samuelson writes with the fresh outrage of someone who has just caught on to the Slick Willie that lurks inside of Bill Clinton's every pronouncement. To read Robert Samuelson here in Arkansas is to be reminded of one's youth, and the outrage that finally erupts after one's loss of innocence.

But even if Bill Clinton runs out of analysts to beguile in the Washington press corps, there is an endless supply of them waiting in the chattering class. Good ol' Ben Wattenberg got the Clinton treatment the other day when the president cornered him on the phone for about an hour, squeezing all the good out of Mr. Wattenberg's latest book — (*Values Matter Most*) before the White House objected to the author's account of their conversation. Still, Ben Wattenberg remains a believer. He is ready to give the president, yes, the benefit of the doubt.

I think I know how he feels, having spent much of the 1980s doing just that. I think I know where Ben Wattenberg is — about the same place I was a few years back, not realizing that Bill Clinton isn't changing his ways but just continuing them. This president, it may only slowly dawn, is one of those politicians who, when he gets to a fork in the road, takes it.

Now watch for the word "values" to start creeping into presidential speeches. It won't be long before the president will be sounding like Bill Bennett. Or Dan Quayle. There is no surer sign of an idea whose time has come than Bill Clinton's parroting it.

It was Robert Samuelson, the *Washington Post*'s Clinton-watcher, who pointed out the big danger with Bill Clinton's easy way with words and principles. It's a danger not so much to the president's budget or his presidency or his party — although all may be in danger — but to the essential American belief that politics matters.

To quote the conclusion of Mr. Samuelson's essay about this president's flip-flops: "The larger danger of his situational speech — designing fictions to fit the moment — is that it vindicates public cynicism of political leadership. Clinton's conceit is that people never notice untruths. But of course, they ultimately do, and in the long run, this makes effective governing harder. Trust diminishes, as it has."

But as long as those who do notice — even supposedly hardened newspaper types like Robert Samuelson and Carl Cannon — can react to Bill Clinton's well-worn ways with new shock, cynicism will not have completely overtaken us. Which is why the president's latest dodges were welcome; the yelps they inspired shows the country still expects better of its politicians.

Chapter 12

ABOUT THE AUTHOR: A WRY SELF-PORTRAIT

GREENBERG AND MYSELF

OCTOBER 22, 1995

It was an honor and pleasure being asked to lecture last week at a university like Auburn in Alabama. But just between us, it made me uneasy.

I will tell you why:

I am afraid they invited the wrong Paul Greenberg.

Really.

You see, it is the other Greenberg that things happen to, that politics still excites, who still looks on the world as new, to whom ideas occur, who pontificates and prophesizes and ponders in public, who composes orations in the shower and loves to hear himself talk.

Me, I just stroll the streets of Little Rock, pausing now and then to study the iron grillwork of the old cemetery, to commune with the graves, to gaze at the scrollwork adorning the top of an old building visible from my office window. . . .

Of the other Greenberg I get news in the mail. The bills are addressed to me; he gets the invitations and compliments, the biting responses to his newspaper column, the single-spaced faxes asking him to use his immense influence on behalf of some invention or panacea or tax reform whose brilliance no one else may have yet recognized, but that will revolutionize American society. . . .

It is he who gets the phone messages, the requests for his autographed picture, the poison pen letters, the urgent communications from the obsessed and litigious and paranoiac, the privately published books and corporate PR and government press releases, the unending mailings from the Right to Work Committee, the White House, the Heritage Foundation . . . and he seems to relish it all. Indiscriminately.

Now and then I get a glimpse of his name in the public prints or on a committee of journalists or other places gentlemen do not frequent.

Me, I like old books, old films, old type faces, the smell of coffee and the taste of Scotch whisky; the origin and connotations of words; Mozart and Telemann, *Carmen* and Patsy Cline . . . all the passions that are safely dead. Like the curious philosophical and historical ruminations of Giambattista Vico (1668–1744), which were outmoded even when they were composed in early eighteenth-century Naples. And the poetry and prose of Jorge Luis Borges of Buenos Aires and the world, a Homer without a Greece.

Perhaps you, too, Gentle Reader, have read and delighted in Borges, and will recognize the theme of this literally self-indulgent Sunday column as having been shamelessly stolen and slavishly copied from Borges's one-page masterpiece entitled "Borges and Myself."

As for the other Greenberg — we are actually quite close — he shares my enthusiasms for the writings of Borges. He, too, admires the historical philosophizing of Ortega y Gasset, the poems of Emily Dickinson, the essays of George Orwell, and the pastoral game of baseball. He also shares my lack of enthusiasm for political polls, modern art, air travel, and pointless violence, including the game of football. I admit it, the other Greenberg shares my tastes and distastes, but in a showy way that turns them into stagey mannerisms.

It would be an exaggeration to say that he and I are on bad terms. Indeed, I fear my purpose in living is so that he can weave together his columns and books and speeches and embarrassing little clevernesses.

When pressed I will admit that he has managed to write a few good paragraphs that may endure till that day's newspaper is discarded, but not even that can save me, because whatever is worthy there no longer belongs to me, or even to the other man, but soon enough becomes part of the conventional knowledge, the static background everybody knows and no longer notices. Its familiarity breeds contempt the way corners do dust.

He has been described, honestly enough, as a perverse and isolated recalcitrant who imagines that character and competence, ideas and imagination, a sense of duty and honor, are more important in the leader of a republic than effectiveness as a mass campaigner. Clearly he is a minor figure out of his time, which is the Age of Clinton.

Some, less than honest, have concluded that he must have something personal against the chief magistrate of the Republic to have opposed a presidential candidate from his own small wonderful province. As if Bill Clinton, except on rare occasions, and only after being provoked, had ever been anything but civil to him.

After election night, 1992, I thought: Now at last we will both be left alone. No such luck. Now, three years later, the speaking invitations proliferate. Publishers make book offers. He is hailed as farsighted, a fashion setter, and among a certain clubby kind of conservative, One of Us. He gets calls from aficionados of conspiracies and the kind of ghouls who still feed on the sad death of Vince Foster. He is made privy to fantastical theories about the Clintons that make even his tasteless, mass-marketed soul cringe.

In short — indeed, in what seems the shortest possible time — he has gone from pariah to prophet. Smug and gregarious, he thinks it is all his due. As someone who was never a joiner, it all makes me want to flee — to take the first bus to Tucumcari, N.M. In another time, I would have booked passage on the first ship to Tarshish, like another ridiculous prophet whose standards were higher than God's.

Is it not boring enough to have spent one's life watching The Rise and Rise of Bill Clinton? Must I be linked to him in history, too? For it begins to dawn that the only mention of my name in the all-swallowing American future that is even now upon us will be in the index of the sort of Clinton biographies that no one reads even now.

(Borges mentions somewhere that Spanish literature has no need of a Ralph Waldo Emerson because it is already sufficiently boring. Somewhere there must be happy little countries already sufficiently boring to have no need of a Bill Clinton.)

The other Greenberg revels in all this. He delights in the Clintonesque. He finds the presidential couple fascinating, the perfect embodiment of the America of the nineties. He is now deep into — not guilt by association — but career by association. It has not yet occurred to him, sophisticate that he foolishly imagines himself to be, that soon enough he will go back to obscurity. And be glad of it. He is convinced that his brilliant insights explain his sudden popularity, but you and I know that his notoriety is only the result of his having been marooned in Arkansas for about thirty years, safely immunized from the fickle fever swamp that is national public opinion. Only by happenstance was he obliged to occupy a ringside seat and watch the making of a president. Simple propinquity may say more about our lives than our egos can bear.

Myself, I preferred the good old days — 1992 — when the presidential election promised to sweep us both away, like two sober soreheads at a pretty good party who can think of nothing but the hangover to come. Those were the days, my friend. Ah, solitude. I've always felt better being in the minority, preferably a minority of one. Then you can be sure you are not just following the herd.

It was wonderful while it lasted. Then came November 1994. The Republican revolution. The Avalanche. The Earthquake. The Volcano. The very Vesuvius of midterm elections. I will spare you the statistical rundown, the usual panegyric about the transformation of both houses of Congress, and the number of governorships and legislative seats and dogcatcher's offices that changed hands. Suffice it to say that *nine million* more of my countrymen voted Republican than had done so only two years before, in 1992, and a million or two fewer voted Democratic, amounting to a seismic shift in American party history of some ten million votes.

Imagine how I felt. I, who have never liked crowds. It is disconcerting when a whole continental mass suddenly seems to share what you had safely assumed to be your own novel insights. I was appalled.

It is the other Greenberg who delights in all this whirl and swirl, publicly noting this or that aspect of the rapidly passing scene like some rude tourist guide pointing his finger at every tall building, as though no one else could see the obvious. It is embarrassing.

Years ago I tried to rid myself of his tiresome presence by taking refuge in the stories of Borges, the travel writings of Rebecca West, or an occasional passage of Talmud . . . but I found that he expropriated even those for his own purposes. My life is running away, and I am left with nothing of my own. I am losing everything — either to oblivion or to the other man. Which one of us has written this column I really don't know.

INDEX

Armey, Dick, 158
Army
    Clinton letter to, 26
    homosexuals in, 33–35, 77
Arnold, Richard, 102, 199
Aspin, Les, 186
Atwater, Lee, 63
Augean Books, 44, 46
Aurelius, Marcus, 213, 269

Baird, Zoe, 151, 274–77, 278
    class and, 276–77
    Clinton euphemisms and, 276
    condescension of, 275
    contempt for, 275
    elitism and, 275
    moral amnesia and, 275
    spiritual emptiness of, 275–76
Baker, James, 240, 254
Baltimore Sun, 245, 299
Bank of Cherry Valley, 80
Bartley, Bob, 212
Becker, Bill, 122
Bell, Clarence, 10
Bennett, Bill, 301
Bennett, Bob, 212
Black, Hugo, 199
Blumenthal, Sidney, 270
Borchert, Martin, 41, 43
Bosnia, 36, 128, 186, 278
    Christopher and, 292, 293
The Boston Globe, 29
bourgeoisie, Calvinism and, 295
Bowen, Bill, 81
Boyer, Peter, 288
    on Clinton, 290
    on Raines, 290
Branch Davidian compound, 164
Brandeis, Louis, 180, 199
Bratton, Sam, 195, 196
Britton, Nan, 215
Brock, David, 203, 210
Broder, David, 8
Brookes, Warren, 296
Brown, Jerry, 19, 63
    Clinton vs., 23
    Hillary Clinton and, 227
Bryan, William Jennings, 271
Buchanan, Pat, 118

Buckley, William F., Jr., 270
Budget, 15, 60, 194, 300
Bumpers, Dale, 7, 30
    Kuwait invasion and, 126
Burden, Jack, 26
Burgess, Joe, 73
Burke, Edmund, 62, 189, 221
Burns, Bob, 93
Bush, Barbara, 230, 237
Bush, George, 22, 240
    broken promise, 30
    1988 campaign, 178, 180
    campaign mistake, 96
    defeat, 96
    imitation of, 75
    last year, 292
    Hillary Clinton on, 229
    NAFTA and, 121
    praise for, 95
    press and, 271
    vision, 180–81, 258
Butler, Jack, 79
Bynum, Preston, 105

Caddell, Pat, 254, 269
Calhoun, John C., 152
Calvinism, capitalism and, 295
Camelot, revival of, 267
Campaign for Military Service, 35
Campaign reform, 36
Cannon, Carl, 299
Cantrell Hill, 83
Cardozo, Benjamin, 199
Carlson, Margaret, 61
Carson, Johnny, 178
Carter, Jimmy, 2, 49, 66
    Europe and, 172
    Georgia and, 91
    in Haiti, 129
    leadership, 189
Carvey, Dana, 75
Carville, James, 295
    Democratic defeat and, 260
    nickname, 261
Cedras, Raoul, 127, 128
Celebrityhood, civility vs., 204
Center for Public Integrity, 38
Chamber of Commerce, 108
Character, sex and, 202